Environmental Security

This student-friendly textbook offers a survey of the competing conceptions and applications of the increasingly prominent notion of environmental security.

The book is divided into three parts. In the first, the key theoretical and practical arguments for and against bringing together environmental and security issues are set out. The book then goes on to reveal how and why environmental issues have come to be framed in some quarters as 'national security' concerns, in the context of the effects of overpopulation, resource depletion, climate change and the role of the military as both a cause and a solution to problems of pollution and natural disasters. Finally, Part 3 explores the case for treating the key issues of environmental change as matters of human security. Overall, the book will provide a clear, systematic and thorough overview of all dimensions of an area of great academic and 'real-world' political interest, albeit one that has rarely been set out in an accessible textbook format hitherto.

Environmental Security: An introduction will be essential reading for students of environmental studies, critical and human security, global governance, development studies, and international relations (IR) in general.

Peter Hough is Principal Lecturer in International Politics, Middlesex University, UK. He is the author of *The Global Politics of Pesticides* (1998) and *Understanding Global Security* (2004; 2008; 2013 3rd edn).

'Peter Hough provides an authoritative and critical analysis of the causes and consequences of environmental degradation, both natural and human-induced, from the tropics to the poles. The helpful "key points" section at the end of each chapter will provide an invaluable navigational aid for those who are new to this subject. Written in a lively and engaging tone, this book will be indispensable reading for students and seasoned scholars alike.'

David Humphreys, The Open University, UK

'This book offers a solid introduction to the manifold linkages between environmental degradation and human, national and international security. Hough's account is particularly strong in drawing out the relationship between human security and environmental problems. Alongside the standardly covered implications of both climate change and resource depletion for human security, it also includes those of pollution and of biodiversity decline.'

Rita Floyd, University of Birmingham, UK

Environmental Security

An introduction

Peter Hough

LONDON AND NEW YORK

First published 2014
by Routledge
2 Park Square, Milton Park, Abingdon, Oxon OX14 4RN

and by Routledge
711 Third Avenue, New York, NY 10017

Routledge is an imprint of the Taylor & Francis Group, an informa business

British Library Cataloguing in Publication Data
A catalogue record for this book is available from the British Library

Library of Congress Cataloging-in-Publication Data
Hough, Peter, 1967-
Environmental security : an introduction / Peter Hough.
pages cm.
Includes bibliographical references and index.
1. Environmental policy- -International cooperation.
2. Environmental protection- -International cooperation.
3. National security. 4. Security, International. I. Title.
GE170.H7 2014
363.7- -dc23
2013032802

ISBN: 978-0-415-51647-1 (hbk)
ISBN: 978-0-415-51648-8 (pbk)
ISBN: 978-1-315-88250-5 (ebk)

Typeset in Times
by Integra Software Services Pvt. Ltd, Pondicherry, India

Printed and bound by CPI Group (UK) Ltd, Croydon, CR0 4YY

To Lisa

Contents

List of tables and boxes xi
Preface xiii
Acknowledgements xvii

PART 1
The environment and security **1**

1 The politicization of the environment **3**
Green shoots: The rise of the science of ecology and the politics of conservation 3
Green revolution? The rise of political ecology 6
The emergence of international environmental policy 8
The globalization of political ecology 11
Global environmental policy in the 21st century 16
Green thinking 17
Conclusion 19

2 The securitization of global environmental policy **21**
Environmental securitization in theory 21
Environmental security in practice 26
Conclusions 32

PART 2
The environment and national security **35**

3 Breeding to death? The threat posed by overpopulation **37**
A growing problem? 37
The globalization and securitization of overpopulation 39
Conclusions 45

4 Fighting over the last drop? Resource wars and energy security **46**
Power politics: The rise of energy security concerns 46
The resource war thesis 48

Resource war sceptics 49
Conclusions 53

5 The spoils of war: Military security and the environment **55**
Introduction 55
Ecocide: The deliberate military destruction of natural resources 56
Collateral damage: Indirect environmental damage by warfare 58
Military securitization of the environment beyond the battlefield 60
Outlawing ecocide 61
Normative progress in curbing military ecocide 65

6 Civilizational security: Global threats from environmental change **68**
Fixing the roof: Ozone politics 68
'Not fixing the thermostat': Climate change 70
When worlds collide: Extraterrestrial security threats 72
Conclusions 73

PART 3
The environment and human security **77**

7 Adapt or die? Climate change **79**
Facing the heat: The human security implications of climate change 80
Feeling the pressure: Those most vulnerable to climate change 81
The international politics of climate change 82
Conclusions 87

8 Messy business: Pollution and human security **89**
Air pollution 89
Water pollution 92
Soil pollution 94
Food pollution 95
Vulnerability to pollution 95
International policy 97
Conclusions 104

9 Running on empty: The human security consequences of resource depletion and biodiversity decline **106**
Desertification 106
Deforestation 111
Loggerheads: International forestry politics 112
Biodiversity 114
Conclusions 117

10 Learning to expect the unexpected: Natural disasters **118**
When the environment bites back 118
Geological disasters 119
Meteorological/climatological disasters 122
Hydrological disasters 125
Human vulnerability to natural hazards 126
The securitization of natural disaster management 129
Conclusions 131

PART 4
Conclusions **133**

11 Conclusions: To securitize or not to securitize? **135**
Objections to securitizing the environment 135
Does securitization help prioritize environmental issues? 140

Bibliography 143
Index 154

List of tables and boxes

Tables

6.1 The Torino Scale 73
8.1 Global deaths due to pollution in 2010 90
8.2 Chemicals subject to the Stockholm Convention 102
10.1 The worst natural disasters in history 119
10.2 Global deaths by natural disaster types 2009–11 119

Boxes

1.1 George Perkins Marsh – *Man and Nature* 4
1.2 Timeline of scientific ecology and political conservation 5
1.3 Rachel Carson – *Silent Spring* 6
1.4 The polluter's dilemma 7
1.5 Timeline of political ecology 17
2.1 Olof Palme 29
3.1 The world's 7-billionth person 37
3.2 End of the world? Wanna bet on it? 42
3.3 Cairo Programme of Action 1994 43
4.1 OPEC 47
5.1 Arthur Westing 55
5.2 UNEP's 'Ecocide day' 2009 65
6.1 Sherwood Rowland and Mario Molina 69
6.2 Key features of the Montreal Protocol 69
7.1 The Intergovernmental Panel on Climate Change 79
7.2 Progress of the Framework Convention on Climate Change 83
7.3 Bjorn Lomborg – *The Sceptical Environmentalist* 85
9.1 The costs of desertification 107
9.2 Lake Chad 109
11.1 UN High-Level Panel Post-2015 Development Targets on the Environment 140

Preface

This book surveys the global politics of the environment through the prism of security studies. 'Environmental security' has featured prominently in the discourse of academic international relations and real-world international relations since both of these arenas came to be shaken up in the aftermath of the Cold War in the 1990s. The apparent passing into history of a conflict which had completely dominated international relations in both the academic and real worlds since the 1940s prompted a reappraisal of the politics of security and provided space for environmental issues to be given greater prominence on the international political agenda. 'Securitizing' the environment – that is, treating issues such as pollution or resource depletion as threats meriting urgent and special political attention – has been advocated by many political ecologists and put into practice by some governments since the 1990s (and even as far back as the early 1970s when the Cold War appeared to be ending and environmental concerns had begun to globalize). Not everyone, though, is convinced of the merits of treating ecological concerns as matters of political emergency, and environmental security as a concept remains highly contested. In addition, environmental security is inconsistently interpreted by its advocates since 'security', in terms of its meaning and the means of achieving it, is viewed differently by different political actors and thinkers. As a consequence of this, the academic literature on environmental security that has evolved over the past few decades has tended to polarize rather than synthesize into clearer thinking, and few comprehensive and accessible texts have emerged to present issues that demonstrably greatly affect and concern the general public.

This book seeks to provide some much-needed clarity to thinking about environmental security by presenting the debate on the appropriateness and meaning of this concept in a systematic and accessible format. Towards this end, two guiding questions underpin this survey of environmental politics from a security perspective:

1. What is the scale of threat posed by the issues of environmental change?
2. Is it appropriate to treat issues of environmental change as matters of security politics?

The complexity and interconnectedness of environmental problems makes precisely determining the scale of their threat a very difficult, if not impossible, task, but it is, nonetheless, important to attempt this. Elements of doubt and an occasional tendency to exaggerate the human impacts of environmental change can be exploited by vested interests unwilling to incur the short-term costs of securing people and the planet in the long term. Scientific and public understanding of the costs of the pollution and depletion of the Earth's resources is, though, improving all the time, and this volume seeks to present this across the range of environmental issues. In addition to the difficulties in quantifying the threat posed by environmental change are concerns over whether describing and treating issues such as climate change as matters of security is merited or helpful. Ontological questions on the meaning of security are invoked: Whose security is at stake? What does being secure entail? Who does the securing? For some – the traditionalists – environmental politics and security politics simply do not go together because security has come to be interpreted as synonymous with the military defence of the state. On the other side of the debate it is not accepted that security has to be about 'national' or military threats – the human impact of environmental change should be enough to merit the treatment of such issues as international political priorities. A middle course between these positions, put into practice by several governments, is to securitize environmental concerns on the grounds that they can have traditional national security consequences in an indirect sense by making conflict and instability in the world more likely. This author allies himself with the second of these three camps – the human or critical security paradigm – but all three perspectives are presented in this volume.

Eleven chapters, examining different dimensions and themes that emerge when bringing 'the environment' and 'security' together, are split into four parts.

Part 1 looks at the big picture, examining, in turn, the evolution of global environmental policy and thought, and then the attempts to 'securitize' such policies, both in academia and 'real-world' politics. Chapter 1 describes and analyses how environmental concerns have evolved from the emergence of scientific appreciation of ecosystems in the 19th century, to political attempts to conserve certain ecosystems and then ecocentric politics – acting against human interests for the good of the environment – in the 1960s. The chapter then goes on to examine how, subsequent to this birth of political ecology, environmental politics has internationalized, globalized and come to be seen as being in various 'shades of green'. Chapter 2 maintains the wider focus on environmental change in the world as a whole but does so by applying the prism of security studies. Attempts to present environmental problems as matters of security, in a variety of ways, in International Relations are appraised along with government securitization initiatives in 'real-world' international relations.

The two chief ways in which major environmental problems have been argued to merit securitization is to frame the issues as matters of (i) national (state) security, or (ii) human security. Part 2, hence, describes and analyses environmental policy as national security, focusing on military dimensions of environmental change and the global-scale threats posed by overpopulation, ozone depletion and climate change. Concerns that an ever-expanding population would eventually eat up and burn the Earth's resources did much to put the environment on the international political map in the late 1960s, but the subsequent application of technology and human ingenuity to the task of increasing food production and making energy usage more efficient ultimately damaged the cause of political ecology by making it appear over-alarmist and pessimistic. But the dwindling of the Earth's resources continues to be a concern to many, and the likelihood that this could, in the future, more readily trigger conflict has attracted some more traditionalist security thinkers to give greater consideration to environmental issues – this is reviewed in Chapter 4. Chapter 5 then examines the military–environmental nexus from another perspective, by evaluating the ecological consequences of war. Prosecuting and preparing for war in the name of security comes at an ecological (and indirect human) cost as well as a more direct human one. Chapter 6 then considers how the global-scale threats posed by ozone depletion and climate change have been responded to in international politics. To date, the former has been dealt with much more effectively than the latter, since more vested interests stand to be affected by acting effectively on climate change, while the problem of 'national security' as a barrier to global environmental security has become ever more apparent.

Part 3 then looks at the environment from the perspective of human security, examining the scale of threat posed by climate change, pollution, desertification, deforestation and biodiversity loss, and attempting to address human vulnerability to these phenomena. The considerable death toll that can be attributed to climate change and pollution is presented in Chapters 7 and 8, along with analysis of how international policy has evolved in response to this. Scepticism and denial remain obstacles in these areas but impartial, transnational scientific understanding and consequent public appreciation offer hope for political progress. In Chapter 9 progressive resource depletion is revisited, this time from a human rather than a national security perspective, and the barrier to progress presented by national interests again becomes apparent. Many governments continue to encourage the felling of more trees than are planted, overfishing and the subsidizing of the overproduction of food because this is economically and politically profitable in the short term, even though unsustainable in the longer term. Chapter 10 provides further evidence for the necessity of a human security approach in appraising international policy on alleviating the impact of natural disasters. The international community, whilst sometimes reacting impressively after a devastating earthquake or tsunami, has been ineffective in addressing the underlying vulnerabilities that render people insecure in the first place. That more difficult long-term proactive, rather than reactive, political task of securing people has been long recognized in the domestic politics of many countries, and the need for global policy to evolve in a similar manner is a recurring theme of environmental security.

Part 4 concludes the book with a chapter appraising the merits and demerits of securitizing the environment. This is not just a case of believing that environmental change is or is not particularly threatening, since many environmentalists resist securitization because of what this is assumed to stand for in terms of militarism and national interests. The line taken by this author is that the human cost of environmental problems is so huge that security status is merited, but that this has to be understood in human rather than national or military terms. The case that environmental problems are already claiming millions of lives is far more compelling than the case that securitization may come to prompt conflicts over dwindling resources or increase flows of migrants or refugees. Environmental change should be securitized but this needs to be done in an appropriate rather than a traditional manner.

Acknowledgements

Two good mates made important contributions to this book – Lloyd Pettiford and Dave Humphreys. Lloyd and I originally contemplated writing this together and I thank him for allowing me to use several of his ideas in Chapters 1 and 5. Thanks to Dave for agreeing to review Chapter 9. His specialist knowledge was invaluable in adding some technical details and helping improve the overall flow of the argument. My thanks also go to Andrew Humphrys at Routledge for putting his faith in me to write this book and then for his patience in waiting for me to deliver it. My appreciation also goes to Lisa, Daisy and Rosie for their endless support and encouragement.

Part 1

The environment and security

1 The politicization of the environment

There is a sufficiency in the world for man's need but not for man's greed.
Mahatma Gandhi (Krech & McNeill 2004: 571)

Green shoots: The rise of the science of ecology and the politics of conservation

The environment – or non-human world – is comparatively 'new' to politics and, as an alternative to human interests, has only been on the agenda of international relations since the late 1960s. That is not to say, however, that problems of environmental change are in any way new. The extinction of certain animal species due to human recklessness and the decline of woodland areas through over-exploitation are centuries-old phenomena. The dodo, moa, and Steller's sea cow, for example, were hunted to extinction before the 20th century. Other notable changes to the natural environment have occurred entirely independently of human action. The 'Cretaceous/Tertiary Impact', caused by either a comet or an asteroid, created the 250 km wide Chicxulub crater in the Gulf of Mexico, widely held to be responsible for the extinction of the dinosaurs and other life forms long before the dawn of humanity. In addition, the temperature of the Earth has periodically naturally warmed and cooled throughout human and pre-human history, with various effects on the natural environment.

The science of understanding such matters of environmental change emerged in the 19th century and was given the name *ecology* by the German biologist Haeckel (Haeckel 1866). The science of ecology brought recognition of natural systemic phenomena linking disparate life forms such as food chains, the carbon cycle and evolution, and an understanding of humanity's place within the environment. Published shortly before this first usage of the term ecology in 1864, George Perkins Marsh's *Man and Nature* is widely regarded as the first *ecological* book in that it used empirical data to prove the effect of human activity on woodlands and waterways (see Box 1.1).

In the wake of this scientific revolution of the 1860s domestic policies to conserve nature and pressure groups campaigning for conservation began to emerge in the US and some Western European states. Yellowstone became the US's first National Park in 1872, and the British Royal Society for the Protection of Birds (RSPB) became the world's first conservation pressure group when it was founded in 1889, as a result of fears that the grebe was in danger of extinction due to the fashion of using its feathers for hats. In the US the Sierra Club, founded in 1892, was the pioneer of non-governmental conservation groups seeking to build upon the idea of national parks to protect the natural environment, established with Yellowstone.

The origins of international policy on issues of environmental change can also be traced back as far as the late 19th century's then unparalleled industrialization and globalization. The year

Box 1.1 George Perkins Marsh – *Man and Nature*

Born into the New England political establishment in 1801, George Perkins Marsh led a varied life as a linguist, lawyer and politician as well as a pioneer of ecologism. After following in the family tradition and serving as a congressman, he became a distinguished diplomat, serving first as ambassador to Turkey before being switched by President Lincoln to Italy in 1861. He stayed in Rome until his death twenty years later; the longest ambassadorial posting in US history.

Drawing on research Marsh carried out whilst posted in Rome, *Man and Nature* begins with an overview of how much of the forested and fertile Roman Empire had become unproductive arid wasteland, through overproduction. Hence, Marsh was discussing desertification over half a century before the term came to be employed. The book was also ahead of its time in foreseeing the links between deforestation and flooding. Whilst *Man and Nature* is more of a scientific than polemical work, in examining the effects of major engineering projects – like the Suez and Panama Canals – on nature, and questioning their legitimacy, there is no doubt that Marsh sowed the seed of political ecology.

- 'Man is everywhere a disturbing agent. Wherever he plants his foot, the harmonies of nature are turned to discords' (Marsh 1864: 36).
- 'We can never know how wide a circle of disturbance we produce in the harmonies of nature when we throw the smallest pebble into the ocean of organic life' (Marsh 1864: 103).
- 'The great question, whether man is of nature or above her' (Marsh 1864: 549).

1889 saw the first international policy dealing with flora, with an international convention to prevent the spread of the disease *phylloxera* in grapes. Then, in 1902, the Convention on the Protection of Birds Useful to Agriculture was the first international legal instrument on animal conservation. These were, however, motivated by economic rather than environmental concerns. Wine and internationally traded food were at stake rather than the flora and fauna themselves. The grapes and birds being protected were the subject of such concern because of their *instrumental* rather than *intrinsic* value. This distinction is the key to determining whether a political issue is truly environmental/ecological (Greens generally prefer the latter term since 'environmental' can be thought to imply that the non-human world is a backdrop to the human world rather than the two co-existing in a single *ecosystem*). In determining whether a given issue is an environmental one the key question is: Is the environment to be protected for its own sake or just when this furthers human interests?

Conservation policies, driven by the aesthetics of loving the countryside or preserving rural lifestyles, permeated the domestic politics of some developed countries in the early 20th century, even including Nazi Germany. The Nazis linked natural and racial German purity, as was encapsulated in their slogan 'blood and soil', and Agriculture Minister Richard Darré enacted some policies in line with this, such as the 1935 Reich Law for the Protection of Nature. Hence, the politics of conservation, whilst giving value to the environment and even restricting human interests as part of this policy, is still instrumental or 'anthropocentric' since it is about preservation for humanity's sake. Conservation is about the preservation of traditional rural culture for human enrichment, be it practical or spiritual. The support for rural preservation by hunting lobbyists is an obvious example of non-ecocentric conservationism (although it is worth noting that the Nazis banned hunting with hounds – so their belief in rural conservation was of a romanticized political conservatism).

National conservation policy gradually internationalized during the 20th century. Since animals are, of course, not confined by state frontiers, the RSPB, Sierra Club and other groups, after the

Second World War, came to orientate their campaigns through the United Nations (UN). Several groups, principally from thc UK and thc US, worked with the newly established United Nations Educational Scientific and Cultural Organization (UNESCO) to found the International Union for the Preservation of Nature (IUPN) in 1948 (Adams 2004: 43–62). The IUPN, a hybrid intergovernmental and non-governmental organization, later changed its title to the International Union for the Conservation of Nature (IUCN) and became a focus of international information exchange on endangered species, based on the compilation of 'Red Lists' of flora and fauna close to extinction throughout the world. A regime specific to the conservation of whales can also be dated back to the 1940s but, similarly, did not become legally significant until several decades later.[1] The International Whaling Commission (IWC) was set up in 1946, due to concerns at the likely extinction of certain species, but was very much anthropocentric as it was guided by the desire of whaling states to continue their practices in a manner that could sustain hunting. Later in 1959, in a prelude to the international ecocentric turn, the Antarctic Treaty established the idea of a conservation park on an international scale, by outlawing industrialization and sovereign claims on the frozen continent in a successful agreement that still holds firm today. The Antarctic Treaty stands as a notable international political achievement, although the inhospitality of the continent meant that no significant potential for national economic development was being stifled in agreeing to its conservation (see Box 1.2).

Box 1.2 Timeline of scientific ecology and political conservation

1798 Thomas Malthus' *An Essay on the Principle of Population* predicts that the world's population growth will exceed its food supply.
1854 Charles Darwin's *On the Origin of the Species* establishes the theory of evolution.
1864 US scientist George Perkins Marsh's *Man and Nature* released – arguably the first book to prove that human activities can harm the environment.
1866 German biologist Ernst Haeckel coins the term *ecology*.
1872 Yellowstone National Park becomes world's first major nature conservation scheme.
1879 Royal National Park established in Sydney, Australia.
1889 Royal Society for the Protection of Birds in Great Britain becomes the world's first conservation pressure group.
1889 First ever international policy on non-human life form agreed – combating the spread of the disease *phylloxera* in wine grapes.
1892 Sierra Club conservation pressure group founded in the US.
1902 Convention on the Protection of Birds Useful to Agriculture becomes the first international policy on animal conservation.
1909 Great Britain (Canada) and the US sign Boundary Water Treaty launching formal cooperation over the Great Lakes.
1911 North Pacific Fur Seal conservation agreement between the US, Great Britain, Japan and Russia.
1915 Ecological Society of America established to promote conservation.
1926 South African statesman Jan Smuts coins the term *holism*, to describe the idea that, in nature, the whole (an ecosystem) is greater than the sum of its parts.
1946 International Whaling Commission established.
1948 International Union for the Preservation of Nature founded by pressure groups and the UN (later became International Union for the Conservation of Nature).
1952 London smog (urban air pollution) kills over 4,000 people in four days.
1959 Antarctic Treaty creates a non-sovereign 'world park' in which industrial development is prohibited.

Green revolution? The rise of political ecology

The emergence of truly environmental rather than human-focused politics – that is, *ecocentric* rather than *anthropocentric* policies – did not occur until the 1960s – around a century after the birth of the science of ecology. A major factor in this development was the publication of Rachel Carson's hugely influential pollution polemic *Silent Spring* in 1962 (see Box 1.3). *Silent Spring* most notably highlighted the polluting effects of the insecticide dichlorodiphenyltrichloroethane (DDT) on wild animals, vegetation and rivers. The book quickly influenced US policy, with the government enacting legislation restricting DDT applications in 1969 and then outlawing its use altogether in 1972.

Box 1.3 Rachel Carson – *Silent Spring*

US marine biologist Rachel Carson is widely feted as having launched environmentalism as a political ideology in the early 1960s with this hugely influential work, the title of which forewarns of a future world without birdsong. The book highlighted the harmful effects of organochlorine insecticides such as DDT on birds and other wildlife, bringing into question the use of newly synthesized chemicals until then near-universally lauded for their role in controlling insects responsible for diminishing crop yields or transmitting diseases.

Carson's determination to present nature's case against profitable and, in many ways, beneficial human practices saw her succeed in getting *Silent Spring* published in 1962 despite a long-standing personal fight with cancer and attempts to block the book's publication by a hostile chemical industry. The book had been serialized in the *New Yorker* magazine prior to its release and caused such interest that chemical companies began fearing a consumer backlash against their products and so mounted vitriolic attacks on the scientific authenticity of the work. The attacks, though, failed to prevent the book becoming a major success commercially and politically, both in the US and across the developed world, such was the scientific rigour of Carson's arguments.

'Can anyone believe it is possible to lay down such a barrage of poisons on the surface of the Earth without making it unfit for all life? They should not be called "insecticides", but "biocides".

Carson (1962: 7)

Transboundary pollution

Soon after the upsurge of political interest in environmentalism prompted by *Silent Spring* it became apparent that, like conservation, pollution had international ramifications and could not be dealt with by domestic policy alone. Most notably, the effects of acid rain became appreciated, and more long-standing problems such as oil pollution by tankers came to command far greater prominence.

Acid rain became a contentious issue in the 1960s, not only through the emergence of evidence that rainwater could become contaminated and the effects of this on groundwater and wildlife, but also because it was a problem in some countries that could not be resolved by that country's government. Sulfur dioxide and other emissions from the burning of fossil fuels (coal, oil and natural gas) which accumulate in the Earth's atmosphere can return to the surface as precipitation, hundreds of miles from where they departed as waste fumes. Hence, countries particularly suffering from this phenomenon, such as Sweden, Norway and Canada, which were at the forefront of the greening of governments that was occurring at the time, found that they could not resolve the problem since the root cause of it lay in other sovereign states. This form of transboundary pollution most graphically demonstrated the need for international cooperation to resolve certain environmental issues, which was already obvious in the case of countries sharing rivers and other forms of water.

The 1967 *Torrey Canyon* disaster, when an oil tanker was wrecked and spilled its load off the coast of the UK's Scilly Isles, was also influential in stimulating awareness and an international political environmental response, this time with regard to marine pollution. This was far from the first of such disasters but it represented the biggest to date and received huge media attention, with telegenic images of blackened birds and beaches fuelling the mood of public protest that was transforming domestic politics in Europe and North America at that time.

Acid rain and maritime oil spills illustrate a basic truism of modern industrialized living; 'pollution does not respect frontiers'. The necessity of a collective international response to such problems is encapsulated in an environmental version of the well-known decision-making game theory the 'prisoner's dilemma' (see Box 1.4).

Box 1.4 The polluter's dilemma

In a fictional scenario suppose that four states share a common sea and for many decades have deposited waste materials in the sea without political restriction. However, pollution levels in the sea have now reached levels that are affecting fish stocks and tourism on the coast, prompting the four governments to convene a conference to discuss the possibility of a coordinated response.

The costs of pollution to each state's income and the costs of enacting restrictions on pollution (by enforcing new regulations on ship owners) are represented below.

State	Cost of pollution	Cost of curbing pollution
A	$2 million per year	$1 million
B	$2 million per year	$3 million
C	$4 million per year	$13 million
D	$6 million per year	$11 million

What policy is in the best interest of each state?

For State A the decision is clear. Curbing pollution makes economic sense with a net benefit arising within a year of action. For State B, also, a net benefit is likely soon enough for this to make political sense. Such gains are, however, contingent on *all* states enacting the reforms so States A and B must also rely on States C and D following suit. For these two states, and particularly State C, the costs of curbing pollution outweigh the costs incurred for several years and possibly beyond the lifespan of its government's terms in office. Although there is a gain to be made in the long term, the decision is more difficult because, as well as imposing short-term and unpopular costs, there is the nagging fear that acting on this might not even work since another state may not also implement the cuts. States A and B also share this dilemma – the polluter's dilemma – since, although their cost–benefit analyses are more straightforward, their fear of States C or D not acting is higher. Any one of the states may conclude that it is worth carrying on polluting and enjoy the benefits of an overall reduction in pollution through relying on the others to enact cuts – the *free-rider problem*.

Ultimately, coordinated action is in the interests of all but short-termism and a lack of trust in other states makes it difficult to guarantee that states will choose this option – *the collective goods problem*. This problem recurs regularly in international environmental politics and is revisited at several points throughout this volume.

All $ figures in the book are in US dollars.

Resource depletion

A global version of the collective goods problem emerged in the late 1960s with the crystallization of the notion that sovereign control over the common 'goods' of water, air and natural resources was unsustainable. In 1968 the ecologist Garrett Hardin used as a parable a warning first aired in the 19th century by the economist William Forster Lloyd on the finite quality of shared resources, known as the 'Tragedy of the Commons'. Forster Lloyd described how the traditional English village green, conventionally open to all villagers, had become endangered because of an abuse of the privilege of grazing their cattle there by the villagers. As the practice had gone on for centuries it had been assumed that it always could, but it had emerged that an increase in the number of cattle above an optimum level was eroding the land and ruining the common resource for all. Hardin argued that the village green was analogous to *global commons* such as clean air, freshwater and high seas fish stocks, endangered by states continuing to exploit or pollute them oblivious to the fact that the cumulative effect of this would eventually be their depletion. 'Ruin is the destination toward which all men rush, each pursuing his own best interest in a society that believes in the freedom of the commons' (Hardin 1968: 1244). Hardin's solution to the problem was population control, and this subsequently became a major international political concern in the late 1960s and early 1970s. As is discussed in Chapter 3, the original 'Green Revolution' – the modernization of agriculture to improve production in the developing world in the 1970s and 1980s – made the widespread prophesies of doom by Hardin and others appear overly pessimistic; consequently, fears of overpopulation and resource depletion diminished. Environmentalism did not disappear but its mass appeal lessened due to the apparent absence of global crisis and the emergence of solutions that were rooted in industrialization, technology and human ingenuity rather than restraints on human freedoms.

The emergence of international environmental policy

The arrival of environmental politics on the international stage was confirmed by the convening of the 'Biosphere Conference' by the United Nations Educational, Scientific and Cultural Organization (UNESCO) in 1968; the first significant intergovernmental meeting in this area. Representatives of 60 states were present at the conference in Paris, including delegates from the US and Soviet governments. Although a barely remembered footnote in diplomatic history, the Biosphere Conference initiated two phenomena which have been central to the progress of international environmental politics ever since. Firstly, the event was organized through collaboration between several groups from within the UN system and civil society. Representatives of the UN's World Health Organization (WHO) and Food and Agricultural Organization (FAO) attended alongside UNESCO staff, and the event was chaired and hosted by the IUCN and attended by several pressure groups and prominent individual activists. A second important legacy of the Biosphere Conference was the idea of improving the understanding of complex environmental problems by building a transnational network of experts – an *epistemic community* – who could share information and seek to reach an *epistemic consensus*.

The Stockholm Conference

The most important legacy of the Biosphere Conference was to pave the way for a bigger UN summit four years later; the 1972 Conference on the Human Environment (UNCHE) at Stockholm. The conference was boycotted by the USSR and its Eastern Bloc allies, over a row about the recognition of East Germany, but was attended by representatives of 113 states from across the world. Notably, Communist China was represented, in line with the thawing in their relations with the US and subsequent re-participation in the UN after diplomatic recognition by Washington. Three influential reports released in the run-up to the conference helped set the tone of proceedings: *Limits to Growth*, *Only One Earth* and the *Founex Report*. *Limits to Growth*, commissioned by the Club of Rome, an international think tank of politicians and industrialists, was influenced by resource depletion concerns and reasoned that economic growth would need to be abandoned as a political holy grail (Meadows et al. 1972). Researchers used computer-modelling techniques to 'prove' their findings that environmental factors would soon place restrictions on growth and/or lead to disastrous consequences for humanity. Excessive economic and population growth was said to be producing a set of inter-related crises. The world was rapidly running out of resources to feed people or provide raw material for industry, and the ability of the environment to absorb the waste products of human consumption and industrial output was being exhausted. Human society, it was suggested, would collapse before the year 2100. Certainly, the model was unable to allow for all possible factors, and it has been discredited on this basis, but its fundamental points about the impossibility of infinite growth on a finite planet and the need to reorientate growth-based, material society have not been lost and still underlie many green political and ethical arguments (Meadows et al. 1972).

Today, such a consensus from a fairly conservative think tank seems surprising and gives a good indication of the scale of threat by overpopulation and overconsumption perceived at the time. The notion of abandoning economic growth was, though, anathema to the world's underdeveloped countries and *Only One Earth* (commissioned by Maurice Strong who was to be Secretary-General of UNCHE) and the *Founex Report* (the product of a conference in Switzerland) took a somewhat different line, stressing more the culpability of the industrialized world with regard to environmental problems, and acknowledging that less-developed countries (LDCs) still had a right to grow. Hence Strong was able to secure the attendance at Stockholm of most developing world governments, including the influential Indira Gandhi of India and the notably environmentally sceptical military government of Brazil (Dodds et al. 2012: 7). This linkage between a right to develop and environmental protection proved to be a forerunner of the concept of sustainable development substantiated over a decade later.

The Stockholm Conference did not produce a new body of international law at a stroke but served to build consensus by getting agreement on several key principles of environmental governance which challenged conventional notions of state sovereignty. The two key outputs were a Declaration and Statement of Principle and an Action Plan, the latter of which listed 109 agreed recommendations. Amongst the Stockholm Conference's most significant legacies were the following:

- Principle 21 confirmed that states retained full sovereign authority over resources located in their own territory but charged them with the responsibility to exploit them with regard to the environmental effect of this on other states.
- The concept of a 'common heritage of mankind' was agreed, whereby resources located outside of territorial borders (such as minerals on the bed of the high seas) should be considered as belonging to the international community collectively.
- The United Nations Environmental Programme (UNEP) was created, to nurture and institutionalize epistemic communities.
- Environmental questions were established firmly on the political agenda by prompting many governments to create new ministers and departments of the environment and greatly deepening and widening a global network of environmental pressure groups.

Common heritage of mankind

The 'common heritage of mankind' principle became more established after Stockholm but did not fully displace the notion of sovereign control over resources. In political practice both the sovereign authority and responsibility sides of Principle 21 have been enacted and two very different solutions to the Tragedy of the Commons parable attempted. Firstly, you can have informed collective management to regulate the use of the 'village green' for the benefit of all. Secondly, you can abandon the idea of common land and divide the 'green' up into individual holdings in the expectation that each plot holder would graze sustainably. Both types of solutions are evident in the development in the 1970s of international law for a 'commons' already subject to many centuries of contention – the high seas (seas outside of any state's jurisdiction). The Third United Nations Conference on the Law of the Sea (UNCLOS III) from 1973 to 1982, included an agreement that minerals on the bed of the high seas would be the property of a new International Seabed Authority. This form of collective management to sustain collective goods can, however, be contrasted with the encroachment on the tradition of the 'freedom of the seas' by the huge growth of waters claimed by states in the legitimization, at UNCLOS III, of 200-mile exclusive economic zones (EEZs). Although EEZs, on the one hand, could easily be accounted for by a conventional realist analysis of coastal states maximizing their power, the rationale offered for their creation was that fish stocks and other resources would be utilized more sustainably if under sovereign jurisdiction rather than subject to a 'free for all' type of governance.

Marine pollution

International political action on marine pollution soon followed UNCHE, and in 1973 the first International Convention for the Prevention of Pollution from Ships (MARPOL) was drafted, which for the first time set standards aimed at preventing accidents and criminalizing the deliberate discharge of oil and other pollutants from ships on the high seas. It took a spate of further tanker accidents in the late 1970s, however, for MARPOL to eventually receive enough ratifications to enter into force in 1983, after modification via a 1978 protocol (an added annex to the Convention).

The 1970s also saw the rise of international cooperation on curbing pollution between states sharing common stretches of water. A series of 'Regional Sea Programmes' emerged, such as the Mediterranean Action Plan and North Sea Convention, whilst many regimes already in operation for riparians (countries sharing a river), such as the world's oldest, the Central Commission for Navigation on the Rhine, began to take on environmental as well as navigational dimensions. UNEP became an important focus for epistemic communities on a range of environmental issues, and assumed responsibility for the stewardship of regimes for common seas, such as the Mediterranean and the North Sea. The study of epistemic communities was pioneered by Peter Haas in the 1980s; he defined the phenomenon as a 'network of professionals with recognized expertise and competence in a particular domain and an authoritative claim to policy-relevant knowledge' (Haas 1992: 3). Haas demonstrated that the creation of the sea conservation regime the Mediterranean Action Plan (MAP) was a consequence of a grouping of like-minded ecologists and marine scientists who gained access to national administrations and the secretariat of UNEP. In particular, North African governments overcame an initial ambivalence to a regime seemingly prioritizing pollution concerns over their development, and smacking of European neo-colonialism. The epistemic community established the principles that came to be accepted by Mediterranean state governments in formulating the norms and rules of the MAP regime, namely that 'Mediterranean currents and wind patterns transmit pollutants across national borders and that these pollutants interfere with other uses of the sea (such as recreation, tourism, fishing and navigation) thereby necessitating coordinated national control policies' (Haas 1989: 381–382).

Atmospheric pollution

In 1979 the Long Range Transboundary Air Pollution (LRTAP) agreement was signed up to by the US, Canada and most Western European states, establishing cuts across the board in sulfur dioxide and other industrial emissions. That it took so long to reach what was a modest agreement between friendly states is testimony to the challenges presented by environmental problems to those traditional determinants of government policy: sovereignty, self-sufficiency, the national interest and economic growth.

Biodiversity

Biodiversity first emerged as a term as recently as 1986, during a 'National Forum on Biodiversity' in the US, but the idea of seeking to maintain the variety of life forms on Earth pre-dates the age of international policy on environment and even the emergence of political ecology that followed in the wake of *Silent Spring*. Prior to the coining of the term, the IUCN had been established in 1948 and then took the lead in drafting the first international policy on biodiversity when it became apparent that the cross-border trading in certain endangered species was a key factor in the reductions of biological diversity becoming apparent from their collation of research. The 1973 Convention on the International Trade in Endangered Species (CITES) restricts the trading of goods derived from flora or fauna identified as being at risk of extinction, such as ivory and certain furs. Eighty states became party to this Convention when it came into force in 1975, and by 2013 it had 178 parties and laws criminalizing the trade in around 30,000 species.

From the 1970s the nature of the IWC was swept along by the ecocentric tide as many states abandoned whaling in the face of concerted pressure group campaigning and public pressure. Hence, in 1986, the IWC framed a moratorium which outlawed the hunting of all whale species apart from for scientific purposes.

The globalization of political ecology

Throughout the 1970s and early 1980s international environmental policy deepened in the developed world but did not significantly widen beyond there. States, principally from the developed capitalist world, became party to numerous new international laws and international regimes as well as developing existing legal instruments in the areas of conservation, pollution and resource management. In the 1980s, however, changes in both the physical and political climate led to closer relations between the First, Second and Third Worlds, and a start in the globalization of environmental politics.

Although transboundary pollution and the management of the global commons were, by the 1980s, firmly on the international political agenda, the majority of the harmful effects of environmental change seemed only to be felt locally and, as such, were of little concern to the wider international community. Domestic legislation in the developed world had banned the use of notoriously polluting chemicals like DDT and curbed the excesses of industrial emissions and waste disposal, leading to visible improvements in atmospheric quality and animal conservation. However, the emergence of evidence that seemingly remote problems, experienced primarily in the global South, had wider repercussions served to reframe some environmental issues and bring others to global political prominence.

Deforestation, seen for a number of years as a problem for forest-dwellers, human and otherwise, came to be cast in new light by the discovery of the 'carbon sink effect' – the result of trees absorbing atmospheric carbon dioxide. Carbon dioxide in the atmosphere above a certain level is poisonous to man and at a lesser level contributes to global warming. It has been estimated that the loss of trees in the world contributes more to global warming than the more frequently cited impact of transport (Stern 2006). The realization that the net loss of tropical rainforest could, ultimately, harm North American and European urban residents as well as Amazonian Amerindians helped bring this issue to the global political agenda. Similarly, seemingly localized issues such as desertification came to be understood as having repercussions beyond the most directly affected peoples, since the world's food supply could shrink due to the removal of once-fertile land from production. Additionally, the increased economic globalization of the world can bring external environmental problems into the domestic arena. Harmful organochlorine insecticides may have been virtually eliminated from use in developed countries by the 1980s but their continued use, promoted by Northern multinational corporations (MNCs) deprived of a domestic market, was seeing them return to their places of origin in imported foodstuffs in a 'Circle of Poison' effect (Weir & Schapiro 1981).

As well as seeing some environmental issues from a wider perspective, in the 1980s it began to become apparent that globalization in general was transforming all environmental issues. The vast majority of environmental problems are related in some way to the processes of economic development and growth, which have dominated how governments frame their policies both domestically and in the global marketplace. Industrialization and urbanization, the classic ingredients of development, put extra strain on a country's resources, whilst changing its pattern of land use and altering the balance between the human and natural environment. Increased industrial and agricultural production invariably brings more pollution as well as more raw materials, food and wealth. The fundamental paradox of how to reconcile economic growth with environmental concerns was apparent at Stockholm but shelved through the desire to demonstrate solidarity, but, by the 1980s, it could no longer be ignored. By then it had become clear that global environmental policy was being stymied because, although the developed world was coming to terms (albeit partially) with the need to put some limits on industrial 'progress', the global South would not compromise economic development since the stakes were so much higher. As Indian premier Indira Gandhi had announced at Stockholm in 1972, 'poverty is the worst pollution'.

Sustainable development

In an effort to get around the economic–environmental paradox, in 1987 the UN General Assembly authorized the establishment of a World Commission on Environment and Development (WCED), chaired by Norwegian Prime Minister Brundtland, which produced the report 'Our Common Future', identifying *sustainable development* as the solution. Sustainable development reconciled environmental and economic interests by framing them as interdependent. The global North would have to take the lead in implementing costly anti-pollution measures and recognize that the South would need more time to follow suit. To the South this was only fair since the North was responsible for most global pollution and had been able to develop without constraints being put on its industrialization. To the North this was a price worth paying as it was the only way to win support from LDCs who would eventually come to be major global polluters also.

Sustainable development is less pessimistic than the *Limits to Growth* thesis, which dominated environmental policy thinking in the 1970s, in that it does not consider economic growth to be anathema to avoiding pollution and the depletion of the Earth's resources. Economic growth, even for wealthy states, can be acceptable so long as it is at a level that can be sustained in the long run and not at the cost of degrading the environment. Hence, sustainable development is less obviously contradictory to the national interest instinct as it merely calls upon governments to be more rationally long-termist in their economic policy. The message is that rapid economic growth today may enrich the present generation but risks impoverishing or endangering future generations if resources are not utilized in a sustainable and responsible manner.

The Rio Summit

The Brundtland Report prompted the UN General Assembly, in 1989, to approve a follow-up conference in Stockholm in 20 years' time to flesh out the concept of sustainable development. As the title indicates, the 1992 UN Conference on the Environment and Development (UNCED), held in Rio de Janeiro, recognized the need to couple together the two issue areas, and was a much larger and more diverse gathering than in 1972. One hundred and seventy-two states were represented, most, at some stage, by their head of government, and some 1,400 pressure groups were also present at the myriad formal and informal meetings that characterized the conference. In contrast, at Stockholm only two heads of government and 134 pressure groups had attended. Although decision-making authority was reserved for government delegates, the pressure groups at Rio played a pivotal role in organizing the event and in the extensive lobbying of the decision-makers.

Amongst 27 general principles agreed to in the 'Rio Declaration' at the summit were two particularly important breakthroughs which served to clarify the meaning of sustainable development.

- Principle 7 identified the 'common but differentiated responsibilities' of developed and less-developed states in environmental protection. The global South was to be part of the process but the North would have to take the lead and incur most of the initial costs.
- Principle 15 acknowledged the legitimacy of the 'precautionary principle' in developing environmental policy. This asserts that a lack of absolute scientific certainty over the harmful side-effects of any form of economic activity widely believed to be environmentally damaging should not be used as an excuse to continue with it. This was an important agreement because issues of environmental change tend to be complex and subject to some level of scientific disagreement. In the face of this, excuses can more readily be found for ignoring environmental demands and choosing the short-term option in polluter's dilemma scenarios.

Like Stockholm, the Rio Summit did not instantly stimulate new international laws but, unlike its predecessor, it did explicitly set the signatory governments on a legislatory path. 'Agenda 21' of UNCED, making up some forty chapters, set out a programme of action for implementing sustainable development across a range of environmental issues. Issues debated in recent years but not yet subject to conventions, such as biodiversity, global warming, deforestation and desertification, were formally given approval for action. A Commission for Sustainable Development (CSD) was established to regularly review progress towards establishing and implementing the conventions that were to follow. In addition, a crucial tenet of sustainable development was realized in the creation of the Global Environmental Facility, a fund subsidized by developed countries, from which LDCs could draw in order to be able to implement agreements. Four specific legal instruments were initiated at Rio:

- *The UN Convention on Biological Diversity (CBD)* entered into force in 1993 and went far beyond the previous most significant regime in this area, CITES, by committing the parties to biannual conferences at which their progress in conserving biological diversity in their countries is opened to scrutiny.
- *The Forest Principles* agreement emerged when negotiations to establish a deforestation convention failed. What emerged instead was a weak, non-legally binding regime which, whilst proclaiming the virtues of sustainable forestry management, in effect gives the green light to states to continue deforestation, by asserting that forests are sovereign resources. A short-termist and selfish response to the collective goods problem had occurred. Effectively regulating deforestation was too much of an economic burden for most prolific 'logging' states to countenance and, despite knowledge of the 'carbon sink effect', was still not seen as sufficiently threatening to the global North for their governments to push harder for action.
- *The Convention to Combat Desertification* was a response to one of the most visible forms of environmental degradation in the world over recent decades, whereby deserts have grown in size at the expense of fertile lands surrounding them. Once land becomes arid in this way it is effectively lost forever in terms of its productive value and so can have food security implications for the local population and, to a limited extent, humanity at large. The Convention, established in 1994, sets out a code of practice for the management of semi-arid lands. The Convention was unusual in global environmental politics in that it was prompted by developing (rather than the industrialized) states. It was principally African states, affected by the spread of the Sahara and Kalahari deserts, who championed the inclusion of this issue in Article 21. The regime has evolved slowly since 1994 and, although it is now virtually global in scope, it lacks the legal rigour of many other global environmental regimes. The effects of desertification remain more localized than global and the level of political commitment has followed suit.
- *The Framework Convention on Climate Change (FCCC)* emerged following a build-up of concern at the implications of worldwide rises in temperature. An epistemic community had, for a few years, been voicing fears that global warming was not natural and was a potential danger, but without any conclusive scientific certainty. However, in the spirit of the precautionary principle the FCCC was signed at Rio and entered into force two years later. The Convention at this stage, however, was also a limited, non-binding agreement without any explicit commitments imposed on states. A rise in appreciation of such threats and recognition that the FCCC was inadequate as a means of countering them prompted a significant revamp of the Convention in the form of the 1997 Kyoto Protocol. The Kyoto Protocol enacted the principle of common but differentiated responsibilities by requiring developed countries to cut emissions of greenhouse gases by 5.2% from 1990 levels by 2012 without any initial commitment from LDCs. Penalties for non-compliance are also included in the regime, along with an imaginative means of meeting overall targets through 'carbon trading'. This idea, initiated in the US in the 1970s, as part of the LRTAP regime,

provides a market mechanism to get round the collective goods problem. Countries exceeding their emissions target can pay countries below their target to acquire their 'carbon credits'.

Ozone depletion

Hard epistemic community evidence was able to prompt perhaps the most influential international environmental regime some five years before the Rio Summit. In 1985 the British Antarctic Survey were able to prove conclusively what had been suspected by scientists for at least a decade – that the Earth's ozone layer had a hole in it. The ozone layer is a protective gaseous shell in the upper atmosphere which absorbs ultraviolet rays from the Sun before they reach the Earth's surface. This is a vital service for humanity (and other life forms) since ultraviolet radiation can kill in the form of skin cancer and other ailments.

The clear danger posed by the loss of this defensive shield prompted an unusually rapid international response. Within a few months of the British Antarctic Survey discovery the Vienna Convention on Protection of the Ozone Layer established a framework treaty, fleshed out two years later in the 1987 Montreal Protocol on Substances that Deplete the Ozone Layer. The 1987 Montreal Protocol saw 24 industrialized states bind themselves to an agreement for major cuts in the future use and emission of chlorofluorocarbons (CFCs) and some other chemicals known to be agents of ozone depletion. In the years since 1987 the regime has been strengthened by a series of amendments deepening the cuts to be made by states and widening its application to most of the world. This was achieved by the application of key sustainable development principles agreed on at Rio, with LDCs allowed to take a slower track towards phasing out CFCs than the developed states and a multilateral fund created to overcome the costs of implementing the agreements. The success of the regime can be proven by evidence that, within 20 years, the ozone layer had begun to repair itself (WMO/UNEP 2006).

In addition to the ozone regime and the four legal instruments initiated directly by UNCED, the rise of sustainable development prompted progress in other key areas of global environmental politics.

Persistent organic pollutants (POPs)

The 1992 Rio Summit was also the catalyst for significant global political action in the area of human health-threatening atmospheric pollution. In 1997 UNEP's Governing Council endorsed the opinion of the UNCED-born Intergovernmental Forum on Chemical Safety: that an international, binding treaty be set up to phase out the production and use of 12 POPs including DDT and several other organochlorine pesticides. The treaty was signed by 127 governments at a diplomatic conference in Stockholm in 2001, initiating a regime that will continue to consider adding new chemicals to the original 12 through a review committee. The production and use of the 12 outlawed chemicals had long ceased in most developed countries but their properties ensured that they remained a domestic hazard to their populations. The listed chemicals are all highly persistent, have a propensity to travel globally in the atmosphere through a continual process of evaporation and deposition, and frequently end up in human foodstuffs through the process of bioaccumulation. Hence, sterility, neural disorders and cancer in peoples of the developed world can be attributed to the use of POPs in other parts of the planet. The political significance of this is such that even President George W. Bush, already known as the 'Toxic Texan' for his administration's lack of enthusiasm for environmental concerns, initially declared the US to be a firm supporter of international political action on POPs.

Global environmental policy in the 21st century

The widening and deepening of international environmental policy in the 1980s and 1990s hit something of a crossroads in the new millennium, with some erosion of the global consensus that had been forged. The First and Third Worlds had been reconciled by the concept of sustainable development and the First and Second Worlds merged together by changing political circumstances but it was a division within the ranks of the First World that came to threaten global solidarity. The US, under George W. Bush, charted a new course in relation to global environmental policy, marked by a return to a military-focused, individualistic foreign policy with a non-collective strategy towards prisoner's dilemma situations. Again, a change in political mindset allied to a change in political circumstances can explain this shift in priorities on environmental issues. The 11 September 2001 attacks, allied to the rise of 'neo-conservative' thinking in the Bush administration, shifted national security policy towards a more traditional path, downplaying the importance of multilateral solutions to foreign policy problems and the more nuanced understanding of national interests evident in the 1990s when the Clinton–Gore administration gave a high profile to environmental concerns.

From 2001, the US backtracked on several commitments to principles and policies accepted by the Clinton administration at Rio. Most notably, the Bush government broke ranks and failed to ratify the Kyoto Protocol, despite the US having signed the framework treaty. The US government sidestepped the precautionary principle and common but differentiated responsibilities concept by citing the lack of scientific certainty over human-induced global warming and concerns over the lesser constraints imposed on LDCs. In addition, they admitted that the treaty is simply not in their 'national interest' because of the economic cost. Similarly, the US delegation at the negotiations of the Stockholm POPs Convention fought hard to ensure that the term 'precautionary principle' did not appear in the final text and declined to ratify a Convention for which they had previously shown enthusiasm.

The exasperation of the international community at the new US strategy became evident at the ten-year follow-up to Rio, the World Summit on Sustainable Development (WSSD) in Johannesburg in 2002. The conference is best remembered for the widespread booing and heckling which greeted the addresses of US Foreign Minister Colin Powell, who had been sent to Johannesburg in place of his President, who was mindful of the hostile reception he would receive. Johannesburg represented the third environmental 'mega-conference' but was more low-key than its predecessor. It was also noticeably more anthropocentric and more focused on development than on the environment. Little progress was made in advancing the agenda on biodiversity established at Rio and, although climate change policy was kept alive, it was not developed in any significant way. New proposals to agree on a framework for phasing in the use of renewable energy sources and improving global South access to developed world food markets were side-stepped but some new goals were set, in line with the recently agreed-upon Millennium Development Goals (MDGs). Under the MDGs, 2015 was set as a target date for the realization of two new human security aims with an environmental dimension: halving the number of people who lack access to clean water and achieving sustainability in global fishing.

Despite US obstruction, global environmental politics in the 21st century has continued to evolve and served to demonstrate the limitations of hegemonic power politics in the contemporary world. Fellow recalcitrant states, like Russia and Australia, were gradually converted to the Kyoto Protocol through pressure by the society of states and non-state actors. Epistemic consensus and global civil society have given such momentum to global environmental politics that it can survive being pushed off the international agenda by displays of national interest against the common good. That the US was out of step with the world became clear when their spokesmen were again booed and, most noticeably, yelled at to 'get out of the way' by the Papua New Guinea delegation at a 2007 UN Climate Change Conference in Bali. The succession of Obama as President saw a return to multilateralism in US foreign policy, but the concurrent economic downturn has kept the US on the fringe of global environmental policy and has threatened the global consensus on sustainable development, with many other countries backtracking on commitments to reduce carbon dioxide emissions and other advances achieved in the 1990s and at the turn of the century (see Box 1.5).

Box 1.5 Timeline of political ecology

1961 World Wildlife Fund (WWF) founded.
1962 Rachel Carson's book *Silent Spring* released.
1967 *Torrey Canyon* oil tanker disaster.
1968 UN Biosphere Conference.
1969 UN Population Fund established.
1971 Greenpeace established.
1972 UN Conference on the Human Environment in Stockholm.
1973 UN Conference on the Law of the Sea initiates process leading to ratification of the UN Convention in 1994.
1973 First International Convention for the Protection of Pollution from Ships (MARPOL).
1973 Convention on the Trade in Endangered Species (CITES).
1974 First UN Population Conference in Bucharest.
1979 Long Range Transboundary Air Pollution (LRTAP) agreement.
1984 Bhopal chemical plant disaster.
1985 Vienna Convention on Protection of the Ozone Layer.
1986 Chernobyl nuclear power plant disaster.
1987 Montreal Protocol to the Vienna Convention.
1987 World Commission on Environment and Development set up by the UN.
1989 Basel Convention on the Control of the Transboundary Movements of Hazardous Wastes and their Disposal.
1991 Iraq sabotages Kuwaiti oil fields in retreat from invasion.
1992 UN Conference on the Environment and Development (Rio Earth Summit).
1992 International Framework Convention on Climate Change (IFCCC).
1993 UN Convention on Biological Diversity.
1994 Convention to Combat Desertification.
1994 Cairo UN Population Conference.
1997 Kyoto Protocol to the IFCCC.
2001 Stockholm Conference on Persistent Organic Pollutants.
2002 UN's World Summit on Sustainable Development in Johannesburg.

Green thinking

Does the politicization and globalization of environmental concerns that has occurred over the past half century really amount to a 'Green Revolution'? Whilst ecocentric politics has undoubtedly made inroads, anthropocentricism is deeply ingrained in contemporary life. However, the current predominant mindset which separates human from nature has not always existed, and is not even a universal feature of thought if we consider the historical and contemporary significance of credos such as paganism, pantheism, Buddhism and

Confucianism. It is principally in the industrialized, modernized world that the natural environment has been constructed and 'naturalized' as an external resource amenable to instrumental use. Nature is viewed, in much political thought in the Western and Communist 'worlds', almost exclusively from a human-use perspective. This anthropocentricism operates paradigmatically – almost unquestioned and unacknowledged. Hence, a jolt of paradigm-shifting proportions may be needed to shake a comfortable human arrogance vis-à-vis the natural environment and our current paradigm of instrumental use. Where significant political progress has occurred, such as with tackling ozone depletion, it has usually been prompted by some sense of crisis.

To what extent, then, are we experiencing an ecological crisis? It is probably fair to say that such a realization has not, as yet, fully dawned on the majority (as opposed to there being a realization of problems amenable to human agency). Most people – and particularly those most powerful in IR – are operating within a set of parameters which are so obvious that they need not be articulated, but merely serve as background reference points through which they can make judgements about how to live their everyday lives. Droughts, 'sinking' islands, an increased number of tropical storms, nuclear accidents, oil spills, species extinctions – these anomalies have not been enough (yet) to deflect us significantly from this course.

For some there is more to a Green Revolution than some measure of ecocentricism in politics. Andrew Dobson argues that most environmentalism is not a separate ideology but a way of 'thinking green' that permits a tack-on of environmental concerns to other pre-existing ideologies. Ecologism, on the other hand, is said to be fundamentally different in its ecocentric basis and therefore a separate ideology in and of itself – a truly radical challenge to industrial society. For Dobson, the 'Limits to Growth' era was revolutionary in its fundamental challenge to economic orthodoxy but green policies before and since then fall short of this (Dobson 1995). Jonathon Porritt suggests that ecology is a 'super ideology' since it is fundamentally different to all other ideologies, be they capitalist or socialist, which he considers represent differing strands of 'industrialism' (Porritt 1984). For some, then, the sporadic implementation of ecocentric policies since the 1960s is not a Green Revolution, and it is only radical ecology that provides a fundamental, revolutionary challenge to anthropocentricism. Such thinking began to emerge as a political current in the 1970s and has taken a number of directions.

Deep Green Ecology, pioneered in 1973 by Norwegian thinker Arne Næss, built on the principle of 'biospherical egalitarianism', assigning equal value to all life forms (or, at least, sentientbeings) (Naess 1973). The animal liberation movement and radical non-governmental organizations (NGOs) like Earth First! have been influenced by this philosophy, which views the 'shallow green' mere consideration of ecocentric values as insufficient and calls for liberal notions of human rights to be extended to the non-human world. Australian philosopher Peter Singer, for example, has controversially and provocatively suggested that, since it has no perception of its existence; 'the life of a newborn [baby] is of less value than the life of a pig, dog or a chimpanzee' (Singer 1979: 123).

Eco-feminism, coined as a term by Françoise d'Eaubonne and developed by several theorists including Rosemary Radford Ruether and Vandana Shiva, views environmental failures as rooted in patriarchy since masculinist attitudes lead to nature being treated as separate and instrumental to humanity. Hence, it is reasoned that only once male dominance of society has ended can the environment be saved (d'Eaubonne 1974, Ruether 1975, Shiva 1988).

Eco-anarchism, most associated with Murray Bookchin, and similar variants of eco-socialism see the innate aggressiveness of capitalism as the root cause of environmental problems and see its overthrow as the key to ecological progress (Bookchin 1971).

The Gaia hypothesis launched in the 1970s by British scientist James Lovelock takes the core ecological notion of holism a stage further, by seeing life on Earth not only as intrinsically interconnected but actually part of a single organism. Despite the titular allusion to paganism (Gaia is the Ancient Greek 'Earth Mother') the approach is science-based but also political in advocating whatever action is best for the Earth as a whole (Lovelock 1991). Hence, Gaia is not necessarily anti-industrialist, and Lovelock surprised many by emerging as a supporter of nuclear energy in the 2000s on the basis that this was a source of power less damaging than burning fossil fuels to the planet's chief threat: climate change.

Environmental thinking thus comes in many shades of green and finds expression in the political mainstream (such as the presence of the Green Party in government in Germany) and its most radical fringes. Whether you think the greening of mainstream political parties and domestic politics in Western countries is evidence of a successful revolution towards universalizing ecocentricism or a dangerous counter-revolution undermining such values by the industrialized establishment probably depends on where you sit on this continuum.

Conclusion

Myriad international regimes have emerged since the high-water mark of environmental governance at Rio in 1992, but global policy today stands in stark contrast to domestic environmental laws in Western European and North American states, which are marked by precautionary consumer standards and ecocentric measures. Where successful international environmental regimes have emerged it has usually been where a clear and unambiguous human health threat is apparent. It is far rarer for the value of environmental protection to be prioritized at the global level than at the domestic level. Global politics is such that international agreements, to which governments remain the signatories in spite of the growing role of pressure groups, are still somewhat reliant on a perception of utilitarian gain. Although it is becoming ever more blurred, a 'high politics–low politics' distinction is still evident in international politics. Governments are still prone to take blinkered decisions informed by short-term economic interest in the face of epistemic consensus and longer-term utilitarian calculations of 'national interest', as has most clearly been seen in the US's stance on climate change.

In the face of this, the short-term and easier response is to play the polluter in the polluter's dilemma. However, only through the holistic management of environmental threats can the prisoner's dilemma scenario be escaped and states be freed to act in their and their people's real interests rather than being compelled by domestic political constraints to conserve harmful human practices. This requires restrictions on governments' and companies' freedom to manoeuvre, which may also be unpopular with the domestic audience. It will require stopping your country's fishermen from fishing at will, or importing your food from abroad rather than paying your own farmers a premium to provide you with your crops and meat, and imposing costs on unsustainable fuel consumption. Seeing the bigger picture in this way is difficult in a politically compartmentalized world but it is slowly happening through the growth of a global civil society and epistemic communities persuading governments and citizens that it is in their own interests to think global. The world as a political arena is evolving beyond a purely state system but politics still tends to be reactive to crises and driven by governmental interests. A global civil society is developing to broaden the traditional agenda but it does not, as yet, have the power to lobby governments and rally citizens to the same extent as seen in the democracies of the global North. From the perspective of governments worrying about an apparently imminent terrorist threat, economic downturn or the next election, global environmental issues often do not get placed near the top of their political 'in trays'.

However, it need not be assumed that short-termist, statecentric and purely anthropocentric thinking on the natural environment in global politics will be inevitable forever. Though faith in human reason to resolve any problems as they emerge has remained strong, along with a continued belief that, overall, the benefits outweigh the weaknesses, in the contemporary period a growing awareness of environmental problems has developed, arising from the sheer intensity of human impacts upon the natural world. We have begun, in other words, to identify various problems associated with the scale of historical development and continuing industrial growth. These problems are providing severe challenges and, to a certain extent, might be said, because of uncertainty associated with them, to be shaking faith in human ingenuity. Ecocentric values are not absent in international politics and have sometimes surfaced in unlikely circumstances. For example, even during the Cold War the US and USSR managed to reach agreement on a regime conserving polar bears (Young 1989). Political ecology might be a minority ideology in today's world but most democratic states have political systems that have evolved over time to act in the public and non-human good, even where this incurs some individual or commercial cost. US environmental policy is robust enough to restrain business interests for the good of the environment and society even though its government has not always behaved this way on the global stage. Whether or not treating environmental problems as matters of security helps in advancing solutions at the international level is considered in the next chapter.

Key points

- Environmental change started to become politicized in the 1960s with emergence of non-human-focused *ecocentric* policies tackling pollution in some Western states.
- Environmental politics internationalized from the 1970s due to fears of cross-border pollution and the consequences of overpopulation in the global South.
- The rise of the global-scale problems of ozone depletion and climate change necessitated a globalization of environmental policies, bringing on board the global South and leading to the development of the idea of sustainable development within the UN system.

Note

1 A wider term than 'international treaty' that includes less formalized agreements.

Recommended reading

Chasek, P.S., Downie, D.L. & Brown, J.L. (2013) *Global Environmental Politics* (6th edition), Boulder, CO: Westview.

Dodds, F., Strauss, M. & Strong, M. (2012) *Only One Earth. The Long Road via Rio to Sustainable Development*, London and New York: Routledge.

Kutting, G. (ed.) (2011) *Global Environmental Politics. Concepts, Theories and Case Studies*, London and New York: Routledge.

2 The securitization of global environmental policy

Climate change is the most severe problem we are facing today, more serious even than the threat of terrorism.

David King, UK Government Chief Scientist 2004 (BBC 2004)

Whilst the end of the Cold War and the rise of sustainable development can be seen to have globalized environmental politics, the scale of political urgency ascribed to such problems varies considerably across both International Relations and international relations (i.e. academia and 'real-world' politics). For some thinkers and statesmen many issues of environmental change are not merely political matters, they are matters of security. This broader approach to conceptualizing global security gained ground in the 1990s when the ending of the Cold War seemed, to many statesmen, academics and members of the general public, to herald a new era of international politics. In this 'New World Order' the threat of global nuclear Armageddon had subsided, allowing previously marginalized issues, such as environmental degradation, to emerge from the shadow of superpower rivalry and register on the international political agenda.

Environmental securitization in theory

Whilst it was the post-Cold War optimism of the early 1990s that encouraged the 'securitization' (i.e. treatment as matters of urgency) of environmental problems, such an approach was being articulated as far back as 1983, when Richard H. Ullman defined a threat to security as:

> *... an action or sequence of events that (1) threatens drastically and over a relatively brief span of time to degrade the quality of life for the inhabitants of a state or (2) threatens significantly to narrow the range of policy choices available to a government of a state, or to private, nongovernmental entities (persons, groups, corporations) within the state.*
>
> (Ullman 1983: 133)

Amongst a range of issues, Ullman argued that states needed to take on board the security implications of demographic pressures and resource depletion alongside more traditional concerns focused on military threats from other countries.

The increased recognition of the threats posed by ozone depletion and climate change in the 1980s lent themselves well to such an approach, but some IR scholars had also been seeking to 'securitize' the environment back in the early 1970s on the basis of resource depletion.

The world-renowned Liberal and arch-critic of Realism, Richard Falk, in *This Endangered Planet,* 1971, articulated that 'We need to revamp our entire concept of "national security" and "economic growth" if we are to solve the problems of environmental decay' (Falk 1971: 185). In a similar vein, Margaret and Harold Sprout's *Toward a Politics of the Planet Earth* trumpeted the need for IR to focus on global as opposed to national security because of the scale of threat posed by resource scarcity and overpopulation (Sprout & Sprout 1971). Going back further still, Fairfield Osborn, in 1948, opined that resource scarcity could be a cause of war nearly half a century before this notion came to be popularized: '… one of the principal causes of the aggressive attitudes of individual nations and of much of the present discord among groups of nations is traceable to diminishing productive land and to increasing population pressures' (Osborn 1948: 200–201). Written before the Cold War had fully begun, this highlights just how that conflict came to dominate the security agenda in the second half of the 20th century.

State securitization

Towards the end of the Cold War such thinking began to permeate the political mainstream and even find the ear of a superpower, through an influential article by US diplomat Jessica Mathews, which highlighted the need for states to give proper concern to the newly apparent threats posed by environmental problems. In a 1989 article for the conservative and influential journal *Foreign Affairs*, Mathews, a former member of the US government's National Security Council, followed Ullman's line of reasoning in a more state-centred analysis. In addition to calling for greater consideration in foreign policy of the effects of resource depletion on the political stability of poorer states, Mathews argued that environmental problems with global ramifications, such as ozone depletion, climate change and deforestation, should become issues of state security concern because they were the underlying cause of regional instability (Mathews 1989). Though less heralded, four years earlier an article by legendary US diplomat George Kennan, in the same journal, had argued that the world faced 'two unprecedented and supreme dangers', which were nuclear war and 'the devastating effect of modern industrialization and overpopulation on the world's natural resources' (Kennan 1985: 216).

From these seeds sown by Kennan and Mathews in the 1980s a new strand of IR enquiry emerged in the post-Cold War New World Order era, positing that increased competition for resources would increasingly be a cause of war, particularly for LDCs. Canadian academic Thomas Homer-Dixon was at the forefront of this area of study, explored in Chapter 4 (Homer-Dixon 1994). Around the same time that the Homer-Dixon thesis was emerging, increased competition for that most precious of all resources, water, heralded a similar and significant 'water wars' literature, highlighting how arid regions, such as the Middle East, could increasingly use access to water as a weapon (Starr 1991, Bulloch & Darwish 1993).

The rise of more expansive interpretations of security in the early 1990s found many critics amongst Realists, who were not shaken from their belief in maintaining a narrower focus on what constitutes security studies by the ending of the Cold War. Stephen M. Walt has forcefully argued this case in stating that: 'security studies may be defined as the study of the threat, use and control of military force' (Walt 1991: 212). Walt and the traditionalists fear that widening the definition of security risks will render the concept redundant by making it too all-encompassing and diluting the important task of analysing military threats and inter-state conflict. Underlying this fear is the belief of many Realists that military threats had actually become more rather than less apparent in a post-Cold War world devoid of that traditional guarantor of state security: the military balance of power. This 'anti-New World Order' thesis was epitomized by John Mearsheimer's lament in 1990 that 'we will soon miss' the Cold War (Mearsheimer 1990).

Some traditionalists consider the demise of the Cold War as signalling a need for security studies to go 'back to basics' rather than broaden its base, since international politics, shorn of the nuclear balance of power imposed by the two superpowers, would need to rediscover the lost arts of multilateral diplomacy, conflict resolution, fighting limited wars and conventional defence (Chapman 1992). The persistence of territorial disputes in places such as Palestine and Kashmir, the resurgence of ethnic conflict in parts of Central Africa and Eastern Europe, and the emergence of a systematic global Islamist terror threat seemed, to many, to bear this out.

Although there is a case to be made that military threats in the 21st century are as apparent as ever, and maybe even greater than during the Cold War, proponents of extending the reach of security beyond national and military parameters contend that they are not the only threats that face states, people and the world as a whole. Indeed, they never have been. Throughout history people have been killed by things other than soldiers and weapons, and states have been weakened or destroyed by things other than military conflict. Ozone depletion, climate change and pollution – alongside other non-military issues like the AIDS crisis and international narcotics trade – come into this category.

Although viewed as unwelcome by traditionalists, such as Walt and Mearsheimer, this 'widening' of security beyond purely military threats did not really undermine the Realist logic of conventional security studies. The focus was still on the state system and seeing relationships between states as governed by power. 'Widening' was simply a case of extending the range of factors which affect state power. An argument for a more profound extension of security than simply tacking on some non-military issues to the range of threats to states, then emerged through the 1990s in a new approach that came to be characterized as the 'Copenhagen School', after the Copenhagen Peace Research Institute. Barry Buzan trailblazed this approach in the early 1990s (Buzan 1991b) but it crystallized later in the decade, when he teamed up with Ole Wæver and Jaap de Wilde to produce the groundbreaking work *On Security*:

> *Threats and vulnerabilities can arise in many different areas, military and non-military, but to count as security issues they have to meet strictly defined criteria that distinguish them from the normal run of the merely political. They have to be staged as existential threats to a referent object by a securitizing actor who thereby generates endorsement of emergency measures beyond rules that would otherwise bind.*
>
> (Buzan et al. 1998: 5)

Hence, the Copenhagen School went further than the 'wideners' in two ways. Firstly, they facilitated the consideration of non-military issues, even if they had no military dimension, so long as they represented 'existential threats'. Secondly, the approach also partially deepened the meaning of security by arguing that issues can be considered matters of security even if they are not threatening states beyond the confines of military and trade affairs:

> *When environmental issues threaten the conditions of human existence on a large scale, as in the case of countries vulnerable to extensive inundation from modest rises in sea level, then casting such issues in security terms is appropriate.*
>
> (Buzan 1991a: 450)

Human securitization

Going beyond the Copenhagen School in extending the domain of security studies is the 'deepening' approach led by Liberals (Pluralists), Critical Theorists and Social Constructivists.

'Deepeners' embrace the concept of 'human security' and argue that the chief *referent object* of security should not be the state or certain sub-state groups, such as stateless nations (highlighted in the Copenhagen School's idea of 'societal security'), but the individual people who comprise these institutions/groups. Richard Falk, for example, considers that security ought to be defined as 'the negation of insecurity as it is *specifically* experienced by individuals and groups in concrete situations' (Falk 1995: 147). This is a significant expansion of widening which, as Falk describes it, 'still conceives of security largely from the heights of elite assessment, at best allowing the select advisor to deliver a more enlightened message to the ear of the prince' (Falk 1995: 146). Norman Myers similarly opined that

> *... security applies most at the level of the citizen. It amounts to human well-being; not only protection from harm and injury, but access to water, food, shelter, health, employment, and other basic requisites that are due every person on earth.*
>
> (Myers 1996: 31)

Most significantly in terms of its popularization, human security came to be adopted by the United Nations Development Programme (UNDP) in the 1990s and informed its thinking on sustainable development and human development.

> *The concept of security must change – from an exclusive stress on national security to a much greater stress on people's security, from security through armaments to security through human development, from territorial to food, employment and environmental security.*
>
> (UNDP 1993)

The clearest case of how environmental change can become an issue of human security is in the threat posed by climate change. The Earth's average temperature has risen consistently over the last century and it is now almost universally accepted that this is more than a natural development and likely to accelerate if not responded to. The central cause of global warming is an exacerbation of the natural phenomenon of the 'greenhouse effect', caused by increased industrial emissions. Increased releases of carbon dioxide and methane over the years, principally through the burning of fossil fuels, have served to exaggerate the natural tendency of the atmosphere to trap a certain amount of infrared sunlight after it is reflected from the Earth's surface. The implications of this are various but include increased desertification, a rising of sea levels due to the polar ice caps melting and more extreme weather events, all carrying significant threats to human life in various forms. The human cost of ozone depletion – in contributing to global warming and heightening the threat posed by skin cancer – also became apparent towards the close of the Cold War and was key in propelling the issue of environmental change much higher up the international political agenda than seen before and, probably, since.

A clear and direct source of human insecurity emanating from environmental change also comes in the form of natural disasters. The 2004 Indian Ocean tsunami claimed over 235,000 lives in a short space of time, whilst the worst ever disaster was the flooding of the Huang Ho river system in China in 1931, which accounted for over three million lives. Natural disasters are often caused by human-induced environmental change. Deforestation exacerbates global warming and can be seen as a causal factor behind natural disasters such as mudslides down once naturally secure hillsides (Humphreys 2006: 1). Human vulnerability to natural hazards has increased in recent years due principally to population growth and movement in the global South. Natural disasters also often occur for rational, natural reasons related to environmental change. Tropical cyclones, for example, can be understood as 'safety valves' which dissipate the build-up of excessive heat in the ocean or atmosphere (Ingleton 1999). This has led many climatologists to suggest that the increased prominence of the El Niño effect in the 1990s, associated with more frequent cyclones and other extreme weather phenomena, could be linked to global warming (Mazza 1998, Trenberth 1998). The 2003 and 2010 heatwaves in France and Russia, unprecedented in history, provided even clearer evidence of a correlation between global warming and natural disasters.

Other issues of environmental change have come to be framed in anthropocentric or human security terms. In 2008 the Economics of Ecosystems and Biodiversity (TEEB), a think tank funded by the EU and German government, gave a new spin to a classically ecocentric issue somewhat put in the shade by the politics of climate change. The TEEB review posited that global GDP would be likely to decline by 7% by 2050 if greater commitment to preserving fish stocks, forests and other species needed by humanity was not forthcoming (Sukhdev 2008). Released against a backdrop of unprecedented rises in global food and energy prices, this seemed a particularly pertinent warning.

For human (and, related, critical) security advocates the root of the problem with the traditional approaches to security politics is what the Critical Theorist Richard Wyn-Jones describes as the 'fetishization of the state' (Wyn-Jones 1999: Chapter 4). This tendency in International Relations is not resolved by the Copenhagen School approach. The latter accepts the idea that non-military issues can be securitized and that the referent object of this can be something other than a state, but maintains the logic that only the state can be the *securitizing actor* (i.e. decide whether the issue is acted upon as a matter of urgency). Hence statecentricism is maintained, if in a subtler form. The practical limitation with this is that not only are the traditional security agents of the state (i.e. the army, externally, and police, internally) often inadequate for dealing with security problems affecting the people of that state, they are often a chief cause of those problems. Buzan accepts that states can be the source of threats rather than protection for individual people but considers that this only applies to certain types of states. 'Strong states' co-existing in 'mature anarchy', which have increasingly become the norm through democratization and the development of international human rights law, can be relied upon to secure individuals (Buzan 1991b: 98–111). Hence, Buzan and Wæver are neo-Realist wideners, albeit of a much more refined form than those who had preceded them.

It should be noted, though, that human security itself is a contested concept, with more and less expansive versions having come to be employed in both academic and political discourse. Wider human security is often characterized as combining 'freedom from want' and 'freedom from fear' (from the UNDP description of the concept), in that it considers any issues with direct or indirect life-threatening consequences for individuals to be matters of security. Concerns among some advocates of an individual-focused approach to security that 'existing definitions of human security tend to be extraordinarily expansive and vague' (Paris 2001: 88) led them to favour a more restricted version based purely on 'freedom from fear'. This narrow version of human security concentrates on direct and deliberate violent threats, excluding less directly human-caused forms of insecurity such as diseases, disasters and environmental degradation. Neil MacFarlane and Yuen Foong Khong, for example, suggest that many environmental and other non-military issues 'fail the "organized harm" test – tsunami waves, traffic accidents, the spread of viruses and crop failure are usually not organized by individuals to do their victims in' (MacFarlane & Foong Khong 2006: 275).

The consideration of environmental issues as matters of security has gathered momentum academically but remains highly contested. This is not only a consequence of environmental issues being given different levels of priority by different ideological perspectives but also a question of appropriateness. Those resisting securitization are not only the environmental sceptics but also environmentalists alarmed at the apparent coupling of the issue area with the politics of national interest and militarism. Lothar Brock, for example, warns that '[t]he securitization of the environment may help to perpetuate the historical practise of justifying the use of force' or 'it may create a sense of urgency that diminishes the space for discourse' (Brock 1997: 20). Although this is not what critical and human security (freedom from want) approaches are advocating, the problem arises because 'security' remains a contentious and loaded political term.

Environmental security in practice

It is clear that designating an issue a matter of security is not just a theoretical question but carries 'real-world' significance. The traditional, Realist way of framing security presupposes that military issues (and certain economic issues for neo-Realists) are security issues and, as such, must be prioritized by governments above other 'low politics' issues, important though these might be. The logic informing this stance is that human needs and ecocentric concerns cannot be addressed unless the country is secure in the first place. Whilst Realism is undoubtedly apparent in real-world ir, some securitization of environmental issues has been evident in corridors of power, mirroring the academic dialectic previously discussed.

National environmental securitization

Many states have taken a widened approach to security since the 1990s. The US Clinton administration made extensive use of academic advisers and a burgeoning literature on the 'national security' imperative of taking on board non-military concerns now that the Soviet threat had receded. The impact of this was made explicit in the 1994 'National Security Strategy', the US's annual foreign policy manifesto:

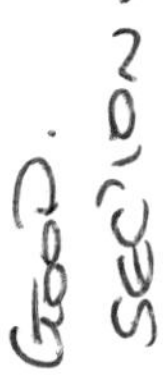

> *Not all security risks are military in nature. Transnational phenomena such as terrorism, narcotics trafficking, environmental degradation, rapid population growth and refugee flows also have security implications for both present and long term American policy … an emerging class of transnational environmental issues are increasingly affecting international stability and consequently present new challenges to U.S. strategy …*
>
> (USA 1994: 1)

Clinton's widening approach to security owed much to his special adviser Strobe Talbott who, in turn, was inspired by Joseph Nye's concept of 'soft power' (Nye 1990). Soft power for Nye denotes the non-military dimension of state power, particularly as rooted in the world of information. For US governments, being 'on top' of information on global issues was useful not only for better comprehending problems like ozone depletion but for advancing the US's standing in the world. The resource wars literature was particularly influential on the Clinton administration in the early 1990s, convincing them that environmental degradation represented a potential source of military insecurity. Homer-Dixon is known to have been invited to brief Vice President Al Gore and the State Department on several occasions (Floyd 2010: 75–76). In 1993 a new government position in the Defense Department was created: with the Deputy Under Secretary for Environmental Security, while the Environmental Task Force was set up as part of Washington's intelligence network.

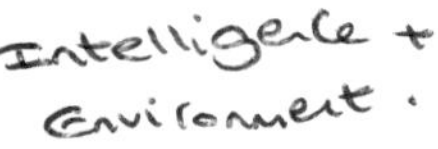

Whilst it was the lifting of the Cold War shadow that permitted some securitization of the environment, such concerns had been periodically aired in international diplomacy in the 1970s and 1980s. Although the 1972 Stockholm Conference did not securitize environmental change and put it at the top of an international political agenda that was still, in spite of détente, dominated by the Cold War and impending global recession, some 'high politics' was witnessed at the conference. Most notably, Swedish Prime Minister Olof Palme used the event to denounce the use of herbicides in war as 'ecocide'. Palme made no explicit reference to the recent American use of the infamous jungle defoliant Agent Orange in Vietnam, but the implied criticism gravely offended to the Nixon administration, which responded by withdrawing the US ambassador from Stockholm. Full diplomatic relations between the two countries were suspended for over a year (January 1973–May 1974).

A less predictable environmental champion than Sweden was the Soviet Union, who chose to play the 'green card' on occasion during the Cold War. In the mid-1970s the Soviets were able to exploit the backlash against the US over Agent Orange and become the unlikely pioneer of international legislation proscribing deliberate environmental destruction in warfare (see Chapter 5). A decade later, a changing Soviet Union under Gorbachev used environmental cooperation in the Arctic as an olive leaf as part of his strategy of accommodation with the West, most notably in his Murmansk address of 1987 (Gorbachev 1987).

In the new Western-oriented Russia that emerged after the end of the Cold War, and the exit of Gorbachev, Moscow, rhetorically at least, appeared to become a full convert to the cause of securitizing the environment. In 1994 the Government Commission on Environmental Security adopted a declaration stating that 'Environmental security is the protection of the natural environment and vital interests of citizens, society, the state from internal and external impacts, adverse processes and trends in development that threaten human health, biodiversity and sustainable functioning of ecosystems, and survival of humankind. Environmental security is an integral part of Russia's national security' (Russia 1996: 55). Similarly, post-Communist Hungary made environmental security an explicitly expressed foreign policy concern in the 1990s.

> *Problems appearing in the context of environmental protection and threats to civilisation spreading across borders constitute some of the largest-scale challenges to mankind. The protection of our natural resources, our natural habitat and values, as well as the preservation of the environmental balance is putting an ever-increasing burden on our societies. Such global problems as the destruction of* rain forests, *damages to the ozone layer, the greenhouse effect and the increase of air, water and soil pollution constitute a threat to our entire Earth.*
>
> (Hungary 1998)

More predictable converts to making the environment the stuff of high politics have since emerged in North America and Northern Europe. Finland's Security and Defence Policy of 2004 recognizes the interlinkages between the environment and security in terms of the extent to which resource scarcity and degradation, allied to unequal access, have increased the likelihood of conflict (Finland 2004). Canada's foreign policy declares one of six core goals to be '[understanding] the interaction among the social, economic, and environment pillars of sustainable development, and of how human security and human rights relate to sustainable development' (Canada 2002). The UK followed a similar path to that of the US over a decade earlier when, in 2008, climate change was referred to in the UK's inaugural National Security Strategy and, a year later, a new role, of climate and energy security envoy, was created. The

Netherlands' 2006 Foreign Policy Agenda also specifically acknowledges the role that environmental degradation plays in threatening global security. The Dutch additionally, though, go beyond national security widening in declaring one of the eight goals of this policy to be 'to protect and improve the environment' (Netherlands 2006).

This ecocentric turn of making the environment the referent object of security has also been advanced in a different political form in recent years outside of the Western World, as part of the 'new left' wave in Latin America in the late 2000s. The critical stance on Western capitalism and focus on indigenous people that marks this political movement has found expression in the empowerment of nature. In 2008 Ecuador's new constitution declared that nature had the 'right to exist, persist, maintain and regenerate its vital cycles, structure, functions and its processes in evolution', and mandates the government to take 'precaution and restriction measures in all the activities that can lead to the extinction of species, the destruction of the ecosystems or the permanent alteration of the natural cycles' (Ecuador 2008). Whilst many countries have cited environmental protection in their constitutions, none have done so in such unambiguously ecocentric terms. This 'rights of nature' approach has also been followed by the Morales government in Bolivia, where the 'Law of Mother Earth' has defended the right of nature 'to not be affected by mega-infrastructure and development projects that affect the balance of ecosystems and the local inhabitant communities' (Bolivia 2011). For both countries this idea of environmental rights has come from the twin impact of indigenous people's empowerment and a legacy of environmental pollution. The rights of long-marginalized indigenous Americans (of which Morales is one) has become an important domestic political concern aided by greater international discourse on this realm of politics promoted within the UN system by the Trustee Council, Working Group on Indigenous Populations, Human Rights Council, Human Rights Council and the International Labour Organization (particularly ILO Convention 169). In addition, the long-standing problem of pollution from oil in Ecuador and tin in Bolivia has heightened environmental concerns beyond those witnessed in most developing countries.

Some states have even securitized the environment in the most explicit and traditional way by sending in troops to tackle ecological disasters. In 2009 Bangladesh deployed armed forces to lead the national response to Cyclone Aila. More significantly, Brazil established the National Environmental Security Force to combat deforestation in 2012, employing a combination of armed forces and police to tackle the huge problem of illegal logging in the Amazon rainforest.

Whilst it could be argued that none of the aforementioned political announcements or initiatives really make environmental change the number one diplomatic priority, it is clearly so for some states affected by climate change. For low-lying island states the prospect of a rise in the level of the oceans is a human and state security threat of the utmost gravity: 'We want the islands of Tuvalu, our nation, to exist permanently forever and not to be submerged underwater merely due to the selfishness and greed of the industrialised world' (Saufatu Sopoanga, Prime Minister of Tuvalu, at the 2002 World Summit on Sustainable Development).

Such governments have sought to emphasize the urgency of international action in diplomatic forums and in media-friendly stunts such as holding a cabinet meeting of the Maldives government underwater in 2009. However, realistic as to the likelihood of their pleas being acted upon, the governments of the Maldives and Kiribati have already made plans to shift their entire populations to other locations.

Intergovernmental environmental securitization

On an international level we can again see the notion of securitizing the environment begin to emerge in the early 1970s, before properly flourishing in the aftermath of the Cold War.

The United Nations (UN)

Swedish Prime Minister Olof Palme (see Box 2.1) was, again, pivotal in securitizing the environment at the United Nations. At the UN Commission on Disarmament and Security in 1982, Palme called on member states to move beyond considering collective security and embrace 'common security', bringing into focus threats emanating from overpopulation, environmental degradation and resource scarcity (Palme 1982). Two years earlier Palme was part of the Independent Commission on International Development Issues (ICIDI) which gave rhetorical support for securitizing the environment, stating that 'few threats to peace and survival of the human community are greater than those posed by the prospects of cumulative and irreversible degradation of the biosphere on which human life depends' (ICIDI 1980).

The onset of the Second Cold War and the creation of the Washington Consensus limited the advance of this environmental security agenda in the 1980s but the mantle was picked up again in the revival of multilateralism from the 1990s, and has found expression from several elements of the UN system. In 2004 the United Nations Secretary-General's High-Level Panel on Threats, Challenges, and Change produced a report, endorsed by many governments at the Millennium Review Summit the following year, setting out a new vision of collective security, reminiscent of Palme's idea of 'common security', that addresses six clusters of threats with which the world must be concerned now and in coming decades, including poverty, infectious disease and environmental degradation (UN 2004).

In 2007, Foreign Minister Margaret Beckett used the UK's presidency of the UN Security Council to push through, with some resistance from other members, the first discussion on an overtly environmental topic, reasoning that climate change carried implications that 'reach to the very heart of the security agenda' (Beckett 2007). A major influence on this British stance was the Stern Report of the previous year, compiled by a British economist on behalf of the UK

Box 2.1 Olof Palme

The world-renowned Swedish Social Democrat politician was twice Prime Minister between 1969 and his assassination in 1986. Domestically, Palme moved the Social Democrats to the left, leading to their defeat in the 1976 elections, which broke the party's 40-year hold on power. Internationally, he was a passionate supporter of decolonization and conducted a firmly non-aligned foreign policy that was, at times, highly critical of both the US and USSR. His fierce condemnation of apartheid led to suspicions that the South Africans may have had a role in his murder (although this has not been proven and the assassin has yet to be caught in spite of 130 individuals claiming responsibility).

Palme was also an environmentalist and a pivotal figure at the 1972 Stockholm Conference, due particularly to his articulation of the idea of the global commons:

> *The air we breathe is not the property of any one nation – we share it. The big oceans are not divided by national frontiers – they are our common property. What is asked of us is not to relinquish our national sovereignty but to use it to further the common good. It is to abide by certain agreed international rules in order to safeguard our common property, to leave something for us and future generations to share.*

Palme, though, was also a somewhat divisive figure domestically. He was not universally liked in the Green movement since he supported nuclear energy as a less polluting source of power than coal or gas. This, though, is a position to which many renowned environmentalists – such as Lovelock – have subsequently converted.

government, which provided an economic security rationale for prioritizing action on climate change. Stern calculated the permanent cost of non-action on climate change as amounting to, at the very least, 5% of global GDP. Set against this, the costs of effective action to curb climate change would cost around 1% of global GDP per year (Stern 2006).

In 2009 the UN General Assembly also took up this theme with a resolution, Climate Change and its Possible Security Implications, calling on all UN agencies to prioritize climate change drafted by the government of low-lying Nauru and unanimously adopted (A64/350).

Linking several elements of the UN system with other IGOs (intergovernmental organizations) is the Environment and Security Initiative (ENVSEC), a partnership of six international organizations – the Organization for Security and Co-operation in Europe (OSCE), Regional Environment Centre for Central and Eastern Europe (REC), United Nations Development Programme (UNDP), United Nations Economic Commission for Europe (UNECE), United Nations Environment Programme (UNEP), and the North Atlantic Treaty Organization (NATO). ENVSEC seeks to promote the idea that the best way to address environmental and security concerns is through prevention and through fostering international dialogue and cooperation, both intergovernmentally and in collaboration with civil society and research institutes. human security approaches, highlighting the necessity of tackling vulnerability to environmental problems, have also been strongly advocated within the UN system by UNDP, secretary-generals and the Human Security Unit of the Office for the Coordination of Humanitarian Affairs within the Secretariat.

NATO

NATO's involvement in ENVSEC and long-standing own involvement in disaster relief represents the clearest intergovernmental expression of the environment becoming the stuff of security:

> *Based on a broad definition of security that recognizes the importance of political, economic, social and environmental factors, NATO is addressing security challenges emanating from the environment. This includes extreme weather conditions, depletion of natural resources, pollution and so on – factors that can ultimately lead to disasters, regional tensions and violence.*
>
> (NATO 2013)

Going beyond rhetorical 'greening', part of the post-Cold War restructuring of NATO saw, in 1998, the establishment of a unit at its Brussels headquarters to utilize military resources to protect citizens from natural rather than military threats. The Euro-Atlantic Disaster Response Coordination Centre (EADRCC) is a tiny cog in the NATO machine but its creation epitomized not only a widening of NATO's notion of security but also a widening of its sphere of operations beyond the defence of NATO member states. The EADRCC is, in fact, coordinated by the Euro Atlantic Partnership Council (EAPC), in which the 28 NATO states are linked to 22 non-NATO partner states, and which emerged from a proposal by one of those partners, Russia. NATO has had a role in disaster relief dating back to 1953, when North Sea floods prompted the initiation of a 'Policy on Cooperation for Disaster Assistance in Peacetime', but the EADRCC has enhanced this role significantly.

The EADRCC helps coordinate international relief programmes responding to natural or industrial disasters occurring in any of the 50 EAPC states.[1] To avoid any duplication of roles with the UN, a permanent Office for the Coordination of Humanitarian Affairs (OCHA)

Liaison Officer is based at the centre alongside EAPC state representatives and permanent NATO staff. Hence, the EADRCC represents a means of assisting UN relief when disaster occurs in a EAPC state, or of coordinating assistance within the EAPC area if the UN-OCHA is distracted elsewhere. In the first year of its operation, for example, the EADRCC helped coordinate an international response to problems caused by flooding in Ukraine at a time when the UN-OCHA was preoccupied with the devastations being wreaked on Central America by Hurricane Mitch. Whenever UN-OHCA is active in an EAPC state, the EADRCC cooperates closely with it and supplies material support, such as vehicles and medical facilities, or logistical support, such as facilitating the waiving of visa restrictions for relief workers. A Euro-Atlantic Disaster Response Unit (EADRU), comprising both military and civilian experts from the EAPC countries, has been despatched by the EADRCC to many prominent recent disasters within the EAPC area, such as to the US at the time of Hurricane Katrina and, most notably, outside of this area, to Pakistan in 2005 when the government requested help with earthquake relief operations.

NATO have additionally looked to address the resource war dimension of environmental security. Through the Science for Peace and Security (SPS) Programme, NATO have sought to help external Partner and Mediterranean Dialogue countries deal with the issue of environmental security through promoting scientific cooperation. For example, a joint NATO-OSCE Science for Peace project has seen scientists carry out monthly exercises to monitor contamination by trace elements, radionuclides and organic matter in several rivers in the Southern Caucasus region, which has been beset by conflict in recent years.

A key spur to the creation of EARDCC was the earthquake disaster in their member states of Turkey and Greece at the end of the 1990s. Disasters and pollution can sometimes provide a basis for intergovernmental cooperation that can thrive even in the absence of cordial political relations. A special edition of the Cambridge Review of International Affairs in 2000 dedicated to 'disaster diplomacy' demonstrated how security communities can emerge between neighbouring states facing a common threat, in which information is shared to minimize a common risk. The warming of relations between Greece and Turkey after earthquakes ravaged both countries in 1999 is a classic case of two governments and societies overcoming cultural and political differences when faced with a common foe. At one level this was a case of basic human empathy at the societal level triumphing over realpolitik and then being reciprocated, but James Ker-Lindsay demonstrates that the case is more revealing than that. The level of cooperation between the two governments, which surprised the rest of the world, was a result of an agreement reached at a meeting of foreign ministers a few months before the earthquake (Ker-Lindsay 2000). Turkish Foreign Minister Cem and his Greek counterpart Papandreou had met principally to discuss the regional military security implications of the crisis going on at that time in Kosovo. Sharing a common concern about the possible spread of conflict to other parts of the Balkans and the flow of refugees from Yugoslavia which was already happening, the two traditional foes engaged in uncharacteristically cordial dialogue. One dimension of this, barely noticed at the time, was to offer reciprocal help in the instance of a deadly earthquake striking either country. Relations between the two governments remain somewhat frosty on certain issues but have certainly continued to be better than for many years prior to 1999, and societal contact has increased since the disasters. This represents a clear case of political spillover, with sectoral cooperation promoting wider cooperation between governments and bringing people closer together through realizing their common interests.

A similar scenario was witnessed in 2001 when the destruction wreaked by earthquakes in India prompted offers of relief from Pakistan and the first contact between the two countries' leaders for two years. However, while such occurrences may assist in improving relations, security communities require more systematic levels of cooperation and information-sharing to be able to develop.

Elsewhere in the world we can also see some seeds of environmental securitization in intergovernmental forums. The success of the EADRCC prompted the emergence of a similar regional international mechanism for the Association of South East Asian Nations (ASEAN), the Agreement on Disaster Management and Emergency Response (AADMER), which entered into force in 2009. ASEAN have also worked on developing strategies for adaptation to the effects of climate change, such as the Asian Cities Networked Resilience Programme. The Gulf Cooperation Council (GCC) similarly held the first in a series of Arabian Gulf Environmental Security Conferences in Muscat, Oman, in 2000, initiating a process of planning for disaster response in conjunction with the US military.

Conclusions

The scale of the human security threat posed by environmental change is difficult to quantify but it is undoubtedly significant and, to a large extent, avoidable, given the political will. Probably the most 'securitized' issues of environmental change, at different times over the past 40 years, have been resource scarcity due to population growth, ozone depletion and global warming. The fact that the first of these 'crises' never really materialized and the second one was partially averted by reasonably effective global political action has served to reinforce the notion that contemporary threats posed by environmental change, such as global warming, are potential rather than actual threats and perhaps exaggerated. As a result, despite gradually becoming more of a feature on the global political agenda, environmental issues have tended not to be treated as matters of urgency by most governments, with the exception of those unambiguously threatened, such as the low-lying island states.

Security threats emanating from the 'environment' present humanity with three key political dilemmas.

1 The threats are usually less clear-cut and direct than the other types of threat considered in this study. They are, as Gwyn Prins describes, 'threats without enemies' (Prins 2002: 107). The threat posed by issues like climate change may be profound but they are, in the main, still perceived as longer-term creeping emergencies rather than imminent disasters and attacks.
2 Countering the threats is usually costly and requires a significant compromising of economic interests.
3 The threats often can only be countered by globally coordinated political action.

Some domestic political systems have evolved to a position where the first and second of the aforementioned dilemmas can be overcome. Pressure group advocacy and government learning have gradually led to long-termist policies being developed, mitigating against threats to both human and non-human state residents. Environmental policies in Western Europe and North America have seen economic interests compromised to limit uncertain threats posed to human health and to wildlife. The third dilemma is, of course, beyond governments acting in isolation but is slowly coming to be addressed by an evolving global *epistemic community* and polity. Transnational pressure groups and scientific communities are simultaneously pushing governments to rethink the first and second dilemmas and provide the means for achieving the third. Central to this process is the slow but inexorable realization by governments that environmental threats are 'real' and the apparent 'national interest' may not always serve their citizens' interests. Political dilemmas can always be resolved when this is understood. The three dilemmas presented here are not, in fact, unique to environmental politics. For most states very similar compromises have been made in the name of military security, since military threats are usually not immediate and require great expense and international diplomatic cooperation to deter.

Environmental problems are the most holistic and long term of all political challenges. Globalization is blurring the distinction between domestic and international politics and encouraging more proactive rather than reactive strategies in managing issues like war, terrorism and human rights, but this shift in thinking is most acutely needed in tackling environmental problems. Securitization represents a way of seeking to push environmental issues up the international political agenda, alongside these more traditional concerns, but, as is explored in the following chapters, the established way of doing this – by invoking national security measures – can risk narrowly defining the problems and deploying knee-jerk and inappropriate solutions. Unless they are seen to represent an imminent and unambiguous crisis – as with ozone depletion – environmental threats are not well served by a sovereign state system set up to operate in terms of national interests rather than human or global security.

Key points

- The idea of going beyond politicization and 'securitizing' the environment emerged academically in the 1970s and then developed after the Cold War had ended in the 1990s.
- For some it was considered appropriate that certain types of environmental problems should be dealt with as matters of 'state security'. For others this was inadequate for dealing with such problems, which necessitate a fundamentally different, human security approach. In a third school of thought on the matter, the idea of securitizing the environment is not appropriate at all.
- Some governments and intergovernmental organizations also came to declare environmental concerns to be security matters from the 1990s.
- The long-termist and global nature of major environmental threats do not always lend themselves well to traditional national security approaches.

Note

1 EADRCC operations have been dominated by natural disasters, particularly floods.

Recommended reading

Dalby, S. (2009) *Security and Environmental Change*, Cambridge: Polity.

Floyd, R. & Mathew, R. (2013) *Environmental Security. Approaches and Issues*, London and New York: Routledge.

Part 2

The environment and national security

3 Breeding to death?

The threat posed by overpopulation

A growing problem?

Box 3.1 The world's 7-billionth person

Danica May Camacho was born in Manila, the Philippines, on 31 October 2011. She almost certainly was not number 7 billion, since precisely calculating this is impossible, but the family naturally treasured this title and enjoyed the notoriety of being selected by the UN to symbolize the latest global demographic milestone (the 6-billionth was a boy from Bosnia Herzegovina in 1999).

Despite this, the fact that, on a global scale this milestone was something to celebrate, was reflected upon after the event when Dr Tayag from the Philippine Department of Health commented 'Seven billion is a number we should think about deeply .... We should really focus on the question of whether there will be food, clean water, shelter, education and a decent life for every child,' he said. 'If the answer is "no", it would be better for people to look at easing this population explosion.'

Source: AP 2011

Can you have too many people? Barring occasional 'blips', such as the Black Death of the 14th century which killed 75 million of the world's people, the Earth's population has always been expanding. The first well-known expression of concern that this phenomenon could lead to the world becoming overpopulated came at the end of the 18th century with the publication of 'An Essay on the Principle of Population' by the British economist Thomas Malthus. Malthus reasoned that the Earth's 'carrying capacity' of resources – particularly food – would soon be exceeded, for '[T]he power of population is indefinitely greater than the power in the earth to produce subsistence for man' (Malthus 1798: 23–24).

A Malthusian doomsday never came, but not because his line of argument was flawed. The world's population and resource consumption grew at a rate greater than ever in history in the following century but so did its carrying capacity as a result of the Industrial Revolution, which served to improve crop yields and resource extraction. Localized hunger and famine have persisted since then due to political failings but, on a global scale, overpopulation has never occurred and there remains enough food and fuel for everyone on Earth today. Malthus' central concern, though, is still valid today, with many reasoning that the planet's carrying capacity is now at around 9 billion, a figure likely to be reached around the middle of this century on current projections. Can technology and human ingenuity again be relied upon to feed the world's people and avoid its degradation or is this a dangerous assumption? This, in many ways, is the quintessential question of environmental politics.

As well as improving productivity and food yields the Industrial Revolution had two other major consequences for the question of population: (i) modernizing health care so that people live longer and the death rate is lowered; (ii) modernizing some societies so that smaller families became the norm, thus lowering the birth rate. The balance between the birth rate and death rate determines population growth (in any given country migration also comes into play). If the two balance out and the number of people entering the world roughly matches those exiting it you have 'replacement-level fertility' and the population remains stable. This was broadly the case in pre-industrial Europe when life expectancy was around 38 (mainly due to a much higher infant mortality rate than today) and the average family featured six children. Today Europe again has replacement-level fertility but with a life expectancy of 80 (for the EU) and 1.6 children per family (EC 2013). In between these eras of demographic stability, though, the European population surged, the early stages of which had alerted Malthus.

The population of the world at the time of Malthus was under 1 billion and by the 1920s had doubled. The rate of increase then accelerated so that it took only 13 years to go from the 5-billionth to 6-billionth person, in 1999, and then a further 12 years until the birth of Danica May. In the developed world, though, population growth has broadly been stable since the 1970s and around 99% of growth today is located in the global South. The standard explanation for this comes from what is known as demographic transition theory, which links population growth to economic development. Whilst developed countries tend to have replacement-level fertility (albeit with exceptions such as the UK and US whose populations are still growing due to immigration, and Germany and Italy whose populations have begun to shrink due to their birth rates lowering further) LDCs tend to have higher birth rates than death rates. This is because increasing life expectancy and lowering infant mortality tends to occur more rapidly than the transition to having smaller families. Medical advances can create rapid health improvements but the social phenomenon of modernization tends to be a slower – and maybe not an inevitable – development. Most developing countries have undergone huge medical advances over the past 70 years but this has often not been accompanied by comparable social change and the adoption of Western-style 'nuclear families'. Despite bearing the brunt of diseases like HIV/AIDS, malaria and tuberculosis the global South has – in comparable terms – actually advanced more than the global North since the 1940s. World life expectancy (at birth) in the second half of the 20th century increased from 46.5 to 64.3, an increase of 38%. Whilst some of this can be attributed to economic growth, great improvements have occurred in parts of the world where economic development and modernization have not significantly advanced. African life expectancy has increased by 36% (from 37.8 to 51.4) whilst US–Canadian life expectancy has increased by 11% (from 69 to 76.9). The highest growths have been in Asia, where both economic and health development has been significant (41.3 to 66.3% and 61% respectively) (WHO 1999). Public health interventions, however, are the major explanation for longer life. In a major study to evaluate the reasons for reduced mortality in the 20th century, Samuel Preston estimated that, contrary to popular assumption, economic development accounted for only 15–20% of the global improvement in life expectancy between the 1930s and the 1960s. Overwhelmingly, this improvement was attributable to better public and professional knowledge with regard to disease prevention and cure (Preston 1975). Subsequent studies by the World Bank (1993) and WHO (1999) have corroborated this finding. Advancements in antibiotics, insecticides and international medical assistance greatly accelerated at the close of the Second World War and have transformed health care, even though much remains to be done in places such as Sub-Saharan Africa. In Sri Lanka in 1946 the death rate – a figure which normally fluctuates by fractions of a percentage – fell by around a third (Karunaratne 1959, Harrison 1978). The reason was a successful anti-malarial campaign led by an international team of medics using the new 'wonder chemical', DDT. Sri Lankan society though, did not suddenly transform in 1946 and this extreme example is illustrative of the bigger picture. Much of the global South has followed the pattern set by the global North in terms of experiencing a fall in death rate due to medical advances but not then replicated the fall in birth rate due to social change. This is because the medical advancement has not necessarily been in line with the countries' economic development. As in the Sri Lankan example, most of the positive health impacts have been exogenous, a consequence of the application of technological advances from outside of the country rather than the country changing in the way that Europe did in the 19th and early 20th centuries. Consequently, the social changes that occurred in industrializing Europe have not all occurred. In particular, the tendency to have fewer children through the use of contraception to avoid 'family overpopulation' and have more room in the house and money in the bank has not arisen in the global South. In countries with much more limited welfare systems, health-care resources and pensions, children will continue to be viewed more as a family resource than a drain on those resources since they represent a future investment. Children will eventually run the family business and look after their parents when they get old.

Hence, much of the developing world still has a growing population, has not progressed through the stages of the demographic transition theory and has the death rate of 20th-century Europe but not the birth rate. Even in cases where developing countries have acted to lower the birth rate, population growth can remain a reality as a consequence of 'population momentum'. Because of their relatively high birth rates, developing countries tend to have a much higher proportion of young people than developed countries, meaning that there are more reproductively active citizens per head. Hence in India, despite some stringent government policies to promote contraception and sterilization to couples, which have seen the birth rate fall significantly since the 1970s, the population is still rising since there are simply so many reproductively active couples. It will take some time until replacement-level fertility is 'achieved' as has occurred in China, which India is likely to overtake as the world's most populous country in the next few decades. The same, though, cannot be said of much of the global South, and hence the world's population is projected to grow to at least nine billion by 2050. In addition, it should be noted that in India and China their governments have had to be particularly strident in pursuing replacement-level fertility as societal norms have continued to favour larger families in spite of economic incentives and some stigmatization of couples choosing to have more than one offspring. Thus, we see the paradox of overpopulation and an illustration of the tragedy of the commons notion highlighted in Chapter 1. A high birth rate at a national level is viewed as a problem but, at a household level, as a source of security.

The globalization and securitization of overpopulation

The neo-Malthusians

In a globalization of the prisoner's dilemma and Tragedy of the Commons paradoxes, global overpopulation became a major international political concern in the late 1960s and early 1970s, more through anthropocentric fear in the North than compassion for the South or ecocentricism. Garrett Hardin's application of the Tragedy of the Commons was the first high-profile neo-Malthusian call for action to relinquish 'the freedom to breed' (Hardin 1968: 1248) and many others followed. A provocative argument from prominent American economists the Paddock brothers, for example, went as far as to argue that India and other countries prone to famine had only themselves to blame and should be left to suffer for the good of the world. Overpopulation, added to endemic poor government, meant that, for some states, food aid was a waste of time and that they should be considered a 'can't be saved' group and ignored by the US and other benefactors. 'Waste not the food on the "can't be saved" and the "walking wounded". Send it to those nations which, having it, can buttress their own resources, their own efforts, and fight through to survival' (Paddock & Paddock 1967: 229). In a similar vein, Garrett Hardin supplemented his Tragedy of the Commons parable by formulating another analogy, likening a situation where there is an insufficient number of lifeboats in the sea after a shipping disaster to states in a world where food supplies will eventually be used up as a result of population growth. Hardin's thesis argued for the application of 'lifeboat ethics' to combat this, which posited that international action to tackle famine was folly as wealthy countries would risk sinking their own 'lifeboats' in doing so. Better to let the overcrowded 'lifeboats' of the Third World sink than ensure everyone drowns (Hardin 1996).

The most high-profile of the new-Malthusians was US biologist Paul Ehrlich whose *The Population Bomb* surpassed *Silent Spring* as the world's biggest-selling environmental book. *The Population Bomb* again used dramatic language and metaphors in the cause of securitizing overpopulation: '[W]e can no longer afford merely to treat the symptoms of the cancer of population growth: the cancer itself must be cut out … The battle to feed all of humanity is over' (Ehrlich 1968: xi). In a subsequent article Ehrlich predicted that 'by 1985 enough millions will have died to reduce the Earth's population by some acceptable level, like 1.5 billion people' (Ehrlich 1969: 28). This message reached even the populist levels of a Johnny Carson US television chat show, where Ehrlich infamously declared that 'I would take even money that England will not exist in the year 2000', an assertion he then repeated to an English audience in a speech the following year (Dixon 1971: 606).

Neo-Malthusian concerns came to influence the White House and, subsequently, the UN. In 1969 President Nixon declared in a speech that 'it is our belief that the United Nations, its specialized agencies, and other international bodies should take the leadership in responding to world population growth' (Nixon 1969). A year after the release of *The Population Bomb*, the UN established a programme specifically to encourage population control in 1969, the Fund for Population Activities (UNFPA) (later renamed the UN Population Fund but retaining the original acronym). The US, together with environmentally pioneering Sweden, were the key architects of this. This was not the start of UN action on overpopulation as there had been, previously, two World Population Conferences, at Rome in 1954 and at Belgrade in 1965, but these had been low-profile, technical events with no real political outcomes. The first high-profile World Population Conference was the third, at Bucharest in 1974. The Bucharest Conference was not a harmonious affair, with the three-way geopolitical division of the world very evident. The First World pushed for action on birth control but a recently emboldened Third World was prepared to stand up against neo-imperialist meddling in their affairs. Hence, the Brazilian delegate at Bucharest declared that 'Brazil will be able to absorb the foreseeable demographic increments … growth is even necessary for economic development and for national security' (Almeida 1974). The Second World also did not share the West's demographic anxieties, since the Soviet Union considered itself underpopulated and, whilst the Chinese were by now pursuing birth control strategies, they saw this as a sovereign, domestic concern and not an international one. Non-aligned, developing and consciously overpopulated India, though, expressed a common view to that of the First World, drawing on demographic transition theory, that 'development is the best contraceptive' (Singh 1974); this subsequently became the slogan by which the event is remembered. Only the Vatican, opposed in principle to contraception, abstained from signing the World Population Plan of Action, which was approved by 137 states and which emphasized the centrality of pursuing economic development by avoiding overpopulation and encouraging the creation of national – rather than international – birth control programmes.

The Fourth World Population Conference at Mexico City in 1984 was more consensual and pragmatic than the third. The global South were less vocal since the high point of Third World solidarity had by this time passed, and the neo-liberal Washington Consensus turn in development policy – emphasizing privatization and export-led growth over international assistance – was in full swing. In addition, many global South countries had followed the Indian line and come to acknowledge that population growth was counter to their primary interest of development. Whilst the Plan of Action from Bucharest was reaffirmed, the Mexico City Conference went back to basics with a renewed emphasis on birth control or what could be characterized as 'contraception is the best contraceptive'! The Mexico Conference, though, was not entirely consensual. At the event, the Reagan administration announced the 'Mexico City Policy' of withdrawing funding for any international programmes that it considered to be encouraging abortions in the name of population control. This was a continuation of a policy heralded in 1976 when the US ceased contributing to the UNFPA on these grounds. The US position on this has periodically shifted since then, with Republican administrations renewing the Reagan position only for it to be repealed under Democratic presidencies. The Republican position was not purely a reflection of the power of the pro-life lobby in Washington but also of the fact that neo-Malthusian anxieties had subsided and population control was no longer perceived in national security terms.

Just as Malthus' doomsday scenario never came to pass, as the Industrial Revolution increased humanity's capacity to utilize resources and feed itself, neo-Malthusian fears were also averted by the Green Revolution, which greatly increased food production in the global South through the utilization of intensive agricultural technology and techniques (such as the use of organochlorine pesticides). The demand for food has continued to rise in the less-developed world and natural disasters continue to blight many of the same countries, creating food shortages, but most contemporary analysts of famine emphasize distributive factors in their explanations of particular cases. Modern governments can insure against future crop shortages by stockpiling reserves of food and protecting the price of agricultural products (Sen 1981).

International political action on population control hence lessened in prominence from the 1980s, when it had become apparent to some Northern governments that growth in the South did not greatly affect their countries and through concerns in civil society and some governments that promoting birth control in global South countries could have human rights implications by encouraging abortions, coerced sterilizations and compromising the reproductive rights of women. To some, the neo-Malthusians, and environmentalists in general, came to be seen as overly pessimistic doomsayers who failed to appreciate humanity's ingenuity in surmounting problems; in consequence a countermovement, the Cornucopians, emerged (see Box 3.2).

Julian Simon and the Cornucopians reasoned that questions of 'carrying capacity' were outmoded since modern economics was too sophisticated to be reduced to a simple supply-and-demand calculation of people versus resources. Their view is that history shows that technological advances can increase the supply and this can happen again. A case in point is the development of genetically modified crops – plants bioengineered (sometimes using genetic material from insects) to make them resistant to pests. This technology has been

Box 3.2 End of the world? Wanna bet on it?

In 1980 Paul Ehrlich and his arch-critic, the economist Julian Simon, agreed to move their academic enmity, until then played out in academic journals, to a new, more populist level by having a wager on the future of the world.

Simon bet Ehrlich that the price of five metals of his choice (of which the remaining reserves in the world were known) would fall over the next decade in spite of population growth, thus disproving the notion that the Earth's resources were going to be put under increasing strain with more people consuming more resources and prices rising as a result. Ehrlich bought $1,000 worth of five metals and they agreed to settle the bet according the price of those metals in 1990, taking account of inflation.

Simon won the bet and Ehrlich was obliged to pay him just over $576. As is the case in economics, numerous factors can explain changes in price and Ehrlich did not consider that this outcome proved population growth not to be a drain on resources. Simon, however, felt vindicated in his Cornucopian belief in human ingenuity and in people *being* a resource rather than a drain on resources.

embraced in the US but so far resisted in Europe, where thinking is more informed by the precautionary principle and fearful as to the environmental consequences of 'messing with nature'. In addition, Cornucopians point out that not all economic activity is about utilizing resources since ideas and services make money as well as manufacturing:

> *It is your mind that matters economically, as much or more than your mouth or hands. In the long run, the most important economic effect of population size and growth is the contribution of additional people to our stock of useful knowledge. And this contribution is large enough in the long run to overcome all the costs of population growth.*
>
> (Simon 1996: 367)

A third school of thought, alongside the neo-Malthusians and Cornucopians, emerged from the late 1980s, as gendered analysis came to have more influence on the academic and real world of politics. Frances Moore Lappé and Rachel Schurman's *Taking Population Seriously* reasoned that the key to reducing the birth rate was empowering women with rights, education and reproductive choices:

> *the powerlessness of the poor often leaves them little option but large families … far-reaching social changes have empowered people, especially women, and provided alternative sources of income, security, and status to child bearing.*
>
> (Lappé & Schurman 1988: 3)

This message of female empowerment was also held by an empowered women's global social movement in the early 1980s, which had demonstrated how traditional development policy often increased the marginalization of women owing to an emphasis on male - employment in new export-focused industries. Women's reproductive rights were also seen as threatened by the overzealous promotion of family planning, such as China's promotion of a one-child policy and mass sterilization campaigns in India.

A further gender dimension of the kinds of population control policies followed in China and India is that it tends to be girls rather than boys who are the victims of the curbs. Mary Anne

Warren first coined the term 'gendercide' to highlight the scale of female-specific abortions and infanticide (Warren 1985). The general preference for male heirs in most societies is exacerbated in countries where overpopulation has prompted government measures to restrict the number of children per family. Though the scale of this phenomenon is uncertain, and the ethics of killing unborn infants unproblematic for many, it is clear that hundreds of thousands of female lives are terminated every year as a result. Baby girls in a number of countries are murdered soon after birth, usually by starvation or wilful neglect when ill, whilst ultrasound scans of pregnant women also make gender-based abortions increasingly common. In China, where families with more than one child are strongly 'discouraged', the 2002 population census revealed a sex imbalance of 116 males to every 100 females. The disparity was as high as 135–100 on the island of Hainan (Gittings 2002). The Chinese government's alarm at the social effects of such an imbalance prompted them to restrict the availability of ultrasound scans. Similarly, the 2011 census in India, where government policy combating overpopulation also encourages single offspring, revealed that the country had 7.1 million fewer girls under the age of seven than boys, mainly due to gender-specific abortions.

Awareness of the gender consequences of promoting birth control ensured that the empowerment of women perspective came to inform the Fifth World Population Conference at Cairo in 1994. As well as reflecting a new focus on women's rights and 'gender-neutral' development, this indicated that the Lappé and Schurman thesis had been taken on board for pragmatic, functional reasons. There was, by now, widespread recognition that empowered women, able to take up careers as an alternative to starting families at a young age, tend to have fewer children.

Box 3.3 Cairo Programme of Action 1994

A total of 179 states pledged to a 20-year Action Plan featuring the following aims:

- Greatly improve female literacy and education.
- Make family planning available in all public health outlets by 2015.
- Reduce infant and maternal mortality.
- Promote economic opportunities for women.
- Promote women's social and legal rights.

The Cairo Conference has been followed up by low-key +5 and +10 meetings in 1999 and 2003 but it is notable that there has not been a Sixth World Population Conference, not even in 2013 at the close of the period of the Action Plan. This is indicative of how overpopulation has slipped down the international political agenda. Population control in international policy has become somewhat politically incorrect due both to alarm at the over-zealous promotion of birth control in countries like China and sensitivity to accusations of neo-colonial meddling. The national security imperative of population control, apparent in the late 1960s, has gone and the issue has been 'desecuritized' to a more routine development/foreign aid concern. Green civil societies have also had to tread more carefully, as epitomized by the pressure group Population Concern choosing to change their name to the far vaguer Interact Worldwide.

The debate that refuses to die

Despite slipping down the agenda, overpopulation has far from vanished as an international political concern. Many neo-Malthusian concerns are still apparent, if in less apocalyptic forms than previously articulated.

Development

The Brazilian position at Bucharest in 1974 is unlikely to be supported since developing countries recognize that more people to feed and protect represents a strain on a pre-modern economy. The setting of development targets in the Millennium Development Goals has provided a clear illustration of how population growth can stifle economic progress. In Sub-Saharan Africa progress has been made in terms of targets such as improving the number of people being lifted out of poverty and having access to clean water, but this has been undermined by the fact that there are far more people to be lifted out of poverty or to be provided with clean water than when the measurements begun.

Migration

The movement of people away from overpopulated to underpopulated areas is a natural and age-old phenomenon but does not sit easily in the sovereign state system. Whilst the countries of the global North may not feel as threatened by population growth in the global South as they did in the 1960s and 1970s, the prospect of mass movements of people heading north, legally or illegally, will often be a source of societal anxiety and remain politically unpopular.

Localized food insecurity

Whilst the Earth's carrying capacity argument is less stark than it appeared to many in the 1960s and 1970s, and there is, for now, still enough food for everyone (in theory at least), localized food shortages and food price rises have increased over recent years and have had knock-on political effects beyond the region directly affected. There is an increasing phenomenon of 'land grab' whereby croplands in the global South are converted to growing biofuels rather than food for domestic consumption, or are sold off to Western or Chinese investors for a quick profit. This risks shrinking the global food supply and creating more localized shortages and political discontent. One estimate suggests that, in the 2000s, over 200 million hectares (eight times the size of the UK) were sold or leased externally (Anseeuw et al. 2011). It should be remembered that food insecurity provided the backdrop for the initiation of the multifaceted 'Arab Spring' revolts in Tunisia in 2010, when a market trader forced out of business and operating an unlicensed store set himself on fire in protest at police brutality.

War

Such instances of heightened resource scarcity may even become a cause of more extreme political instability, in the form of war. This concern has attracted increasing concern and is addressed in the next chapter.

Environmental degradation

Population pressure can be viewed as a contributory factor behind all of the issues of environmental change considered in this volume. The sheer existence of more people increases the probability of there being more pressure placed on biodiversity, pollution, desertification, deforestation and climate change. Again, though, there is a danger of oversimplification in seeing people and resources as the two ends of a see-saw. Blaming overpopulation overlooks the fact that most of the growth in demand for food and resources comes from rising consumption in the global North rather than rising populations in Africa, Asia and Latin America. Nevertheless, there must be some correlation between the world's people and the resources they utilize.

Conclusions

The Green Revolution may have saved the world (or, at least, some of it) but has it also served to give us a false sense of security and blinded us with science? Human ingenuity has proved its worth but there is a danger that this can lead to complacency in addressing environmental questions. The Cornucopians came to be a major influence on a new breed of climate-change deniers and environmental scepticism in general, burying their heads in the world's rapidly expanding sands. Winning the wager with Ehrlich does not invalidate all of the neo-Malthusian concerns nor validate all of the Cornucopians' arguments. Ehrlich's hyperbole makes him an easy target but many of Simon's assertions sound equally foolish today. In *The Ultimate Resource* Simon actually argues that 'Our energy supply is non-finite, and oil is an important example' (Simon 1981: 49), and goes on to deny that deforestation and desertification are occurring. This neatly illustrates the dangers of hubris in politics. Whilst the extent of the world's oil reserves remain uncertain, the notion that the world has a limitless supply of a substance that takes millions of years to form is about as flawed as an argument can be. Population is an emotive subject that has tended to polarize opinion. Thinking has swung to extremes and so hampered a reasoned appraisal of the implications of a world with eight or nine billion people. The world, obviously, *does* have a carrying capacity even though history shows us that this capacity can be extended. People *can* be a resource but can also be a drain on resources. The implications of a growing world population should neither be ignored nor exaggerated.

Key points

- On current projections the world is set to have more people than it can support by the middle of the 21st century.
- For neo-Malthusians this projection necessitates action to curb global population growth.
- For Cornucopians a growing world population is not a problem, as history shows us that technological advances can meet growing demands.
- Global policy on population control has shifted in emphasis from (i) encouragement of development to (ii) a more pragmatic focus on promoting birth control and then to (iii) a more sociological approach which addresses the status of girls and women.
- Overpopulation has somewhat fallen off the international political agenda in recent decades but there remain several important implications of the phenomenon which cannot be ignored.

Recommended reading

Kegley, C. & Blanton, S. (2012) *World Politics. Trend and Transformation* (12th edition), Boston: Cengage, Chapter 12.

Lappé, F. & Schurman, R. (1988) *Taking Population Seriously.* San Francisco: Institute for Food and Development Policy.

4 Fighting over the last drop?

Resource wars and energy security

The next war in the Middle East will be fought over water, not politics.

Boutros-Ghali 1985 (BBC 2003)

Power politics: The rise of energy security concerns

As has been seen in the first three chapters, the two major geopolitical shifts that affected the world in the 1970s and then at the end of the 1980s served to bring the environment into widened security purview due to heightened fears over resource depletion, and then allow the opportunities to deal with such concerns to eventually emerge from the shadow of superpower rivalry. For many, a link between resource depletion and military power politics calculations began to become apparent in the economic downturn of the 1970s and then became firmly established after the conclusion of the Cold War.

The economic downturn that accompanied the oil crises of the 1970s shook international relations practically and academically. The US and global economies thrived under the Bretton Woods monetary system centred on Washington through the 1950s and 1960s, but it all came unstuck in the 1970s, amidst the global economic recession of 1971–4. The sudden rise in oil prices, instigated by the Organization of Petroleum Exporting Countries (OPEC) (see Box 4.1) taking advantage of having secured political control of this crucial commodity from multinational corporations (MNCs), allied to the spiralling costs of the Vietnam War, led to the US budget deficit (amount of debt acquired through borrowing) getting so large that bondholders and other governments began to lose faith in the dollar holding its value in relation to gold. Importantly, the revival of European economies and emergence of Japan as a major player in the international economy meant that the US's hegemony was not what it had been; other currencies were emerging to rival the US dollar, leaving it ill-equipped to be a world currency any more.

In light of these changes the academic dominance of classical Realism, which stressed the uppermost primacy of military power in calculating the 'national interest' by which state foreign policy should be guided, was toppled by a recognition of the importance of economic power in state relations. Neo-Realists, such as Kenneth Waltz (1979), revamped the old paradigm to accommodate non-military components of power into its framework of analysis based on competitive state–state relations. At the same time, a new breed of Liberal thinkers, Pluralists such as Robert Keohane and Joseph Nye (1977), felt vindicated that a more cooperative-based and multifaceted model of how politics is conducted at the international level was shown to be needed by the rise to prominence of military dwarfs but resource-rich countries, such as the OPEC countries, in the global arena. In the 'real' world of international relations, the 'Carter doctrine', announced by the US President in 1980, made it plain that

Box 4.1 OPEC

The most influential international economic cartel – an organization seeking to control the price of an export – has been the Organization of Petroleum Exporting Countries (OPEC), which was set up in 1960 and initially comprised five states: Saudi Arabia, Iran, Iraq, Kuwait and Venezuela. Its membership has now expanded to 12, with the addition of Algeria, Angola, Ecuador, Libya, Nigeria, Qatar and the United Arab Emirates. The OPEC countries produce around 45% of the world's crude oil and represent around 55% of exports. The organization shot to prominence in the early 1970s when its members began to take control of the North American and Western European MNCs, who had previously dominated their oil-extraction and petroleum-manufacturing industries, giving OPEC the means to raise prices. Crucial to OPEC, as with many economic organizations, is the hegemonic role played by one of its members, Saudi Arabia. Saudi oil exports have generally been three times that of the next biggest exporters, Iran and Venezuela, allowing Saudi Arabia to call the shots. OPEC sets quotas for oil production amongst its members so that it can control the supply vis-à-vis the rest of the world's demand and so manipulate the price in its favour. The flaw in such a strategy is the temptation likely to present itself to any of the members to break ranks and exceed their quota in order to sell more and make a quick profit – an example of the collective goods problem. The Saudi government is in a position to sanction that by being able to adjust its level of production if any country does fall out of line, an action it has taken on several occasions.

OPEC has continued to be an influential actor in the international political arena but has yet to relive its 1970s heyday when it effectively held the global North to ransom and many of its members underwent rapid economic growth on the back of burgeoning oil prices. From the 1980s, the global North countries coordinated their position as oil consumers, looked to alternative suppliers, such as Mexico and Azerbaijan, and learned to be more efficient with their consumption, reducing OPEC's control of the oil supply. However, OPEC is far from a spent force and it seems inevitable that it will rise again in prominence as the world's oil supply starts to shrink. There are alternatives at present for Northern consumers but OPEC controls around 80% of proven oil reserves, which means that its influence cannot be avoided in the medium term. Despite the emergence of alternative power sources in Europe, overall demand for oil is rising, due to the growth of markets like China, India and Brazil. Additionally, OPEC have developed an increasingly close relationship with prominent non-member exporters Mexico and Russia and would be likely to absorb any other state that happened to strike it lucky and start exporting oil.

questions relating to the economic resources of distant states would enter into the calculations of the American national interest, by stating that military action to secure oil imports and other economic interests was a possibility:

> *An attempt by any outside force to gain control of the Persian Gulf region will be regarded as an assault on the vital interests of the United States of America, and such an assault will be repelled by any means necessary, including military force.*
>
> (Carter 1980)

The rise to high politics of oil pricing prompted greater scrutiny of the importance of threats to the supply of key economic resources to states. This became allied to the rise in concerns that global overpopulation could drain the world's resources, as discussed in the previous chapter, and greater recognition that resources could be threatened by environmental degradation as well as through political action. It was not until the 1990s, however, when the agenda of international politics was allowed to broaden, that environmental degradation as a potential state security threat began to take prominence in academia and mould the thinking of foreign policy makers. Economic statecraft had been revived as an instrument of foreign policy by the oil crises, but it was not until the strategic constraints of the Cold War had been lifted that a full manifestation of the Carter doctrine was put into practice with the US-led action against Iraq in the Gulf War. A Just War and long-awaited display of collective security it may well have been, but few would dispute that securing oil supplies was a key additional motivation for the allied forces' action.

The resource war thesis

The post-Cold War era was ushered in with a war motivated, at least at some level, by resource interests and demonstrating that the Soviet–US power balance was no longer the determinant of war-making decisions. In this context, a new strand of IR enquiry emerged, to consider whether threats to stability due to changes in resource access were possible and hence something that should be of concern to Realist-minded foreign policy makers. Canadian academic Homer-Dixon has been at the forefront of this area of study, leading teams of researchers since the 1990s in exploring the possibility of causal links between environmentally induced resource depletion and military conflict. His extensive research led him to claim that links can be shown to exist: 'Environmental scarcities are already contributing to violent conflicts in many parts of the world. These conflicts are probably the early signs of an upsurge of violence in the coming decades that will be induced or aggravated by scarcity' (Homer-Dixon 1994: 6).

Homer-Dixon's research focused on LDCs, since his belief was that such states were less likely to adapt to the social effects of environmental degradation than developed countries and thus are more prone to this form of conflict. Hence, Homer-Dixon does not postulate that environmental scarcity leads directly to conflict but that it can be a root cause of social unrest that can spill over into violent unrest. In line with explanations of famine, environmental scarcity (of, for example, fish or fertile soil) occurs through the interplay of three factors: the supply of resources, the demand for resources, and changes in the distribution of resources. Two phenomena, emerging from changes in the three factors, are identified by Homer-Dixon as the key link between environmental scarcity and social unrest: 'resource capture' and 'ecological marginalization'. Resource capture occurs when elites within a state respond to falls in supply or rises in demand by appropriating more resources for themselves and leaving the poorer sections of society to bear the brunt of scarcity. Ecological marginalization is said to occur when population growth and/or changes in access to resources for certain sections of the populus produce migrations which cause the over-exploitation of resources in certain areas (Homer-Dixon 1994: 10–11).

Case studies, undertaken by colleagues of Homer-Dixon to illustrate his thesis, included the Senegal River conflict of 1980, and the 1980s civil war in Peru between the government and Shining Path. The Senegal River conflict was considered an illustration of how 'resource capture' can lead to conflict. An ethnic conflict between the politically dominant Arabic Mauers and black Mauritanians followed the expropriation of blacks' land by the Mauers. This land grab was in response to scarcity resulting from a rise in land prices due to a dam project. Ethnic Senegalese lived among the black Mauritanian population and Mauers numbered among the population of neighbouring Senegal, causing the ethnic unrest to become internationalized. In Peru the rise of the Shining Path leftist insurgency was reasoned to be more attributable to the 'ecological marginalization' of their support base of peasant farmers in the mountainous areas of the country than any ideological conversion to Maoism (Homer-Dixon & Percival 1996).

The spillover of conflict from Mauritania to Senegal led Homer-Dixon to his belief that river water is the only renewable resource likely to precipitate inter-state conflict; his research has generally concluded that environmentally inspired conflict is most likely to be civil rather than international. He contends, however, that the weakening of states contributes to regional instability and can still be construed as a security issue for other states (Homer-Dixon 1994).

In the same year as Homer-Dixon's breakthough article on scarcity, the prominent US journalist Robert Kaplan created a similar impact with *The Coming Anarchy*, which also painted a pessimistic picture of the post-Cold War world as a dangerous place characterized by 'disease, overpopulation, unprovoked crime, scarcity of resources, refugee migrations, the increasing erosion of nation-states and international borders and the empowerment of private armies, security firms and international drug cartels' (Kaplan 1994: 144).

Many others have come to link scarcity with war, and a subsequent strand of the resource war literature has emerged specifically in relation to climate change. Alan Dupont and Graeme Pearman, for example, posit that a warming world has increased the likelihood of conflict in five key ways: resource scarcity, land being rendered uninhabitable due either to water scarcity or inundation, the effects of disasters and disease, greater refugee movements and an increased scramble for remaining resource sources (Dupont & Pearman 2006). In an empirical study by Columbia University, similar in style to the Homer-Dixon research, it was found that countries affected by the El Niño–Southern Oscillation extreme weather phenomenon between 1950 and 2005 were twice as likely to experience major civil or international conflict (i.e. those with at least 25 fatalities) as those unaffected. Cases in point highlighted in the study included the fact that El Niño struck Peru in 1982, in the same year as the Shining Path insurgency took off, and that civil wars in Sudan had flared up in parallel with the emergence of extreme weather conditions. The study concluded that 'when crops fail people may take up a gun simply to make a living' (Hsiang et al. 2011).

The work of Homer-Dixon and others in his wake certainly convinced the US government of the early 1990s that environmental degradation represented a potential source of military insecurity. In 1993 a new government position in the Defense Department was created, the Deputy Under Secretary for Environmental Security, and the Environmental Task Force was set up as part of Washington's intelligence network. The introduction to the 1994 National Security Strategy Document, an annual government statement of foreign policy aims, states that '… an emerging class of transnational environmental issues are increasingly affecting international stability and consequently present new challenges to U.S. strategy …' (USA 1994: 1). Other countries have followed suit in stating that environmental change is a foreign policy concern, as was highlighted in Chapter 2.

Resource war sceptics

Despite its influence on the thinking of the US government and others, the approach of framing environmental scarcity as a military security matter has not been without its critics. The empirical evidence linking environmental degradation and political conflict is, by Homer-Dixon's own admission, not straightforward, prompting scepticism as to whether other variables are the real causes of conflicts in situations where environmental scarcity can be demonstrated. Dan Smith, for example, points out that the Senegal River conflict was more about ethnic and class conflict than access to river water (Smith 1994). Marc Levy criticizes the Homer-Dixon-led research on the grounds that the fact that only LDCs are chosen as case studies is a tacit admission that general poverty, rather than environmental change, is the root cause of the conflicts analysed (Levy 1995: 45).

As with the critics of neo-Malthusianism discussed in the previous chapter, the assumption that changes in the balance between resources and people creates political problems is viewed as flawed logic by the resource war sceptics. It is easy to link droughts in Sudan to the Darfur Crisis and other civil conflicts in the country but such events are unfortunate facts of life in the Sahel, and the responsibility for the bloodshed lies squarely with the Janjaweed insurgents and the Sudanese government for giving a green light to their murderous campaigns (Brown & McLennan 2009: 297). History can also provide plenty of evidence of environmental disasters and extreme weather conditions *not* prompting conflict. The devastating dustbowls that struck the US Great Plains in the 1930s did not trigger conflict (Brown & McLennan 2009: 296). Neither was conflict a consequence of the 2010 earthquake in the far more politically volatile state of Haiti, in spite of widespread assumptions that it would. Australia has been as much affected by El Niño as Sudan or Peru but has not been struck by civil war for obvious economic and political reasons. The cited cases suggest a correlation between conflict and underdevelopment and a lack of democracy, more than between conflict and environmental scarcity.

The environmental scarcity literature focuses on the competition for non-renewable resources as a new, destabilizing trend in post-Cold War international relations, referred to by Paul Rogers as 'prologue wars' heralding a new era (Rogers 2000: 79), but the 'newness' of such conflicts is questionable. There is a long history of conflicts over land. The 1969 'Football War' between El Salvador and Honduras, despite its linkage to a volatile World Cup qualifying match between the two national sides, echoed the River Senegal dispute in that its main cause was ethnic tension created by migration and its effects on land rights. In respect to the much vaunted coming of 'water wars', Peter Gleick points out that such conflicts go back 5,000 years and lists a number of them including an ancient 'dambuster' raid by Alexander the Great against Persia between 355 and 323 BC (Gleick 1994). If the focus is narrowed to domestic upheaval then it is probably fair to suggest that most popular revolutions have had questions relating to access to productive land at their core. 'Who gets what?' is widely held to be the essence of all political contention. Equally, abundance can be a source of contention as much as a scarcity, in what has come to be termed 'the resource curse theory'. Iraq's oil has made it the foremost international military battleground of recent years, and the geological fortune of possessing rich diamond reserves has been the political misfortune of countries such as the DR Congo and Sierra Leone. Of course access to resources causes political upheaval. It was ever thus.

Not only are 'water wars' nothing new, they barely register in an analysis of modern military history. Despite a spate of publications warning of the likelihood of conflicts fought to secure freshwater supplies, particularly in the arid and volatile Middle East (Starr 1991, Bulloch & Darwish 1993), no war of this kind was fought in the 20th century and water has played little part in Arab–Israeli hostilities (Libiszewski 1995). Consequently, a bourgeoning 'anti-resource war' literature has emerged, providing empirical evidence that cooperative responses to increased resource scarcity are more common than conflictual ones (Nordas & Gleditsch 2007, Reuveny 2007, Salehyan 2008). As Jon Barnett concludes, 'on the basis of existing environment and conflict research there is simply insufficient evidence and too much uncertainty to make anything other than highly speculative claims about the effect of climate change on violent conflict' (Barnett 2003: 10).

A three-year empirical project carried out by a team at Oregon State University provides solid grounds for suggesting that international quarrels over water resources are invariably dealt with cooperatively rather than inducing conflict. The study found that there had been 1,831 international political interactions over water in the previous 50 years, of which none had produced war and only 507 instigated a dispute (two-thirds of these disputes were purely verbal and only 37 had any armed dimension). In contrast, 1,228 of those international water interactions produced cooperative responses including 157 treaties (Wolf 2007). There is no evidence that fighting over depleting resources is in any way a distinguishing feature of the contemporary world. Indeed, scarcity may even be a source of greater peace by giving a spur to more cautious and cooperative diplomacy.

Shlomi Dinar observes that, 'In general, the history of hydropolitics is one of negotiation and cooperation rather than militarized conflicts' (Dinar 2011: 185), and offers supporting evidence from a region marked by aridity, poverty, ethnic tension and limited democracy. The Helmand River Agreement of 1973 occurred when Iran gave trade concessions to the Afghan government in order to guarantee water supplies. Relations between Syria and Turkey improved rather than deteriorated after a diplomatic dispute over the effects of the latter's Southeastern Anatolian dam project on the Euphrates in the late 1980s, culminating in a 1987 bilateral accord guaranteeing downstream Syria a specified share of water. Syrian concerns on this issue were channelled through the European Union and the World Bank instead of ratcheting up the stakes vis-à-vis Ankara, and this multilateralism worked in their favour given the Turks' Western orientation. A reassured Syria then struck a similar deal of their own with their downstream riparian Iraq over the Euphrates in 1989 (Dinar 2011: 184).

Christopher Fettweis similarly suggests that 'there has never been a war over offshore oil deposits' (Fettweis 2011: 224) and 'cooperation rather than conflict is the rule concerning even the most vital of national interests' (Fettweis 2011: 201). Despite the rise to prominence of oil politics and the Carter doctrine this resource never featured in the Cold War. The USSR never attempted to interfere with the transit of Gulf oil despite the obvious strategic potential this held (although this could also be explained as a successful case of deterrence by the US). After the Cold War, the Gulf War, on an intergovernmental level, was about as uncontroversial as any international conflict in history, in spite of (and perhaps because of) its oil dimension. Similarly, there has been no new 'Great Game' over the rise of Caspian oil in the 1990s, or anywhere else. Securing oil supplies undoubtedly factors in the national interests of most states but there is no precedent for fighting over supplies amongst oil consumers.

The Arctic 'Great Game' that never was

The high stakes of energy security viewed through the pessimistic prism of Realism tend to prompt hyperbole that rarely manifests itself in reality. A recent case in point is the rise of geopolitical interest in the Arctic, prompted by surveys revealing greater reserves of oil and gas than previously envisaged, and the apparent opportunities presented by melting ice sheets and assertions of sovereign control, epitomized by a submarine mission in which a robot planted the Russian flag on the North Pole below the ice, in 2007. A 2008 article in *Jane's Intelligence Review*, widely cited in the UK popular press, reasoned that Russia's recent war against Georgia and the general high stakes could see them, and possibly other Arctic states, 'make pre-emptive military strikes' to secure resources in advance of the UNCLOS adjudication of 2020 (Galeotti 2008: 11). Similarly, another widely cited article by a former US coast guard officer in the journal *Foreign Affairs*, warned of 'armed brinkmanship' due to the anarchic nature of the emerging Arctic political landscape. 'Decisions about how to manage this rapidly changing region will likely be made within a diplomatic vacuum unless the United States steps forward to lead the international community toward a multilateral solution' (Borgerson 2008: 73). Across a range of publications, Cold War stereotyping came out of cold storage, with a special edition of the *Eurasian Review of Geopolitics* on 'The Polar Game' similarly declaring that 'Russia's decision to take an aggressive stand in the polar area has left the US, Canada and the Nordic countries little choice but to forge a cooperative High North strategy and invite other friendly countries, such as Great Britain, to help build a Western presence in the Arctic' (Cohen 2008: 36).

Seemingly supporting such reactions was a notable reassertion of energy security interests in a series of foreign policy statements and initiatives by the Arctic states in the late 2000s.

The Russian North Pole submarine's mission appeared to symbolize Russia's renewed preparedness to assert itself in its own backyard after the humiliations of Western incursions into its Slavic periphery through NATO expansion and the 1999 war with Yugoslavia. Although the North Pole robot was a private rather than government mission, a subtext was that Moscow was, at the time, asserting that the Lomonosov submarine ridge, upon which the North Pole lies, was part of its continental shelf claim lodged with UNCLOS, which was later articulated in a 2009 strategic document. In Canada, securing sovereign rights in the Arctic was a key plank of Stephen Harper's successful nationalistic election campaign of 2006, and under his government an annual military patrol of the Arctic region, known as Operation Nunaliuut ('This Land is Ours'), has become well established. In the US, energy interests and a desire to focus Congress on the potential offered by the Arctic prompted the Bush (Jr) government to release a Homeland Security Directive for the region in one of its last acts in the White House. The Norwegians and Danes similarly released new strategies of Arctic foreign policy in the late 2000s and, following up on this in 2009, Norway moved their national military headquarters from Jalta near Stavanger to Reitan, near Bodo in the north, whilst the Danish Folketing (parliament) voted to authorize the establishment of an Arctic military command and task force by 2014. NATO also joined the apparent new 'Great Game', holding its first major Arctic seminar at Reykjavik in January 2009, and then trumpeting its Arctic presence in a 2012 'Cold Response' military exercise in northern Norway (see Hough 2013: 17–47).

However, despite such developments it is clear that, whilst the Arctic natural environment is undoubtedly changing, the economic and political climate is not heating at anything like the rate widely predicted in 2007 and 2008. In April 2010, whilst President Medvedev was visiting Oslo, the Russians and Norwegians concluded an agreement ending a low-level 40-year diplomatic dispute over how to partition the Barents Sea, amicably splitting it in two. In a joint communiqué that followed, the two foreign ministers announced that: 'We firmly believe that the Arctic can be used to demonstrate just how much peace and collective interests can be served by the implementation of the international rule of law' (Store & Lavrov 2010). This initiative took much of the world by surprise but should not have, given that it was a win–win result. Doggedly sticking to their divergent claims had created a 'grey zone' amounting to some 12% of the sea in which neither side could prospect for oil. Russian policy in the Arctic has actually consistently been far less belligerent and more cooperative than portrayed in the West since the thaw evident in Gorbachev's 1987 Murmansk speech, when he declared that 'What everybody can be absolutely certain of is the Soviet Union's profound and certain interest in preventing the North of the planet, its Polar and sub-Polar regions and all Northern countries from ever again becoming an arena of war, and in forming there a genuine zone of peace and fruitful cooperation' (Gorbachev 1987). Russian overtures to the West on the Arctic have been consistently conciliatory, whilst maintaining their claims to the seas to their north in a purely legalistic manner.

Maritime disputes still exist but this is far from unusual in international relations and there is little precedent for fighting over fish and water. Areas of contention remain in the Bering Sea between the US and Russia and between the US and Canada over the Northwest Passage and Beaufort Sea but these are lower-level disputes than that of the Barents Sea – which was amicably resolved. The continental shelf claims are being pursued in a distinctly legalistic manner, with the Russians, Canadians, Danes and Norwegians patiently presenting claims to UNCLOS and showing every indication that they will abide by its arbitration. This was made public with the 'Ilulissat Declaration', which followed a meeting of the 'Arctic five' in Greenland in 2008, and which stated that 'We remain committed to this legal framework [UNCLOS] and to the orderly settlement of any overlapping claims' (Ilulissat 2008).

Foreign policy statements assert national interests and zero-sum characterizations of energy security because that is what foreign policy statements are supposed to do and what most of us expect to read. Formal Realism, though, often masks a truer discourse of cordial cooperative relations and this is the case with the Arctic five. The toughest posturing has come, not from the Russians or the Americans, but from Canada, but this, nonetheless, is still more rhetoric than reality. Shelagh Grant suggests that 'claims of protecting Arctic sovereignty seem little more than paper sovereignty' (Grant 2010: 418) given that no new icebreakers have been constructed and a much-vaunted Resolute Bay military base has not materialized in spite of the tough talk. In addition, Canadian public opinion is much more sensitive about their Arctic hinterlands than the rest of the world generally appreciates, and the Harper government has actually been playing to this audience rather than an international one. This was confirmed in cables released in 2010 by Wikileaks, which, whilst in the case of the Middle East revealing geopolitics perhaps hotter than envisaged, revealed the opposite for the Arctic case, with Harper being forced to admit to cordial relations with Russia (Wikileaks 2010).

Rhetoric and reality are often not the same thing in international relations and particularly, it seems, in the politics of the Arctic. The cordial intergovernmental diplomacy that characterizes the Arctic five and Arctic Council, and the energy-seeking ventures bringing together Western MNCs and the Kremlin, represent cases of transnational symbiosis rather than new Cold War nationalism. Far from the lucrative scrambles produced by the discoveries of Yukon gold of the 1920s or Alaskan oil of the 1960s, future energy exploration in the High Arctic is set to be much more long-term and speculative or, as Charles Emmerson terms it, a 'slow rush for Northern resources' (Emmerson 2010). Whilst global warming is rightly bringing much-needed attention to the needs of its indigenous populations, whose lives are being transformed by a changing physical and economic climate, a great deal of hot air has been spoken about an Arctic oil rush, territorial scramble and new Cold War.

Conclusions

Securing access to resources is becoming more critical, with parts of the world experiencing a depletion of life-supporting foods and fuels. It does not follow from this, though, that the people most affected will be forced to fight over them. Responsible management and cooperation is a more rational and fruitful political response to scarcity and ensuring supplies than conflict. Democratization and interdependence leaves room for optimism that we are not entering an era of resource wars. Democracies are forced to confront resource allocation questions as a matter of course and, increasingly, act on environmental degradation even if no obvious human side-effect is apparent. In addition, democracies (and some non-democracies) long ago came to the conclusion that resources are more easily secured through trade and common management than conflict. There is a compelling pessimistic Realist logic to the resource war thesis but it does not stand up to much academic scrutiny. In time, this influential line of thinking may come to be seen as being as excessively pessimistic, as were the similarly influential overpopulation concerns of the late 1960s. Equally, though, it could be dangerous to entirely dismiss the possibility that the thesis could come to have some relevance in the future on the basis that it is not yet supported by evidence. The allocation of resources is the fundament of all politics, and desperation or bloody-mindedness sometimes manifest themselves in political violence. It would be foolish to entirely dismiss the possibility that the much-increased likelihood of scarcity due to global warming could yet see the resource wars scenario become a reality, but there is scope for optimism that common resources can be managed amicably by most states in the present state system.

Key points

- Energy politics in international relations rose to prominence in the 1970s with heightened concerns about securing oil supplies.
- Changes in the international political landscape with the ending of the Cold War, allied to changes in the literal landscape owing to global warming, led many academics and governments to believe that increased competition for resources would be an increasingly likely trigger for war.
- The 'resource war' thesis remains speculative and unproven and contrary evidence of more cooperative, rather than aggressive, diplomacy being invoked by resource stress is emerging.

Recommended reading

Dinar, S. (ed.) (2011) *Beyond Resource Wars. Scarcity, Environmental Degradation and International Cooperation*, Boston: MIT Press.

Homer-Dixon, T. & Percival, V. (1996) *Environmental Scarcity and Violent Conflict: Briefing Book*, Population and Sustainable Development Project, American Association for the Advancement of Science and University of Toronto.

5 The spoils of war

Military security and the environment

Using trees as a symbol of peace is in keeping with a widespread African tradition. For example, the elders of the Kikuyu carried a staff from the thigi tree that, when placed between two disputing sides, caused them to stop fighting and seek reconciliation. Many communities in Africa have these traditions.

Wangari Maathai, Nobel Peace Prize winner, acceptance speech, 2004

Introduction

The relationship between the military and the environment is a complex one, although superficially very simple. Clearly, bombs can have a detrimental effect, whether exploding and destroying urban environments or by not exploding (especially landmines) and making agricultural land unusable. Wars pollute rivers, contaminate soil and obliterate landscapes. The nature of modern weaponry only exacerbates some of these problems. It is not difficult to see how military activities cause environmental stresses. However, the complication emerges initially in the sense that it is doubtful whether extensive defoliation in the Vietnam War, the destruction of oilfields in Iraq, uranium contamination in Kosovo and all the other war damage combined adds up to the environmental destruction caused by the normal practices of modern industrial society (including, of course, the production and maintenance of military hardware in peacetime). More complicating still is the fact that war can even have some environmentally positive impacts, with countries 'putting themselves on a war footing' by becoming more frugal, resourceful and so, in some ways, ecological. So in assessing 'the spoils of war' we need to consider a variety of environmental consequences of conflict on and off the battlefield, as well as the whole process of preparing for such eventualities (see Box 5.1).

Box 5.1 Arthur Westing

Few would dispute that US academic Westing is the leading name to have emerged in the subject of environmental damage by war over the past 50 years. Westing was one of four experts appointed by the American Association for the Advancement of Science to participate in the Herbicide Assessment Commission. This was created in 1969 to investigate the effects of the controversial defoliation programme Operation Ranch Hand, carried out by the US to expose enemy forces throughout much of the Vietnam War. Westing's background was as a botanist and forest ecologist but the fact that he had also served in the US military, seeing action as an artillery officer in the Korean War, equipped him with insights on both sides of the military–environment equation.

Westing has gone on to direct the UNEP project Peace, the Environment and Security, was appointed as a Peace Messenger by the UN Secretary-General in 1988 and has served as a consultant to the Red Cross, World Bank and the government of war-torn Eritrea. He has a huge publications record and is the most cited source on the impact of Operation Ranch Hand, which he described as causing 'widespread, long-lasting, and severe disruptions of perennial croplands, and of farmlands – that is to say of millions of hectares or the natural resource base essential to an agrarian society' (Westing 1989: 337). Westing's writings have also advocated the need to criminalize and prosecute such acts, notably highlighted in the 1974 article *Proscription of Ecocide*:

> *... what is urgently required at this time is the establishment of the concept that widespread and serious ecological debilitation – so-called ecocide – cannot be condoned. I would first limit it to ecocide caused by military activities, although it might well be argued that such a limitation is shortsighted.*
>
> Source: Westing 1974: 26

Ecocide: The deliberate military destruction of natural resources

The wilful destruction of nature in the course of war can be witnessed as either an offensive or defensive strategy.

Offensive ecocide: Attacking the natural resources of an enemy

Operation Ranch Hand was probably the most infamous systematic military assault on the environment. Swedish Prime Minister Olof Palme denounced the US's Vietnam defoliation programme as 'ecocide' at the 1972 United Nations Stockholm Conference on the Human Environment, prompting a diplomatic spat between the two normally friendly countries. The US, though, have never been held accountable for this act of ecocide and, despite increasing recognition of these sorts of acts as unlawful, the tendency has been for military necessity to hold sway over moral norms.

This *scorched earth* tactic of destroying the crops and livestock of the enemy has been deployed in wars since ancient times, whether in the context of international conquests, as by the Romans against Carthage, or in the course of domestic military subjugation such as in William the Conqueror's 'Harrying of the North' after annexing England in the 11th century. Ahead of Operation Ranch Hand the British were the first to undertake a strategy of chemical defoliation in wartime in the early 1950s during the 'Malayan Emergency', when the acid formulations 2,4,5-T and 2,4-D (later combined in Agent Orange) were used to clear lines of communication and wipe out food crops in the struggle against the communist uprising. Imperial Chemical Industries (ICI) provided the technical advice for the British and Malayan governments, and in 1952 fire engines spraying sodium trichloroacetate (STCA) and trioxane, mixtures of the aforementioned herbicides, were sent along a number of key roads. After seven months it proved more effective, both economically and practically, to remove vegetation by hand and the spraying was stopped. In 1953 the use of herbicides as an aid to fighting the guerrillas was restarted, as a means of destroying food crops grown by the communist forces in jungle clearings. Helicopters despatched STCA and trioxane, along with pellets of n′-chlorophenyl-n, n-dimenthylurea onto crops such as sweet potatoes and maize (Connor & Thomas 1984). However, since this pre-dated the environmental era, the sorts of studies which highlighted the environmental and health damage resulting from similar spraying operations ten years later in Vietnam never took place in Malaya.

The use of herbicides was far more widespread in Vietnam, with an estimated 80 million litres of 2,4,5-T, 2,4-D, picloram and cacodylate sprayed, in a variety of mixtures, on jungle foliage and enemy crops by the US Air Force between 1962 and 1971. American scientists – including Westing – have estimated that 10% of Vietnam's inland forests, 36% of her mangrove forests and 3% of cultivated land were affected by the programme (NAS 1974: 5–6). This scale of ecological disruption indirectly affected the health of the Vietnamese populus by reducing the quality of their nutritional intake and creating refugees who were susceptible to disease, but most dramatic were the alleged cases of direct toxification by herbicides. Dioxin, which arises as a contaminant in the manufacture of 2,4,5-T, is one of the most toxic chemicals known to man. An estimated 170 kg of this poison was sprayed over Vietnam and the neighbouring countries of Laos and Cambodia, amidst the applications of Agent Orange (NAS 1974: vii–9). Dioxin is toxic in several dimensions – teratogenic (causing birth defects), hepatoxic, mutagenic, carcinogenic, a skin-irritant, and responsible for increasing cholesterol levels in blood. Many studies have linked instances of such symptoms amongst South Vietnamese residents and their offspring with the Agent Orange sprayings between 1962 and 1971 (Franklin 2003). As is in the nature of toxicology, and particularly carcinogenicity and teratogenicity, proving what are the causal factors is extremely difficult, but numerous instances have come to light of spontaneous abortions and infant deformities. The evidence, though, is unambiguous with regards to liver damage resulting from dioxin exposure. A study led by Do Thuc Trinh (and utilized by Westing), found that 'Chronic hepatitis was more than ten times as prevalent among those subjects who had been directly exposed to military herbicides (more than a decade previously) than among those who had not' (Westing 1984: 166).

Whether or not Vietnamese birth deformities, liver damage or any other ailments can be attributed to Operation Ranch Hand, no compensation has been forthcoming for any of the victims. The Cambodian government attempted to claim compensation for damage done to the Kampong Cham province during the American herbicide campaign, but the case dissolved with the overthrow of that government in 1970. The only people who have been compensated for illnesses attributable to Operation Ranch Hand are soldiers who fought on the same side as those responsible for the spraying. War veterans in the US, Australia and New Zealand, who have suffered subsequent skin and liver disorders or birth defects in their offspring, won a long battle for compensation in 1979, when a US Federal Judge ruled that they could sue the companies responsible for manufacturing Agent Orange, led by Dow Chemicals. Over 45,000 people have since claimed a share of the $180 million in damages from Dow and six other chemical firms. Dow agreed to the settlement in the face of public pressure and mounting legal costs, but have always maintained that the various illnesses incurred by the veterans are not related to the Agent Orange sprayed in Vietnam.

Despite some uncertainties in the scientific data relating to Agent Orange exposure, the US's defoliation campaign in Vietnam, Cambodia and Laos was roundly condemned by America's scientific community and many international statesmen. Continued pressure by the Herbicide Assessment Commission (HAC), including a petition signed by 5,000 scientists (of whom 17 were Nobel Prize holders), led to the termination of the campaign in 1971 amidst growing public horror at the evidence of horrific birth defects occurring in the South Vietnamese population (Hay 1982: 151).

Following the tactics used in Vietnam (and with equal effect), the government of Indonesia in the late 1960s conducted what has been asserted to be the biggest deforestation in history to quell insurgencies in Borneo and West Kalimantan (Peluso & Vandergeest 2011). Similarly, the 1980s civil war in El Salvador saw the government bomb villages, agricultural lands and forests, seeking to deny guerrilla forces a base and sustenance. As a consequence, El Salvador today finds itself virtually deforested. Some of this is a consequence of the country's high population density and economic inequality, leading landless peasants to chop down trees for survival reasons, but it is also to do with explicit military policy during the 1980s. During a decade-long civil war, the military sought supremacy over leftist guerrillas of the Farabundo Marti National Liberation Front (FMLN) through a scorched earth policy. In an echo of Vietnam, the forests were seen as the sea in which the guerrillas swam and were therefore to be removed; few trees escaped. Social pressures led to deforestation and war; war caused further deforestation and social pressures and therefore further incentive to fight.

In a different form of domestic ecocide Saddam Hussein added to his notable list of environmental and human crimes deliberate desertification, by diverting the courses of the rivers Tigris and Euphrates in order to drain marshland areas that were home to the Shia 'Marsh Arabs', who had initiated an uprising against his rule after the Gulf War in 1991. This act of ecological ethnic cleansing drained around 90% of the region's marshes and also depleted its population from 250,000 to about 40,000 (Weinstein 2005: 715).

Defensive ecocide: Environmental self-destruction

The 'backs to the wall' tactic of preventing the enemy making use of your resources in retreat is also a well-established military strategy. In 1812 Russian forces retreated from Napoleon's invading French army whilst destroying their own arable lands in an ultimately successful strategy that paved the way for the disastrous 'retreat from Moscow', which sowed the seed of Napoleon's downfall. The Russian strategy was learned from British military leader Wellington, who, in alliance with Portuguese guerrilla forces, had resisted French invasion in the Peninsular War in a similar manner two years earlier. French military power was built on its arable supremacy, allowing her to feed the biggest army in Europe, and this had come to be realized by those on the receiving end of its autarky.

Whilst, by the 20th century, industrial might had become the main determinant of military power, scorching the earth could still serve its purpose. During the Second World War the British took responsibility for rendering uninhabitable the islands of Norway's Svalbard archipelago (Spitsbergen), to limit German interest in its coalfields, despite Norwegian opposition. Consequently, the German presence on the Arctic islands was limited to the manning of some weather stations. In a different and more dramatic form of defensive ecocide, the deliberate flooding of the Yellow River was carried out by the Chiang Kai-shek government when resisting the Japanese invasion of Manchuria in 1938. In destroying dykes the Chinese slowed down the invaders by creating a bigger barrier and destroying farmland but also sacrificed hundreds of thousands of their own citizens and left millions more homeless in an act both desperate and appalling.

More recently, 'defensive ecocide', more spiteful than strategic, featured in the Gulf War. Saddam's forces, retreating from Kuwait in 1991, set fire to several oil wells, some of which continued to burn for much of the rest of the year. Oil was also deliberately leaked into the Persian Gulf by the Iraqi troops.

Collateral damage: Indirect environmental damage by warfare

Environmental degradation due to war can also occur more indirectly as a result of the general destruction of battle or the knock-on effects of targeted strikes.

Wartime pollution

The 1938 Manchurian War was, in fact, a multifaceted environmental (and human) horror show. The Japanese used chemical and biological weaponry in a brutal invasion and then, once their defeat in the Second World War became apparent, left much of the remaining munitions scattered across north-eastern China to prevent them falling into Allied hands. Japanese troops buried shells containing chemicals including mustard gas and phosgene in fields, lakes and streams, prompting a slow-burning public health disaster in which thousands of Chinese people have died or been disabled as a result of exposure to toxins leaking from the weapons for more than 70 years.

The Second World War 'total war' bombings were of such a scale and nature that environmental catastrophes were inevitable, but 'collateral ecocide' has still been apparent in the supposedly more strategic strikes of recent wars. In one well-chronicled episode, between 20,000 and 30,000 tonnes of oil polluted the Mediterranean Sea and coastline as a result of the bombing of Jiyeh Power Station by Israel in the 2006 Lebanon War (CoE 2011). In the 1999 Kosovan War NATO included in its strategic targets chemical plants and fossil fuel facilities, a tactic that inevitably led to the pollution of waterways and other forms of environmental damage. The bombing campaign led to significant pollution of the Danube, among other places, and, as these sites burned, toxic and carcinogenic chemicals were released into the ground and air. Most notorious was the targeting of the petrochemical and fertilizer plants at Pančevo. NATO acknowledged the environmental consequences of the strike but asserted that the military necessity of taking out a key source of the Serb regime's power justified some collateral fallout.

Longer lasting, although more uncertain forms of environmental and human damage from the Kosovan War bombings and other recent campaigns, such as in Iraq, have come from contamination resulting from the use, by the US and UK, of the radioactive and highly persistent chemical 'depleted uranium' to coat shells. Greenhouse gases, CFCs, mercury, sulfur dioxide and nitrous oxide emissions are also common forms of collateral damage as a result of contemporary bombing campaigns (Sanders 2009: 71–72).

Land degradation

Battlefield destruction can also render arable land and other natural resources useless to humanity and other life forms. Millions of craters today mark the agricultural belts of Vietnam and Laos as the result of a combination of deliberate and collateral military actions by the US in the late 1960s. Many of the First World War battlefields in France and Belgium remain barren nearly a century later. Degradation can also occur more indirectly as a result of sudden influxes of refugees fleeing war. Thirty-eight square kilometres of forest in Kivu Province, in the Democratic Republic of the Congo, were lost within three weeks of the arrival of Rwandan refugees fleeing genocide in the mid-1990s (UNEP 2002).

Over-exploitation of resources

Resource depletion through over-utilization is another typical consequence of war. The appropriation of food and fuel by invading troops is the most predictable form of this phenomenon, but excessive strain may also be put on the home resources of the invaders. Indeed, this may even extend to non-participating allies of a fighting force. Before their entry into the First World War, the US transformed much of their rural territory into arable land in order to intensify production in support of the British and French.

As well as being worsened deliberately, deforestation can be accelerated as a consequence of countries trying to literally rebuild their country after a conflict. Many Iraqi city trees were felled for fuel in the aftermath of the US-led invasion of 2003 (Sheehan 2003). It is also known that Afghan water supplies and vegetation have been seriously damaged and depleted since the onset of war in 2001 (CoE 2011).

Biodiversity can suffer both as a consequence of animals being killed in conflict and as a result of the trade in illegal fauna commodities being used to fund the war effort. Gorilla numbers in the Democratic Republic of the Congo are known to have fallen as a consequence of that country's persistent civil conflict, through being directly killed and through deforestation (Kalpers 2001). In peacetime, NATO naval exercises off the south coast of Spain are known to have killed at least fifteen beached whales in 2002 (CoE 2011).

Military securitization of the environment beyond the battlefield

Preparatory pollution

As the NATO exercise case illustrates, it is not just actual war which can prompt pollution and environmental damage but the whole phenomenon of defence and preparing for war. As with many other dimensions, the process of Cold War defence greatly intensified the traditional ecological side-effects associated with this. The rise of nuclear weapons testing, mass military exercises and the global proliferation of military bases came with significant costs, many of which are continuing to be counted.

The Soviet testing of nuclear weapons and dumping of nuclear waste was particularly extensive in its peripheral regions, such as the northern reaches of Siberia. One hundred and thirty tests were carried out in the Soviet Arctic between 1955 and 1970, prompting landslides and other geomorphological changes as well as depositing radioactive material in the soil, water, ice and air (Glasby & Voytekhovsky 2010: 20). Similar environmental damage was inflicted on parts of the Soviet Empire during the Cold War. The Soviet military left behind significant pollution in Estonia on their withdrawal in 1994 (three years after Estonian independence). Soviet military camps had taken up nearly 2% of the country. No compensation for soil and water pollution by oil, cadmium, lead, uranium and general waste was ever paid for in a clean-up that the Estonian government claimed cost them $4 billion (Auer 2004: 119–121).

US militarism at home and particularly in its overseas outposts has also carried significant environmental costs. Realpolitik and imperial neglect saw the huge naval base at Subic Bay in the Philippines become the scene of an ecological disaster owing to wilful pollution, as sewage treatment was sidestepped and waste dumped directly into the sea. The Philippine government claimed compensation but the Americans never obliged and abandoned the base in 1991 whilst pointing to the 1947 Military Bases Agreement between the two countries that cleared them of any responsibility. In domestic politics American military exceptionalism is also apparent, with the Pentagon exempted from being reported on by the Environmental Protection Agency (EPA), and hence never held accountable for known instances of water and soil pollution well above state limits by solvents, fuels and the by-produce of munitions near military bases (Schettler 1995).

In a more general sense, there is a significant ecological side-effect to the sheer existence of the military–industrial complex. A study in the 1990s found that the military accounted for around a quarter of the world's jet fuel, 9% of its iron and steel consumption, and employed 20% of its scientists (Ostling 1992: 8). Given that, two decades on, global military expenditure has significantly increased, it must be assumed that this ecological footprint is now even Larger.

Environmentally positive impacts of war

Perverse as it may seem, war has myriad effects on the environment and sometimes the overall impact on particular countries can be viewed as ecologically positive. Reduced production and transport usage on the home front is likely to lead to less pollution and waste and biodiversity depletion. Atlantic fish stocks replenished themselves during the Second World War and some wild animal stocks revived as fishing and hunting declined (Westing 1980, Reuveny et al. 2010). At least on the home front, countries on a war footing are often frugal, resourceful and localized, in line with ecological principles. In an empirical analysis of the environmental impact of wars since the late 1960s, Rafael Reuveny, Andreea S. Mihalache-O'Keef and Quan Li conclude that warfare reduced carbon dioxide emissions and (away from the warzone) promoted forest growth and reduced nitrous oxide emissions (Reuveny et al. 2010).

The conquest of nature

The military securitization of the environment can also take the form of a kind of nationalization of nature by force, as wild badlands are symbolically tamed. In addition to being depleted in wartime, tropical woodlands have featured prominently in the security politics of the past 70 years as symbols of resistance. Much of the resistance to the Japanese invasions in South East Asia during the Second World War was jungle based, and this also came to be the arena of resistance to European colonial rule after 1945. As well as carrying out deforestation for tactical reasons, many governments came to denote their woodland as 'jungle' so as to invoke notions of lawlessness, danger and insecurity requiring the assertion of sovereign control through enforced land purchases, forced population movements and the establishment of military bases (Peluso & Vandegeest 2011). This was very much the case with the Indonesian and El Salvadoran government deforestations referred to previously.

Outlawing ecocide

International law is unambiguous on the illegality of military ecocide but, in a predictable illustration of traditional national security trumping environmental concerns, there is little, if any, precedent for enforcing existing legislation.

The Just War tradition

The word 'environment' did not appear in the Geneva or Hague Conventions on war prior to the 1970s, despite their extensive evolutions since the 19th century. A 1909 annex to the 1899 Hague Regulations does, though, state that it is forbidden 'to destroy or seize the enemy's property, unless such destruction or seizure be imperatively demanded by the necessities of war' (Hague Convention 1907: Article 23(g)). In more general terms the centuries-old tradition of Just War, upon which the Geneva and Hague Conventions are built, can be seen as helping safeguard the environment, since the notion of 'limited war', which proscribes the escalation of conflicts beyond their specific purposes, and acts of pure retribution and spite, must apply to the destruction of nature beyond military necessity. It can similarly be suggested that international arms control law proscribes ecocide, in principle at least. The 1925 Geneva Protocol on Chemical Weapons (and its contemporary successor, the 1993 Chemical Weapons Convention), whilst driven by humanitarian rather than environmental concerns, by outlawing the military use of toxins inherently makes wilful pollution illegitimate.

That the wanton destruction of buildings and land is contrary to customary international law was confirmed at the Nuremberg War Trials at the close of the Second World War, even though no actual prosecutions were made. German General Lothar Rendulic was tried by the International Military Tribunal for ordering the scorched earth destruction of several villages in Finnmark, Norway, when in retreat from the Russian army. Rendulic was acquitted of the charge of wanton destruction, as the Tribunal accepted that he genuinely perceived the destruction to be militarily justified, but the precedent for such acts amounting to an international crime was, nonetheless, established (Boas & Schabas 2003: 293). Military ecocide was more acute in during the war in the East, but military security, the national interest and an early manifestation of Cold War realpolitik ultimately trumped humanitarian concerns when it came to prosecuting Japanese war crimes. The Tokyo War Crimes Trials did not properly address the Japanese deployment and testing of chemical and biological weapons in Manchuria, China, due to the US desire to keep such knowledge to themselves and out of the hands of the Soviet Union.

The rise of international law

Japan's actions in Manchuria were clearly counter to the Geneva Protocol and Hague Convention but the will to implement these instruments was not apparent – nor, likewise, had it been when appeasement saw Mussolini's chemical assault on Abyssinia overlooked by the League of Nations in 1935. The death knell of the Geneva Protocol came when it became apparent that huge advances in chemical synthesis in the 1940s and 1950s had rendered it redundant by the time an attempt came to prosecute the US for Operation Ranch Hand. In response to a General Assembly request, US Secretary of State Rogers, in 1969, stated that 'the 1925 Geneva Protocol does *not* cover chemical herbicides'. The US government defended Operation Ranch Hand on the grounds that the chemicals used were not known in 1925 and that their intention was to kill plants not humans.

The simultaneous rise of environmentalism and the Vietnam War proved the twin catalysts for the emergence of international law specifically dealing with military ecocide. In the spirit of détente, the Soviets and Americans actually cooperated in formulating a draft for what would become the 1976 Convention on the Prohibition of Military or Any Other Hostile Use of Environmental Modification Techniques (ENMOD Convention). Moscow, able to capitalize on the controversy that had emanated from Operation Ranch Hand, initiated the idea of an 'ecocide convention' and Washington, having terminated the strategy in 1971 and then abandoned the whole war in 1975, had no strategic need to risk the reputational loss of being the world's environmental pariah (which was particularly galling since, domestically, they were amongst the greenest of countries and certainly far more so than the Soviet Union). ENMOD was adopted by Resolution 31/72 of the United Nations General Assembly in 1976 and opened for signature the following year.

Simultaneous to the negotiation of ENMOD, a Protocol to the Geneva War Conventions dealing with ecocide was agreed. Protocol I Additional to the Geneva Conventions, added in 1977, includes two provisions dealing directly with the dangers that modern warfare poses for the environment:

> *Article 35 – Basic rules*
>
> *3. It is prohibited to employ methods or means of warfare which are intended, or may be expected, to cause widespread, long-term and severe damage to the natural environment.*

Article 55 – Protection of the natural environment

1. Care shall be taken in warfare to protect the natural environment against widespread, long-term and severe damage. This protection includes a prohibition of the use of methods or means of warfare which are intended or may be expected to cause such damage to the natural environment and thereby to prejudice the health or survival of the population.

2. Attacks against the natural environment by way of reprisals are prohibited.

By 2013 the Protocol had been ratified by some 172 states, but notable non-parties included the US, India, Israel, Iran, Pakistan, Turkey and Libya.

Parties to the ENMOD Convention similarly undertake not to use environmental manipulation that would have 'widespread, long-lasting or severe effects as the means of destruction, damage or injury to any other State Party' (Article 1). Far less universal than Protocol I, ENMOD had, by 2013, 76 parties (though this does include the US).

Parties to the twin instruments are prohibited to attack, destroy, remove or render useless objects indispensable to the survival of the civilian population, such as foodstuffs, agricultural areas and drinking water supplies. Protocol I is the more ecological of the twin instruments since its aim is protecting the environment from war, whilst ENMOD is really humanitarian as it seeks to prohibit the use of the environment (land, sea, atmosphere or space) as a weapon in war. ENMOD is limited by the stipulation that such manipulation of the environment must be 'widespread, long-lasting or severe' (WLS) to be deemed illegal but, nevertheless, has the advantage of being worded in such a way that gives it the potential to outlaw war-making methods not yet invented (Roberts & Guelff 2000: 407–418). Hence, the US defence against persecution for Operation Ranch Hand under the Geneva Protocol would not stand up in the event of a country being prosecuted under ENMOD. It was international concern that the US strategy in Vietnam could evolve to include tactics such as deliberate flooding and the manipulation of the weather that did much to inspire ENMOD.

Post-Cold War developments

The oil and ordnance pollution that marked the Gulf War, and the general multilateral optimism that permeated international relations in the aftermath of the Cold War, reinvigorated international efforts to prevent ecocide. New World Order 'widening' was evident when the Security Council held Iraq liable for ecocide in their Kuwaiti invasion through the adoption of Resolution 687, confirming that they were

> *liable under international law for any direct loss, damage, including environmental damage and the depletion of natural resources, or injury to foreign Governments, nationals and corporations, as a result of Iraq's unlawful invasion and occupation of Kuwait.*
>
> (S/RES/687 (1991) 8 April)

On the basis of this, the Kuwaiti government filed claims concerning the damage to its natural resources and related public health concerns. The UN Compensation Commission (UNCC) was subsequently established by Security Council Resolution 692 in May 1991 to adjudicate the amount of damage claims; its Governing Council then approved, in December 1996, an award of $610 million to Kuwait. Hence, the Iraqi government became the first and, to date, only international entity to be charged for environmental damage in war. As a corollary of this prosecution, the UN General Assembly, in November 1992, adopted a resolution on 'The protection of the environment in time of conflict', which stated that the 'destruction of the environment not justified by military necessity and carried out wantonly, is clearly contrary to international law' (A/RES/47/37).

In further developments, in 1992 and 1993 the UN Secretary-General submitted two reports on the protection of the environment which paved the way for a General Assembly resolution (A/RES/49/50). Under this, the International Committee of the Red Cross (ICRC) was mandated to encourage the inclusion of their guidelines on the protection of the environment during conflict in military manuals and other materials of information on the laws of war. Consequently, many countries have adapted ICRC drafted principles into the rules of engagement they provide for their armed forces. The international legal impact of this can also be seen in the 1994 San Remo Manual on International Law Applicable to Armed Conflicts at Sea, which declares that environmental damages that are not collateral are unacceptable.

A further legal milestone came with the adoption of Article 8(2)(b)(iv) Statute of the International Criminal Court (ICC), which lists as a war crime the launching of an attack that may cause excessive damage to the natural environment. Whilst this makes individual criminal responsibility for ecocide more clearly established under an international treaty, the statute suffers from the same lack of precision as the Geneva Protocol and ENMOD in terms of evaluating 'excessive damage' (Peterson 2009). Consequently, to date, no individual or government has been prosecuted for military ecocide under the Hague Convention, ENMOD or the ICC. A case presented to the International Criminal Tribunal for Yugoslavia (ICTY) (a special UN court set up to try crimes committed in the wars of the Yugoslav secession) by the Serbian government against NATO bombing raids in the Kosovan War was dismissed by the ICTY committee on the basis that it did not exceed the WLS threshold.

In some other international laws potentially limiting ecocide, military necessity is explicitly cited as an exemption. The 1993 Prevention of Major Industrial Accidents Convention, for example, does not apply to military installations. The Arctic Council, an intergovernmental organization that has produced a burgeoning range of soft and hard laws on environmental and shipping issues covering the region since the mid-1990s, has it explicitly written into its rules of procedure, at the insistence of the US, that military activities are off-limits.

In a microcosm of IR as a whole, the international solidarity against Saddam Hussein in the early 1990s has proved something of a false dawn for prosecuting military ecocide, and efforts since then have focused on improving the implementation of existing legislation and developing new instruments. Through its Environmental Cooperation for Peacebuilding programme, UNEP has worked with the International Committee of the Red Cross seeking to strengthen international laws protecting the environment during times of conflict. This work was showcased in 2009 in an International Day of Action (see Box 5.2).

A campaign for a more comprehensive and unambiguous UN treaty on ecocide, led by lawyer Polly Higgins and picking up the mantle from Westing and Falk in the early 1970s, has gathered momentum over recent years. The campaign, launched in 2008, seeks to end the ambiguities of military (and industrial) necessity by establishing it as customary international law (like genocide and torture) and opening it up to ICC prosecution. Celebrities, members of parliament and the Morales government of Bolivia are amongst those who have pledged their support to this cause, which has set a deadline of 2020 for the codification of this new treaty (Higgins 2010). This is an ambition unlikely to be achieved, but the popular support and attention gathered by the campaign is probably as important as establishing a legal platform for prosecution. The precedent for enforcing the conventions on genocide, torture and (anthropocentric) war crimes is pretty limited but the (fairly) unambiguous universal acknowledgement of these crimes has made them less likely to occur than in the 'total war' era of the 20th century.

Box 5.2 UNEP's 'Ecocide day' 2009

UNEP held an International Day for Preventing the Exploitation of the Environment in War and Armed Conflict on 6 November 2009. The event emphasized the need to clarify and enforce existing laws and made some particular recommendations, including the following:

- Give greater clarity to the '*widespread, long-term* and *severe*' (WLS) threshold; *severe* should be taken to mean environmental impacts over several hundred square kilometres and *long-term* be considered a period of several months or over a season.
- Recommend new law to demilitarize important ecosystems – determined at the outset of conflict.
- Laws should deal with civil as well as inter-state wars.
- The Permanent Court of Arbitration should be empowered to deal with environmental crimes.

Normative progress in curbing military ecocide

Whilst the idea of environmental security as a race against time is powerful and apt, there is some scope for optimism that time can be a healer on the issue of ecocide. Implementing moral international laws is inherently and inevitably difficult in a sovereign state system but few deny that overall progress has been made in advancing human rights and environmental principles over recent decades. Huge gaps and problems with implementation remain, but as humanitarian and ecological values have been crystallized in the form of laws and regimes, sovereign states have come to be restrained. The stance that military ecocide is unacceptable has, in line with this, come to be much more widely acknowledged. This has been reaffirmed at several high-profile intergovernmental forums. Principle 24 of the 1992 Rio Declaration at UNCED states that 'warfare is inherently destructive of sustainable development. States shall therefore respect international law providing protection for the environment in times of armed conflict and cooperate in its further development, as necessary.'

This normative evolution can actually be traced back to the late Cold War era once détente had advanced humanitarian law and the backlash against Operation Ranch Hand had occurred. Long before New World Order optimism had come to inform international relations, General Assembly Resolution 36/150, in 1981, condemned Israeli plans to construct a canal linking the Mediterranean and Dead Sea, because of its environmental impact on Jordan as well as the political ramifications for Palestinian independence, with only the US and Israel voting against this view. On the basis of this, UNEP's Governing Council adopted several decisions in the 1980s condemning Israeli actions that led to environmental damage against the Palestinians and their Arab neighbours, including reaffirming the General Assembly position on the canal in 1983.

As well as promoting legal measures, UNEP has also contributed to this normative wave by advancing the *idea* of environmental protection in war. Its Disasters and Conflicts Programme has four core services of post-crisis environmental assessment, post-crisis environmental recovery, environmental cooperation for peacebuilding and disaster risk reduction to improve the resilience of war-torn communities such as in Afghanistan, the Democratic Republic of the Congo and Sierra Leone. UNEP also lead the initiative ENVSEC, which includes the UNDP, OSCE and other intergovernmental organizations which, in 2006, carried out a scientific assessment of the environmental impact of the Israeli invasion of Lebanon in 2006, submitting a detailed report just four months after the ceasefire.

Intergovernmental forums outside of the UN system have also taken up the cause of stigmatizing military ecocide. The Parliamentary Assembly of the Council of Europe have called for the environment to be more specifically cited in Geneva Protocol I and argued that conflicts in Bosnia-Herzegovina and Chechnya should have seen prosecutions mounted on the basis of that legal instrument (CoE 2011). This body, representing all of Europe bar the dictatorship of Belarus, have also called for the strengthening of existing international legislation and for greater funds to be given to UNEP in order to improve implementation by allowing it to carry out environmental impact assessments on conflicts. Similarly, the IUCN has a Specialist Group on Armed Conflict and the Environment, which has also called for a strengthening of international law as well as increased understanding of the military's environmental footprint.

Aside from the one 'concrete' legal case with Iraq and Kuwait, we can also see some small steps being taken by governments to make amends for historical environmental war crimes. The Japanese government, having for over half a century denied knowledge of the chemical weapons used in Manchuria, in 1997 finally entered into talks with the Chinese government over how to remedy the damage, leading to a memorandum in 1999 committing them to a plan to locate and destroy some 700,000 abandoned weapons at a cost of over $500 million (BBC 2004). Whilst accepting no international legal liability for Operation Ranch Hand, President Ford in 1975 issued Executive Order 11850, after the US had ratified the Geneva Protocol, renouncing the military use of herbicides 'as a matter of national policy'. Thirty years on, the US position, articulated by the specialist Judge Weinstein, was still claiming that 'there is no basis for any of the claims of plaintiffs under the domestic law of any nation or state or under any form of international law, the case is dismissed' (USDC 2005: 233), in response to a persistent campaign by Vietnam War victims. However, the fact that US war veterans suffering from Agent Orange exposure received compensation amounting to $180m from the chemical manufacturers in 1984 for injuries inflicted, and international support for the Vietnamese victims, made this a weaker position and maintained pressure on Washington. Hence in 2012, whilst still not accepting liability, the US initiated a clean-up of ecological damage in Vietnam. Washington has given $43 million to two American firms working in conjunction with the Vietnamese Defence Ministry. Continuing in this theme of partial atonement, in the same year the US returned to Subic Bay. However, in re-establishing military relations with their former colony, the US was now cooperating with a government now party to MARPOL and not prepared to turn a blind eye to being literally 'crapped on' as a price of their protection.

Realpolitik could still be argued to underpin these cases, since 21st-century US foreign policy still values its South East Asian influence, and a flatlining Japanese economy cannot ignore the resuscitating possibilities offered by its growing neighbour, but moral pressure has also played a part. Global civil society has been vocal with groups like the Alliance for Bases Clean Up (formerly the People's Task Force for Bases Clean Up and featuring Princess Caroline of Monaco) and the Vietnamese Association of Victims of Agent Orange (who have led the legal campaign) have presented the US with a soft power incentive to change. The Manchuria case presents a clear illustration of how normative forces can influence governments both by shaming and encouragement. The Chinese came to be more enthusiastic about the Chemical Weapons Convention than was anticipated, recognizing that abandoning their own stockpile would be a price worth paying to secure a moral victory over their old adversary and remedy a festering environmental and health sore. The Japanese, as champions of arms control on the international stage, were forced to confront their past demons and make reparations for the sins of their grandparents (Frieman 2004).

Military necessity will probably always be argued to trump environmental concerns at times of crisis, as is still regularly seen in compromising democracy and human rights on the grounds of national interest, but this is not to say that moral restraints cannot advance. Just War principles continue to be sidestepped in contemporary conflicts but they have, nevertheless, advanced in the years since the end of the Cold War. Reputation is more important than ever and illegality and immorality are more easily exposed than ever. In this way, moral laws and norms tend not to unravel once established. The passage of time, both in terms of the building up of moral pressure in support of victims and in creating 'distance' for the perpetrator, can permit small, initial steps to be taken in making amends for historical crimes.

However, as is the case in many facets of environmental politics and the politics of securitization, the high-profile catastrophes are only the tip of the iceberg. We may be unlikely to witness another Operation Ranch Hand or episode of Saddam Hussein-style despoiling, but beneath the surface of international political attention lies a huge military–industrial complex eating up the Earth's resources and spitting and belching some of them back out. As with security politics in general, the reflexive focus on international military conflict can tend to miss the bigger picture.

Key points

- The environment can be degraded by war; either deliberately in 'scorched earth' strategies or collaterally.
- International law proscribing deliberate environmental damage in war emerged in the 1970s.
- There is little legal precedent for prosecuting ecocide but normative progress on stigmatizing this has been made.

Recommended reading

Higgins, P. (2010) *Eradicating Ecocide: Laws and Governance to Prevent the Destruction of our Planet*, London: Shepheard-Walwyn.

Reuveny, R., Mihalache-O'Keef, A.S. & Quan Li. (2010) 'The Effect of Warfare on the Environment', *Journal of Peace Research* 47(6): 749–761.

6 Civilizational security

Global threats from environmental change

It is no good squabbling over who is responsible or who should pay. Whole areas of our planet could be subject to drought and starvation if the pattern of rains and monsoons were to change as a result of the destruction of forests and the accumulation of greenhouse gases. The environmental challenge which confronts the whole world demands an equivalent response from the whole world. Every country will be affected and no one can opt out.

Margaret Thatcher, speech to UN General Assembly 1989

This speech from the arch-Conservative UK Prime Minister and 'Iron Lady' of the Cold War gives some indication of how, in the late 1980s, environmental questions were being framed not only in national but also in global security terms. In the previous year this had been demonstrated at the World Conference on the Changing Atmosphere: Implications for Global Security, held in Toronto, which pledged significant action from the international community on climate change, along with a commitment to strengthen the already established policy measures on ozone depletion and acid rain. That 'thinking global' had gone mainstream was then highlighted when *Time* magazine in January 1989 declared the endangered Earth to be their 'planet of the year', in place of the usual selection of an individual person. At that point in time, global solidarity was possible with the passing of the Cold War and widely seen as necessary in the face of new, global-scale threats. In the years since 1989 these global threats have become even clearer but, unfortunately, the same level of global solidarity has not always been apparent.

Fixing the roof: Ozone politics

UNEP took up the issue of ozone depletion by CFCs, launching a World Plan of Action on the Ozone Layer in 1977 which initiated four years of monitoring of the stratosphere. After this, UNEP's Governing Council called for an international treaty to curb ozone depletion to be established. This call manifested itself in the 1985 Vienna Convention for the Protection of the Ozone Layer, with states agreeing in principle to take 'appropriate measures' to combat the problem. As no consensus on specific targets could be agreed at Vienna, it was decided that it would be a 'framework treaty' to be fleshed out in the future and that work would start immediately on a protocol indicating a timeframe for phasing out CFCs and other ozone-depleting chemicals. The 1987 Montreal Protocol to the Vienna Convention then became the key component of a new ozone regime (see Box 6.2).

Such was the rigour of the argument initiated by Rowland and Molina and taken up by UNEP that much of the chemical industry was won over, ahead even of the Montreal

Box 6.1 Sherwood Rowland and Mario Molina

In 1974 US Scientists Sherwood 'Sherry' Rowland and Mario Molina produced an article for the journal *Nature* warning that chlorofluorocarbons (CFCs), the synthetic chemicals used in aerosol sprays and refrigerators, were damaging the Earth's ozone layer. The research built on previous findings by James Lovelock which had detected CFCs in the atmosphere above the Atlantic (Lovelock 1971). Predictably, the research was, at first, rubbished by the chemical industry, but patient and persuasive lobbying by Rowland, Molina and other scientists began to convince the US government, public opinion and, eventually, even some chemical companies, that CFCs were eroding the ozone layer through the release of chlorine, so allowing in dangerous amounts of ultraviolet rays from the Sun.

In 1985 the British Antarctic Survey were able to prove Rowland and Molina to be correct by photographing a large hole in the ozone layer in the stratosphere above the frozen continent. This discovery and the causal role of CFCs were corroborated by NASA and others and by 1987 – rapid in IR terms – international law was in place committing countries to phase out the chemicals.

Rowland and Molina were awarded the Nobel Prize for Chemistry in 1995.

Box 6.2 Key features of the Montreal Protocol

- Nearly 100 chemicals with ozone-depleting properties to be targeted, in accordance with agreed timelines.
- Parties are required to report annually on the production, import and export of the chemicals they have undertaken to phase out.
- An Implementation Committee (consisting of ten Parties) reviews data reports submitted by Parties, assesses their compliance status, and makes recommendations on how to deal with non-complying states.
- Parties are prohibited from trading in ozone-depleting chemicals with non-Parties.
- Developing countries are allowed an extra 10–16 years beyond the dates established for industrialized countries to phase out ozone-depleting chemicals.

Protocol. In 1986 the world's biggest CFC producer, DuPont – along with other corporations in the newly formed Alliance for Responsible CFC Policy – gave its support for limits on production.

In 1990 the Parties agreed to aid the implementation of the Montreal Protocol by the establishment of a Multilateral Fund, in coordination with the World Bank, to help developing countries meet their compliance obligations under the treaty. By 2012 $2.9 billion had been allocated to the fund, most of which had been used on a variety of programmes phasing out of over 400,000 tonnes of ozone-depleting substances (World Bank 2011).

An important further development came in 1992 when the soil fumigant pesticide methyl bromide was confirmed as a significant agent in the depletion of the ozone layer and added to the chemicals covered in the treaty. A UNEP report concluded that around half of all methyl bromide applications to the soil are ultimately emitted into the atmosphere and that, once there, their capacity for ozone destruction is at least 30 times greater than that of the CFCs. The report also estimated that between 5% and 10% of annual global ozone depletion was attributable to methyl bromide (UNEP 1992). Hence a global agreement concerning methyl bromide use and production was reached in November 1992 at the Copenhagen Meeting of the Parties. The Copenhagen meeting decreed that methyl bromide production and consumption levels should be frozen at 1991 levels from the start of 1995. In September 1997 the ninth Meeting of the Parties to the Montreal Protocol committed 160 governments to a timetable for a complete phasing out of methyl bromide production and use. In line with the 'common but differentiated responsibilities' principle agreed upon at UNCED, developed countries agreed to end use of the chemical by 2005 after a series of intermediate cuts, whilst developing countries agreed to a deadline of 2015 to eliminate its use following a freeze in 2002. As with other areas of environmental and humanitarian global governance, however, the US position backtracked under the Bush Jr administration from seeming to support a complete phase-out and the US has maintained a significant level of methyl bromide use since 2005 by exploiting a 'critical use exemptions' clause to the agreement, far more than had been anticipated. The Californian strawberry industry, mindful of the costs of switching to alterative soil fumigants, lobbied hard for US delegates to argue that previously agreed-upon alternative fumigants were not adequate for the West Coast climate, much to the irritation of most other Montreal Protocol parties (Gareau 2008). Hence methyl bromide continues to be used, principally in the US but also in several other states. A global phase-out is still proceeding, but more slowly than was originally envisaged.

By 2013 there were a 196 parties to the Montreal Protocol, making it one of the most universal treaties in existence. By 2012 these countries had collectively phased out more than 98% of the production and consumption of the chemicals controlled by the protocol. Whilst the remaining 2% still represents a significant problem, UNEP estimate that the ozone layer is expected to return to its pre-1980s state sometime between 2050 and 2075. Without the protocol, ozone depletion would have risen to around 50% in the northern hemisphere and 70% in the southern mid-latitudes by 2050. This would have resulted in twice as much harmful ultraviolet radiation (UVB) in the northern hemisphere and four times as much in the south. The estimated implications of this are striking: 19 million more cases of non-melanoma cancer, 1.5 million cases of melanoma cancer, and 130 million more cases of eye cataracts (UNEP 2012).

The Montreal Protocol stands as the greatest achievement of global environmental governance and, given the aforementioned statistics, one of the greatest achievements of international relations as a whole. The sense of urgency engendered by solid scientific evidence of the environmental change occurring and its human health impact united the world. Unfortunately, it is an achievement that has yet to be replicated in other issues of environmental security and, most notably, climate change.

'Not fixing the thermostat': Climate change

The sense of urgency and global solidarity that prompted the ozone regime was apparent also for climate change at the time that the Montreal Protocol was being developed. Prior to the World Conference referred to at the start of the chapter, Toronto also hosted the 1988 G7 summit where the issue was discussed at the high table of the world's leading economic powers. In stark contrast to later US intransigence, the Reagan administration was instrumental in putting climate change on the summit agenda, alongside the more conventional concerns of Soviet relations, the state of the global economy and terrorism. As discussed in Chapter 2, climate change then became a primary case for security 'wideners' in the 1990s, featuring in foreign policy statements of national interest of the US, Russia and many other states.

However, in spite of increasing clarity on the causes and consequences of climate change, the solidarity and sense of urgency has not been maintained, and international political and legal progress has been slow, as is analysed in the next chapter.

The slower development of the climate change regime compared to its ozone 'sister' is not for the want of trying to get it prioritized at the global political level by some states. In 2007 the UK government used their chairmanship of the UN Security Council to put climate change on the agenda for the first time, citing the following security implications of the phenomenon: border disputes due to the melting of ice sheets and rising sea levels; increased migration with the 'the potential for instability and conflict'; conflict over energy supplies; conflict due to scarcity; conflict due to poverty; and conflicts related to extreme weather events (UNSC 2007). The British position was backed by her EU partners Germany and Slovenia, also present in the Security Council at the time, and supported by many others in the ensuing debate. The Namibian representative Kaire Mbuende, for example, notably referred to greenhouse gas emissions as tantamount to 'low intensity biological or chemical warfare' (Namibia 2007). However, this securitization move was not supported by all, and China and South Africa objected to climate change being debated in the Security Council, arguing that it was not appropriate since it was a development rather than a security issue.

This approach of invoking traditional military concerns to highlight the threats posed by climate change is related to the widening literature which had developed and continues to evolve in academic circles. The prominent Homer-Dixon, for example, has described the phenomenon as 'just as dangerous – and more intractable – than the arms race between the United States and the Soviet Union during the Cold War or the proliferation of nuclear weapons amongst rogue states today' (Homer-Dixon 2007: 1). That year also saw mainstream acknowledgement of this line of thinking with the awarding of the 2007 Nobel Peace Prize jointly to Al Gore and the Intergovernmental Panel on Climate Change (IPCC) for making the threats of climate change much better appreciated.

The momentum for securitizing climate change has been maintained at the UN over recent years. In 2009 the General Assembly passed Resolution 63/281 acknowledging the impacts that climate change has on security but, cautious of allowing the issue to be hijacked by the great powers in the Security Council, reaffirmed that the FCCC was the key instrument for addressing global warming. The Resolution also requested the Secretary-General to submit a comprehensive report to the General Assembly on the possible security implications of climate change. The subsequent report, released later that year, highlighted the 'threat multiplier' dimension of climate change in exacerbating the threats posed by extreme weather events and disasters and the need to focus on the most vulnerable in strategies of mitigation and adaptation. The report focused much less on the military or power implications of climate change, highlighted in the Security Council debate, and was a much clearer expression of a human security approach (General Assembly 2009).

In 2011 a second UNSC debate on climate change took place, culminating in a non-legally-binding document reaffirming that peace could be threatened by resource stress. This time, though, the debate also noted the non-military security implications of climate change in the context of the problem of land losses for low-lying island states, after successful lobbying by the delegations of Nauru, the Maldives and the Seychelles. Also distinct from 2007 was the greater unity in the Security Council with the US, now under the Obama regime, which was notably more engaged. However, the G77 and Non-Aligned Movement global South lobbies were still resistant to securitization through fear that the issue could come to be framed in a way that neglects the importance of aid and global economic reform. Developing countries, in general, are wary of being even more dominated by the 'big five' permanent members through the continued encroachment by the Security Council on the functions and powers of the more egalitarian General Assembly and UN programmes.

Global warming is a global problem, in both cause and effect, but the scale of human security threat is not equal across the globe. For low-lying island states the prospect of a rise in the level of the oceans is a human and state security threat of the utmost gravity. The governments of the Maldives and Kiribati have already made plans to shift their entire populations to other locations. For other states the threat is seen as far more remote, both geographically and chronologically, and the urgency to act, which is generally needed for governments to ratify costly environmental agreements, is not there. Indeed, it should be noted that the Stern Review, which formed the basis of the British securitization push, was very much a cost–benefit analysis and, whilst noting that globally the balance is undoubtedly weighted in favour of the former, it makes clear that some parts of the world could experience net gains from fewer cold-related deaths, and the increased revenue from tourism and improved agricultural fertility (Stern 2006). Even in the part of the world most dramatically affected by climate change, opinion in divided. Prominent Greenlandic politician Aleqa Hammond has articulated this: 'Because of the warming of the sea the halibut are multiplying faster, and the fisheries have never been so good as they are now .... Because of global warming our rivers and lakes have never been so full. We have lots of water and we want to use it for hydro power' (Cathcart 2007). It is also apparent that many of the threats could be averted by human adaptation to a changing landscape and the Cornucopian arguments, highlighted in Chapter 3, on human ingenuity and technological innovation as a way of countering threats have gathered momentum. The acceptance of 'common but differentiated responsibilities' amongst the states of the world has been limited by their 'common but differentiated insecurities'.

National security threats from climate change continue to be asserted, most notably the threat of sudden influxes of environmental refugees or of conflicts induced by increased competition for depleting resources. These concerns, though, lack the urgency and certainty of the consequences of increased ultraviolet radiation penetrating to the Earth's surface. In addition, the costs of phasing out carbon dioxide and methane are much greater than the cost of phasing out CFCs. DuPont may have been producing a quarter of the world's CFCs, but that still represented less than 2% of their earnings. The stakes are much higher with carbon dioxide emissions.

When worlds collide: Extraterrestrial security threats

Although they have yet to greatly impact human society, natural phenomena emanating from beyond the Earth must also be seen to represent a civilizational security threat. 'An asteroid of size 1 km or more hitting our world at the minimum possible velocity (11 km s^{-1}, the escape velocity of the Earth) would release at least as much energy as 100,000 one-megaton hydrogen bombs' (Kitchin 2001: 54). Asteroids are minor planets within our solar system which vary in size from a diameter of over a thousand to less than 1 km. Most lie between the orbits of Mars and Jupiter but some, the 'Earth-crossing asteroids' (ECAs), can cross this planet's orbit of the Sun. The ECAs, together with comets and meteoroids (debris from asteroids or comets) which pass close to the Earth, are collectively referred to as 'Near-Earth objects' (NEOs). The possibility of one of these celestial objects striking the Earth, and the likely effects, has been the subject of increasing speculation in recent years and some measures have been taken to improve the capacity to predict such a collision and initiate thinking on how it could be avoided. The 'Torino Scale' has been devised to rationalize the likelihood of asteroid collision (Peiser 2001) (see Table 6.1).

Table 6.1 The Torino Scale[1]

0	Events having no likely consequence	collision will not happen
1	Events meriting careful monitoring	collision is extremely unlikely
2		collision is very unlikely
3	Events meriting concern	1% chance of localized destruction
4		1% chance of regional destruction
5	Threatening events	significant threat of regional devastation
6		significant threat of global catastrophe
7		extremely significant threat of global catastrophe
8	Certain collisions	localized destruction (occur every 50–1,000 years)
9		regional destruction (occur every 1,000- 100,000 years)
10		capable of causing global climate catastrophe (occur less than once per 100,000 years)

There are no validated records of human deaths due to NEO collisions, but there is evidence that such collisions have occurred. Meteoroids regularly enter the Earth's atmosphere (what are referred to as meteors), where most burn up and disappear, but some survive long enough to strike the surface (meteorites) or explode close to the surface (bolides). Evidence that comets can collide with planets was provided in 1994 when Shoemaker-Levy 9 was observed crashing into Jupiter. The 'Cretaceous/Tertiary Impact', caused by either a comet or an asteroid, 65 million years ago created the 250 km wide Chicxulub crater in the Yucatán Peninsula and is widely held as being responsible for the extinction of the dinosaurs and various other life forms. A bolide is believed to be responsible for the 1908 phenomenon around the River Tunguska in Siberia when over a 1,000 square kilometres of uninhabited forest were flattened. In 2013 this threat was put in the spotlight when a 17 metre wide meteor from the Apollo asteroid group exploded directly above Chelyabinsk in the Russian Urals, 32.5 seconds after entering the atmosphere, resulting in around 1,500 people being injured (of which over 60 were hospitalized), along with $33 million worth of damage (Smith-Spark 2013).

Surveillance of the night sky for early detection of NEOs has increased since the launch of the 'Spaceguard' initiative by NASA in the early 1990s and its subsequent linking-up with other national schemes. What could be done, though, if an NEO was set for collision with the Earth remains to be established. As typifies traditional securitization, military solutions have figured prominently in discussions. The possibility of destroying an NEO by nuclear strike has been aired regularly, particularly in the US, the state most likely to be able to attempt such an action. Nuclear deterrence is always a divisive security measure, however, and a less dramatic strategy of deflecting an NEO off course by crashing an unmanned spacecraft into it is now more commonly suggested.

Conclusions

The notion that the whole world's security could be imperilled by environmental catastrophe is less prominent in intergovernmental circles today than it was in the 1980s. The threat of ozone depletion appears to have been tackled (although there is still some way to go) and – despite the Chelyabinsk bolide – extraterrestrial collision still appears more of a theoretical than a real threat. Ultimately, climate change has not been treated as an issue of civilizational security and made the world's number one political priority, as appeared possible in the late 1980s.

The lack of consensus on securitizing climate change is a consequence of governments and academics failing to speak the same language in the debate. They have been talking at cross-purposes and engaging in distinct simultaneous discourses rather than a genuine dialectic from which a consensus on how to respond could emerge. This is a consequence of the referent object question in securitization, as discussed in Chapter 2. Ozone depletion was successfully securitized because it was a global security issue and every state's national security issue. The diverse threats posed by climate change, whilst important to all, undoubtedly matter more to some states than others. However, there is more to the lack of consensus than this. Climate change is an 'ultimate' security threat to the low-lying island states faced with submersion, but the threats to other states seeking to securitize the issue are less clear-cut and existential. In the short-termist perspective that characterizes international political interactions for most states, a variety of national interests are invoked by climate change but not imminent national survival. UK advocacy of action on climate change at the UN Security Council in 2007 was as Realist as the Chinese and South African resistance to this. The British had been won over by the resource war thesis of Homer-Dixon and others to believe that mitigating global warming was a route to peace and also calculated that it made economic sense given the conclusions of the Stern Review they had convened, which concluded that the costs of inaction on climate change greatly exceeded the price of action. Compassion for the fate of peoples most affected in arid, low-lying or polar regions doubtless played a part in the thinking of Beckett, Blair and the Labour government, but a clear self-interest was considered apparent and British permanent membership of the Security Council provided a good opportunity to attempt a 'tactical securitization' of the issue. The Chinese and South Africans, in disputing this securitization move, were not rejecting the notion that change was an important concern but calculating that it was not in their national interests to debate this in the Security Council.

The playing of the national security card over climate change by some countries is instinctively treated with suspicion by others because of what national security is understood to stand for in the discourse of the international relations all have been engaged in over the past century. It invokes a militarization of politics with an aggressive interference in the affairs of others or a defensive retreat behind strengthened armed borders, neither of which are relevant for the multidimensional threats posed by climate change. The rhetoric of climate change securitization has done little to dispel this notion. The debates in the Security Council in 2007 and 2011, the foreign policy statements of the US, UK and others, plus the academic arguments of the likes of Homer-Dixon, have highlighted national security threats of failed states, resources conflict and mass migration. Tightening up borders to deter environmental migrants is directly contradictory to the human interest, and the solution of armed humanitarian interventions to lawlessness deployed in other contexts is unlikely to be either welcomed or useful. As Prins and Stamp memorably put it, 'you can't shoot an ozone hole' (Prins & Stamp 1991:12).

The misgivings of the Chinese and South Africans over debating climate change in the Security Council doubtless have something to do with their determination not to have to compromise their economic development, but there is some merit in the argument that it is an issue better tackled elsewhere. In theory it is appropriate that climate change be debated at the high table of global high politics, but the problem with this in practice is that the UN Security Council has always been an arena of Great Power realpolitik. It is the arena where Soviet and US Cold War adventurism was ignored and, in the present age, where violations of international law by countries like Israel and Syria continue to be ignored because of their continued sponsorship by Washington and Moscow. A precedent for tackling non-military issues in the Security Council was established in 2000 when the HIV/AIDS crisis was debated but this, in fact, was inspired not by the human security threat of a disease claiming around 3 million lives a year, but was driven by national interests concerning the implications for

UN peacekeeping troops or the creation of power vacuums in Sub-Saharan states most affected by the pandemic. There is a danger of a securitized discourse on climate change in the UNSC framing the global South as dangerous 'badlands' in need of control, as with other issues debated there like HIV/AIDS and narcotics. This was evident in the intergovernmental discussions and media reporting on the Haiti earthquake in 2010 which focused on looting, lawlessness and conflict when, in fact, none of these things were occurring, nor did they to any great extent.

Whilst, at one level, the idea of giving issues of 'civilizational security' the ultimate political spotlight seems welcome and appropriate, this is not necessarily the case since this is the arena of Great Power national interests rather than global interest. Securitizing ozone depletion, after all, did not involve Security Council resolutions or any grand national security gestures, it was dealt with in a transnational, technical and legal manner. As discussed in the chapters of Part 3, new, lower-key approaches are generally what is needed for dealing with the human problems induced by environmental change.

Key points

- Effective international political action to curb the erosion of the ozone layer occurred soon after evidence of this threat to global security became apparent.
- Climate change is widely regarded as of at least a comparable scale of threat as ozone depletion, but has been less successfully 'securitized' due both to it being more differentially threatening to states and being addressed in contradictory ways.
- A major extraterrestrial collision with the Earth is, as yet, a theoretical threat but is a real one with the potential to be the ultimate of all civilizational security threats.

Note

1 This scale was devised by Professor Richard Binzel.

Recommended reading

Gareau, B. (2013) *From Precaution to Profit: Contemporary Challenges to Environmental Protection in the Montreal Protocol*, Yale: Yale University Press.

Webersik, C. (2010) *Climate Change and Security. A Gathering Storm of Global Challenges*, Santa Barbara: Praeger.

Part 3

The environment and human security

7 Adapt or die?

Climate change

Here is the truth: The Earth is round; Saddam Hussein did not attack us on 9/11; Elvis is dead; Obama was born in the United States; and the climate crisis is real.

(Al Gore 2011)

Climate change is undoubtedly complex, since it invokes myriad interconnected issues of the already complex subject areas of meteorology, environmental change, economics and politics. However, in essence, the phenomenon is actually quite straightforward and unambiguous, belying the contention that surrounds it. 'Greenhouse gases' in the atmosphere raise temperatures by trapping a proportion of solar radiation reflecting off the surface of the Earth. The amount of greenhouse gases in the atmosphere has been rising and the world's mean temperature has been rising. Greenhouse gases and temperatures have risen and fallen in the past, but have never risen at the rate that they currently are and have been since industrialization began adding carbon dioxide emissions into the atmosphere beyond that which occurs naturally in the carbon cycle. As discussed in the previous chapter, this reality has yet to be reflected in international policy, despite concerted efforts to communicate the message from the likes of Gore and, in particular, the IPCC (see Box 7.1).

Box 7.1 The Intergovernmental Panel on Climate Change

Established in 1998 on the recommendation of UNEP and the World Meteorological Organization (also a UN Specialized Agency) by Resolution 43/53 of the General Assembly, the IPCC represents a classic example of an epistemic community, a concept defined in Chapter 1. It is not a think tank or a political actor, in an overt sense. The IPCC is an inclusive forum for presenting evidence from specialists and has brought together around 1,200 independent scientific authors and 2,500 reviewers from around the world.

The IPCC has a Chair and a Bureau to coordinate business and a secretariat based in Geneva. Its work and findings are coordinated through three working groups and one task force. The first working group evaluates scientific literature on climate change. The second considers the consequences of climate change and possible options in terms of adaptation. The third working group appraises strategies for mitigating climate change. A National Greenhouse Gas Inventories Programme is coordinated by a Task Force. The IPCC have published four Assessment Reports in 1990, 1995, 2001 and 2007, and the fifth is due in 2014.

Inevitably, thinking in the IPCC is not uniform, but they have achieved much in building an epistemic consensus to assist in the politics of climate change mitigation and adaptation. Amongst the notable contributions of the panel has been the clarification of the following facts:

- The 100-year linear warming trend (1906–2005) was 0.74°C, with most of the warming occurring in the past 50 years.
- Global greenhouse gas emissions have grown since pre-industrial times, with an increase of 70% between 1970 and 2004 (24% between 1990 and 2004).

Facing the heat: The human security implications of climate change

The human implications of climate change are myriad, complex and interlinked. In human security terms climate change is a 'threat multiplier', serving to exacerbate a series of existing problems:

- *More frequent and lengthy heatwaves.* One obvious consequence of a warming world is an increase in heatwaves and it is notable that the two deadliest recorded instances of this phenomenon were recent events: in 2003 in France and 2010 in Russia, both claiming over 50,000 lives.
- *Increased incidences of wildfires.* The 2010 Russian heatwave was accompanied by wildfires. The deadliness of the twin phenomena was, of course, heightened by the fact that Moscow and St Petersburg were not used to dealing with such hazards and there was insufficient knowledge of how to control the spread of the fires.
- *More frequent droughts.* A heightened drought threat is another inevitable consequence of a progressively warming world. The IPCC estimate that the number of people affected by water scarcity will increase from around 1.7 billion to 5 billion by 2025 (IPCC 2001).
- *Coastal flooding due to sea level rises.* Short of the national security total submersion scenarios discussed in Chapter 6, the encroachment of the sea brings heightened human security threats for coastal communities through increased soil erosion, loss of fertile land, settlement dislocation, saltwater intrusion into freshwater sources and storm surges. In a glimpse of the future most of the Maldives were submerged during the worst storm surges that accompanied the devastating 2004 Indian Ocean tsunami.
- *Reduced crop yields due to reduced rainfall.* The production of staple foods is forecast to decrease by up to 50% as early as 2020 in several African states (WHO 2012). Crop yields should increase slightly in the highest and lowest latitudes but arid, semi-arid and tropical countries, where food scarcity is already most acute, will suffer from lower precipitation rates.
- *Spread of tropical diseases north and south.* Tropical diseases associated with insect vectors native to equatorial areas are becoming increasingly common in areas with traditionally more temperate climes. The warmer the weather the more readily mosquitoes breed and bite, and malaria and other diseases have recently become a health threat in countries away from the insects' usual habitats. The US, for example, has been hit by West Nile virus as far north as New York every summer since 1999. A record number of cases of the bacterial lung infection Legionnaires' disease in the UK in 2006 led the Health Protection Agency to claim that the country had suffered its first casualties from infectious disease due to global warming (Laurence 2006). The WHO estimate that climate change is responsible for 3% of malaria and diarrhoea fatalities (Hughes et al. 2011: 93).

- *Water cycle disruption*. Climate change affects the natural recycling of water in contradictory ways. On one hand there are hazards relating to more frequent and stronger riverine flooding in wet seasons due to glaciers melting, whilst, on the other hand, progressively higher temperatures mean that there will be reduced water supplies in dry seasons. The flow rate on the great Siberian rivers has already increased by between 15% and 20% since the mid-1980s (Usher et al. 2010).
- *Increased rate of water-borne diseases in flooded areas and pollution in urban areas*. Flooding brings disease as well as destruction, as is analysed in Chapter 10. Schistomiasis, transmitted by water snails, is forecast to become more prevalent in China, despite its rapid economic development and sophisticated health system (WHO 2012). There is already a huge death toll attributable to atmospheric pollution, highlighted in the following chapter, and, since higher temperatures are associated with higher levels of pollution, this is likely to worsen. Overall, the WHO estimate that climate change already costs 140,000 lives a year and, in economic terms, will invoke an extra $2–4 billion costs by 2030 (WHO 2012).
- *Ocean acidification*. Oceans and seas absorb around half of the carbon dioxide emitted by fossil fuel-burning which forms carbonic acid when it combines with seawater. On the plus side this serves to counter temperature rises in the atmosphere but this acidification has consequences for sea, the sealife and humanity. The world's oceans have already acidified by 30% and, at current rates of carbon dioxide emissions, this will be a rise of 150% by the end of the century (UKOA 2013). Fish and shellfish stocks will inevitably decline in the face of this due to the effects of acid on the calcium carbonate in their bones and shells.
- *More frequent and stronger windstorms*. The fact that storms increase in frequency and intensity when temperatures and atmospheric pressure increases is already established by observing weather phenomena such as El Niño. The idea that storms could also come to affects parts of the world previously unaffected was given some credence in 2004 when the first ever recorded cyclone in the southern hemisphere of the Americas, Catarina, struck southern Brazil killing three people.

Feeling the pressure: Those most vulnerable to climate change

The effects of climate change vary from locality to locality and from person to person but the following localities and groups of people can be considered to be amongst the most vulnerable.

Low-lying territories

Over half of the world's people live within 200 km of the coast and population growth rates are significantly higher in these areas. One-tenth of the world live below ten metres above sea level including much of rapidly developing Asia and megacities like Shanghai (O'Brien & Leichenko 2008: 21). Hence, low-lying islands have been amongst the most vociferous campaigners for global mitigating action on climate change.

The Arctic

The world's most profound form of environmental change is being felt most profoundly of all in the Arctic. The IPCC have reported that average Arctic temperatures had increased at nearly twice the global average rate over the past century and that Arctic sea ice had shrunk by 3.3% over the previous decade (IPCC 2007). Many of the previously referred to human security impacts are coming to be felt most dramatically in the Polar North due to its differentially rapid rate of warming. Pollution is being exacerbated as northerly winds become more intense, precipitation increases and the flow rate on rivers accelerates. Further effects on pollution and the food supply will then be experienced since melted ice entering the sea affects the salinity and the ocean circulation patterns. Together with its Antipodean counterpart, changes in the Arctic also contribute to the exacerbation of climate change for the world by altering the albedo effect (reflectiveness) of the Earth since sea ice reflects sunlight.

In addition to such polar dimensions of environmental change brought on by warming, a particular Arctic aspect of the phenomenon could come from the effects of the thaw on the atmospheric supply of methane. There are pools of the greenhouse gas in the ground below the tundra which already account for 20% of the world's non-industrial emissions of a gas more than 20 times as powerful an agent of warming as carbon dioxide (Wille et al. 2008). The Western Siberian peat bog is estimated to contain around 70 billion tonnes of methane, the equivalent of 73 years of manmade carbon dioxide emissions at current rates (Pearce 2005).

Women, children and the old

Children and pregnant women are particularly vulnerable to water-borne diseases, which are set to become more prominent in a warmer world. In non-industrialized societies it is usually women who access water and look after children for their families. Children's immature respiratory, neurological and immune systems leave them particularly vulnerable to pandemics and heatwaves. The elderly are also amongst the most vulnerable of people and the world's average age profile is getting older. The 2003 French heatwave prompted a 20% spike in mortality in the 45–74 age group compared to a 70% rise in the 75+ age group (O'Brien & Leichenko 2008: 26).

The poor

As with most human security threats, it is poverty that is the primary underlying cause of vulnerability to the multiple threats associated with climate change. The poor are the most affected in the short term by heightened scarcity, extreme weather events and hazards, and the least able to adapt to the increased prevalence of these changes in the long term. It is the gravest environmental injustice of all that it is those people least responsible for climate change who are most negatively affected by it.

The international politics of climate change

Climate change first appeared on the international political agenda in the 1970s, with the first UN Conference held in 1979. The IPCC was initiated in 1988 and its first report, in 1990, prompted a General Assembly Resolution setting up an Intergovernmental Negotiating Committee to draft a binding treaty for reducing the emission of greenhouse gases, comparable to the ozone regime. This was then presented and opened for signature at UNCED in 1992, initiating a regime which has subsequently evolved slowly through annual Conferences of the Parties (CoPs) establishing binding rules on emissions cuts. In line with the 'common but differentiated responsibilities' principle agreed at Rio, there is a funding mechanism for assisting LDCs in this aim, which also are given a longer timeframe for making cuts. This process is summarized in Box 7.2.

Box 7.2 Progress of the Framework Convention on Climate Change

1990 UN General Assembly Resolution establishes Intergovernmental Negotiating Committee

1992 Framework Convention on Climate Change

1995 FCCC Conference of the Parties 1 in Berlin
'Common but differentiated responsibilities' principle reaffirmed for curbing greenhouse gas emissions.

1996 FCCC Conference of the Parties 2 in Geneva
Call for legally binding protocol to FCCC with specific targets.

1997 FCCC Conference of the Parties 3 in Kyoto
Kyoto Protocol commits some developed countries to a 5.2% cut in aggregated greenhouse gases (on 1990 levels) by 2008/2012.

1998 FCCC Conference of the Parties 4 in Buenos Aires
Market mechanisms for achieving Kyoto target fleshed out – emissions trading, joint implementation and a Clean Development Mechanism.

1999 FCCC Conference of the Parties 5 in Bonn
Timetable for implementing Kyoto Protocol agreed.

2000 FCCC Conference of the Parties 6 in The Hague
Talks break down and US withdraws support. Talks completed in Bonn in 2001.

2001 FCCC Conference of the Parties 7 in Marrakech
Marrakech Accords agree more funding for LDCs.

2002 FCCC Conference of the Parties 8 in New Delhi
Developed world (including US) pledge to help LDCs in adapting to climate change through technology transfers.

2003 FCCC Conference of the Parties 9 in Milan
Funding for LDCs extended.

2004 FCCC Conference of the Parties 10 in Buenos Aires
Russian ratification allows the Kyoto Protocol to come into force in February.

2005 FCCC Conference of the Parties 11 in Montreal
US attempt to derail FCCC process but rules for emissions trading set and Clean Development Mechanism strengthened.

2006 FCCC Conference of the Parties 12 in Nairobi
Limited progress prompts criticism from UN Secretary-General Annan.

2007 FCCC Conference of the Parties 13 in Bali
Bali Road Map sets course for new Framework Convention to be signed at Copenhagen in 2009.
EU propose deeper cuts than Kyoto but these are opposed by the US. LDCs start to make general commitment to their own cuts.

2008 FCCC Conference of the Parties 14 in Poznan
New funding mechanism for LDC adaptation discussed.

2009 FCCC Conference of the Parties 15 in Copenhagen
Failure to agree new binding instrument to succeed Kyoto Protocol. A more limited Copenhagen Accord brought US, China and India on board to pledge to act to avoid global temperature rising beyond 2°C. Further aid pledges also made.

2010 FCCC Conference of the Parties 16 in Cancun
Copenhagen Accord pledge reaffirmed and adaptation fund agreed.

2011 FCCC Conference of the Parties 17 in Durban
Durban Platform for Enhanced Action pledged that a new legally binding treaty would be concluded by 2015. Extension of Kyoto Protocol to 2020 signed up to by EU, Australia, Norway and Switzerland but not the US, Canada, Japan or Russia.

2012 FCCC Conference of the Parties 18 and Climate Change Conference in Doha
Compensation mechanism for victims of climate change discussed.

As can be seen in Box 7.2 strategies for adapting to climate change have become more prominent as hopes for successful mitigation have lessened. Technological solutions have also come to be suggested in the emerging science of geoengineering. One example of this is solar radiation management through measures such as releasing reflective aerosols into the atmosphere. The technical and economic feasibility of such measures, though, remains to be established.

International policy on climate change has been stifled by global and human security concerns being trumped by assertions of national interest by some countries, most notably the US. President Bush Sr's announcement at Rio in 1992 that 'The American lifestyle is not negotiable' is as clear an example of 'beggar thy neighbour' in the face of a collective goods problem as you could find. The administrations of Bush Sr and Bush Jr originally disputed the science of anthropogenic climate change but, recognizing the Canute-like futility of such a stance, the position shifted in the 2000s to a more brazen but honest admission that acting on climate change was against US national interests because of the costs incurred.

Climate change scepticism

A dwindling band of climate-change deniers still exists but they now hold little credibility in the face of the epistemic consensus that has emerged from the – admittedly – 'broad church' that is the IPCC. Former UK Chancellor of the Exchequer Nigel Lawson, for example, strangely sought to add his thoughts to the debate with a book which epitomizes a stance of denial in the face of what Gore termed 'The Inconvenient Truth'. Lawson's book confuses 'weather' with 'climate' in asserting that temperature rises are 'not, at the present time, happening' (Lawson 2008: 91) and blames alarmism over this on the 'new religion of eco-fundamentalism' (ibid. 104) epitomized by the IPCC, which he labels a 'politically correct alarmist pressure group' (ibid. 11). The book proceeds to argue that the world's ice-sheets are not melting, windstorms are not linked to rising temperatures and then scoffs at the worst heatwave in history by commenting; 'I spent the summer of 2003 in south-west France myself, and found it perfectly tolerable' (ibid. 34). It is arrogance of the most breathtaking kind for an economist to dispute scientific evidence reached consensually by an inclusive gathering of the world's leading experts in the subject, but that is what the 'debate' on the science of anthropogenic climate change is now reduced to. In a survey of a sample of 928 articles on climate change in refereed scientific journals between 1993 and 2003, published in *Science* and quoted by Gore in *The Inconvenient Truth*, it was found that none could be classified as taking a sceptical position, in contrast to around half of all press reports (Oneshes 2004).

A more refined sceptical position on climate change has emerged that does not dispute the evidence but asserts that the threats have been exaggerated and can be adapted to and that other, more pressing human security threats are being sidelined because of the prominence given to the issue. The best-known exponent of this line of thinking is the self-styled 'Sceptical Environmentalist' Bjorn Lomborg (see Box 7.3).

Lomborg followed up the Sceptical Environmentalist by seeking to build up a rival epistemic consensus to the IPCC-based climate change orthodoxy he termed the 'Copenhagen Consensus' The Copenhagen Consensus emerged from a 2004 conference panel of eight economists influenced by the Cornucopian thinking described in the earlier chapter on population. The economists produced cost–benefit analyses for international policy tackling climate change alongside a range of other major global issues including combating malaria, HIV/AIDS and poverty. The Copenhagen Consensus findings suggested that more good could be done

Box 7.3 Bjorn Lomborg – *The Sceptical Environmentalist*

Lomborg's 2001 work *The Sceptical Environmentalist* attracted great interest (and great derision from ecologists) for questioning whether implementing international policy on global warming made any rational sense. The Danish academic claims that he was converted to a sceptical view of the Kyoto Protocol and other international environmental policies he had previously supported by an exercise in one of his classes at the University of Aarhus in which he asked his students to consider the most efficient way to allocate money to solve the most pressing global problems. The students' results and Lomberg's subsequent research suggested that, when set against other global problems, the costs of acting to curb global warming exceeded the gains. Lomborg did not deny that climate change was a human-caused problem, but suggested that it is not as significant a threat as it had been painted and that the expenditure to be allocated to tackling the problem would be better spent on addressing global poverty.

by prioritizing issues other than climate change. The Kyoto Protocol was argued to be a misallocation of global resources since

> *A tenth of the annual cost of the Kyoto Protocol – or a tenth of the US budget this year for the wars in Iraq and Afghanistan – would prevent nearly 30 million new infections of HIV/AIDS. The same sum could similarly be used to help the four million people who will die from malnutrition this year, the 2.5 million killed by indoor and outdoor air pollution, the two million who will die because they lack micronutrients (iron, zinc, and vitamin A), or the two million whose deaths will be caused by a lack of clean drinking water.*
>
> (Lomborg 2008)

Lomborg's *Cool It* built on this argument and reasoned that adaptation to climate change, through geoengineering, was a more efficient strategy than mitigation. Lomborg also argued that mitigation was not cost-efficient because by the time the worst effects of climate change are being felt, people in developing countries will be as wealthy as people in the developed world today and so able to adapt to the changes (Lomborg 2007).

Whilst the rise of the Copenhagen Consensus has more rigour than Lawsonesque denial we again see economists reducing complex, technical arguments to purely economic matters. There is some compelling logic in arguing that aid is not always directed at the most deserving causes and it is worth being pragmatic in deciding how to help the most people. However, positing that more good could be done in tackling malaria than mitigating climate change overlooks the facts that a comparatively large amount of global money has been allocated to malaria without coming close to eradicating the disease and that malaria and many other health problems are, and will increasingly be, exacerbated by climate change. The threat multiplier point about climate change is sidestepped and it is assumed to be a separate problem from disease or development, which is an unsupportable abstraction. Even the economic analysis of the Copenhagen Consensus lacks rigour since it is difficult to find any basis to assume that Bangladeshis at the end of this century will be like Dutchmen today, as they assert. Similarly, assuming that geoengineering is a more efficient strategy for tackling climate change can hardly be proven since none of these techniques have yet been tried and tested, let alone costed.

'Alternative' international policy on climate change

Despite the impasse on effective intergovernmental policy on climate change (and also because of it) progress has, nonetheless, been made in transnational climate governance in which strategies of mitigation and adaptation at the local level have been promoted by IGOs and NGOs. The EU, for example, has promoted initiatives such as the Energy Cities Network European Covenant of Mayors which links over 2,600 metropolitan authorities in a variety of initiatives and pledges to reduce carbon dioxide emissions. In the US, embarrassment at federal inaction prompted the Regional Greenhouse Gas Initiative involving Connecticut, Delaware, Maine, Maryland, Massachusetts, New Hampshire, New York, Rhode Island and Vermont. These states have vowed to reduce CO_2 emissions from their power stations by 10% by 2018. On a wider level the C40 Cities Climate Leadership Group, Cities for Climate Protection Programme and International Council for Local Environmental Initiatives have also developed largely non-governmental schemes and promoted information-sharing (Connelly 2012: 372–374).

Within the UN system, the Human Security Unit has advanced 'community-based adaptation and mitigation plans to address gaps in national and international strategies (UNHSU 2013: 5)'. Amongst such schemes are early warning systems and strategies for adaptation and coping with climate change focusing on local empowerment. A project in Lesotho, for example, has promoted climate-sensitive agricultural practices in the face of greater water scarcity, including techniques for improving the storage of grain and fodder, and a greater emphasis on growing more drought-tolerant crops. A successful precedent for such adaptation has occurred in Rajasthan, India, where a switch from the rearing of livestock to the production of cumin, mustard seeds and herbal medicines has boosted local agriculture in spite of more regularized droughts (Chatterjee et al. 2005, O'Brien & Leichenko 2008: 32). Such schemes empower citizens through giving them greater self-reliance by explaining how to grow 'backyard gardens' to extend cultivation knowledge beyond farmsteads into the whole community and involving them more in early warning systems. Climate change epitomizes the ecologist's maxim of 'think global, act local', and sustainable adaptation and mitigation is enhanced by localized schemes working in tandem with the bigger picture of cutting and offsetting global carbon and methane emissions.

Local empowerment has raised the diplomatic profile of some of the most vulnerable countries and nations in the low-lying states and the Arctic. The combination of advancing local knowledge and increased awareness of the human dimension of environmental change has also been prominent in climate change diplomacy. Inuvialuit from Banks Island, Northwest Territories, presented a video recording showing the effects of climate change on their local environment and community at the 2000 Conference of the Parties (COP) of the UN Framework Convention on Climate Change (UNFCCC) in The Hague. ICC Greenland have, since 2005, been running the 'Sila-Inuk' project which documents findings from Inuit hunters around the island on changes in the availability of resources and the Siku-Inuit-Hila (Sea Ice, People and Weather) Project which monitors sea ice changes (Lynge 2011: 194). In 2005 the 'Many Strong Voices' programme on climate change was established linking the ICC with the Small Island Developing States (SIDS) – containing many low-lying tropical islands vulnerable to sea level rises and, hence, fellow 'barometers' of global warming. The programme is not really non-governmental in that it is coordinated by UNEP/GRID Arendal and the Center for International Climate and Environmental Research funded by the Norwegian government, highlighting the ICC's capacity for constructive engagement with the international community. Many Strong Voices has articulated its three central aims: an effective global agreement on climate change, respect for the use of traditional knowledge in understanding climate change and financial and technical assistance from the world's most wealthy and culpable for the problem (MSV 2012). Building on this initiative and utilizing contacts established through the UN Forum for Indigenous Peoples, in 2009 the ICC organized the Indigenous Peoples Global Summit on Climate Change in Anchorage which attracted 300 participants from over 70 countries.

More localized strategies have the advantage, in human security terms, of being more likely to empower communities and deal with the question of differential vulnerability. In a microcosm of the global picture, the poor tend to incur the costs of rich profligacy whilst those largely responsible are better equipped to cope with the shared consequences. Localizing food production may shrink carbon footprints but also the profits of small-scale LDC exporters. The shift from fossil fuels to biofuels in countries like Brazil is at one level 'green' but at another not since it has led to pollution, habitat destruction and the dislocation of small farmers (O'Brien & Leichenko 2008: 29).

Sustainable mitigation and adaptation therefore includes a variety of strategies including improved transport and communications in vulnerable regions, construction of safer housing in vulnerable regions, and more flexibility in state/regional provision such as altering school times to avoid periods of drought (O'Brien & Leichenko 2008: 31). On a wider scale, sustainable adaptation could also involve states relaxing border controls to allow for the migration of livestock herders such as in East Africa (O'Brien & Leichenko 2008: 32).

Legal avenues are another way for questions of environmental injustice to be raised. The UN High Commissioner Refugees (UNHCR) has suggested that neglecting to mitigate climate change is contrary to the Covenant of Economic, Social and Cultural Rights and, given the question of vulnerability, also to 'second generation' global human rights instruments such as the Conventions on women, the disabled and the child and the rights of indigenous peoples (UNHCR 2009). The Inuit Circumpolar Council (ICC) in 2005 attracted global attention by serving a petition with the Inter-American Human Rights Commission against the US government, for their negligence in combating the problem. The legal case predictably came to nothing but the episode served its purpose in highlighting the human consequences of climate change through wide media coverage of the story.

Conclusions

In spite of the difficulties in progressing meaningful international policy on climate change, due to the traditional barrier of narrowly defined, short-term national economic interests, a discourse on the need for action has, nonetheless, advanced significantly. The US government has had to cease being in denial on the issue for its own credibility on the world stage, and short-sighted economists, industrialists and politicians denying there is a problem are increasingly preaching only to a constituency of the wilfully ignorant. Public opinion is now convinced of the reality of anthropogenic climate change and the necessity of acting to mitigate its effects. This is the case even in the US, the home of climate change scepticism. Annual polls by Pew between 2006 and 2010 revealed that an average 40% of US citizens consider climate change to be a 'very serious' and 32% a 'somewhat serious' problem, as opposed to 13% seeing it as not a problem at all (Pew 2010). British public opinion is now so convinced of the need to act that, in 2006, even a UK Conservative Prime Minister-to-be chose to campaign for election on a husky-drawn sledge in Spitsbergen to emphasize his credentials on the matter. Getting over the hurdles of vested economic interests remains a major problem, but the normative change that has occurred on climate change provides at least hope that effective, sustainable mitigation and adaptation in the human interest is possible.

Key points

- Climate-change is a 'threat multiplier', exacerbating existing human security threats such as those from extreme weather events, natural disasters and the spread of disease.
- Amongst the people most vulnerable to the effects of climate change are those living in low-lying territories, arid areas and the Arctic and, more generally, women, children, the old and the poor.
- Climate-change denial and scepticism persists but holds little credibility in the face of IPCC evidence and has little public support.
- Formal intergovernmental policy on climate change has been stifled by displays of national interest but more informal transnational schemes offer hope for enhancing human security.

Recommended reading

Gore, A. (2006) *An Inconvenient Truth. The Planetary Emergency of Global Warming and What we can do About it*, Emmaus, PN: Rodale Press.

O'Brien, K. & Leichenko, R. (2008) *Human Security, Vulnerability and Sustainable Adaptation*, Human Development Report 2007/2008, United Nations Development Programme.

Stern, N. (2007) *The Economics of Climate Change.* The Stern Review (UK Government), Cambridge: Cambridge University Press.

8 Messy business

Pollution and human security

The chemicals to which life is asked to make its adjustment are no longer merely the calcium and silica and copper and all the rest of the minerals washed out of the rocks and carried in rivers to the sea; they are the synthetic creations of man's inventive mind, brewed in his laboratories, and having no counterparts in nature.

Rachel Carson (Carson 1962: 7)

Pollution kills and, in spite of significant improvements in combating the harmful contamination of the air, water, soil, flora and fauna through political efforts over recent decades, it continues to do so in huge numbers. A breakdown of pollution mortality for 2010 revealed that air pollution alone is a bigger killer than anything in the contemporary world (killing over 6 million in 2010), representing a far greater human security threat than war, terrorism, human rights abuses and crime combined (which have claimed just over 700,000 annual casualties in recent years) (see Table 8.1).

Air pollution

The pollution of the air occurs as a result of the introduction into the atmosphere, or formation there, of chemicals or fine particles (traces of chemicals below 2.5 micrometres). There are myriad of these that have health consequences but amongst the most significant are carbon monoxide, sulfur dioxide and a variety of nitrogen oxides.

Pollutants can be dispersed in the atmosphere through convective or turbulent movement (i.e. heat or wind). They may be directly hazardous but can also have secondary effects through combining and reacting, particularly when exposed to sunlight, such as with photochemical oxidants produced when hydrocarbons combine with nitrogen. For example, tropospheric ozone, which is a human and plant hazard (distinct from the stratospheric ozone layer), is formed in this way.

Indoor

As is evident from Table 8.1, indoor pollution presents a huge human security threat. Smoke from domestic combustion, such as cooking and heating, is a much bigger killer than has been appreciated until recently. The 3.5 million annual fatalities represents a big increase on previous estimates largely due to increased recognition of the contribution of indoor pollution to cardiovascular diseases. The link with respiratory diseases has been much longer established.

Table 8.1 Global deaths due to pollution in 2010

1.	Household air pollution (smoke)	3,546,399
2.	Outdoor air pollution (ambient particulate matter)	3,223,540
3.	Lead poisoning	674,038
4.	Water / sanitation pollution	337,476
5.	Ozone	152,434
6.	Residential radon exposure	98,992

Source: Lim et al. (2012).

It is a recurrent theme of human security threats that they tend to be much closer to home than popularly perceived and, despite the focus on the long-range transmission of toxins, the same is true of pollution. Alongside combustion, significant health impacts also accrue from domestic contamination by lead water pipes, chemicals used in pest control or cleaning and accumulations of radon resulting either as a consequence of better insulated homes retaining subsurface sources or from the use of granite as a building material. Biological agents such as moulds and allergens represent further domestic pollution threats.

Outdoor: Urban

High temperatures and the use of tall chimneys for industrial emissions and waste incineration help to disperse pollutants widely, meaning that it is the low-level pollution from motor vehicles and domestic chimneys that account for most urban pollution. The biggest source of outdoor pollution is from motor vehicle emissions, which include carbon monoxide, hydrocarbons and nitrogen oxides. In many developed countries, though, this has lessened in significance through the redesign of engines.

There have been several notorious historical events which have served to graphically illustrate urban pollution in the form of smog. The 1952 'pea souper' in London killed over 4,000 by the inhalation of sulfuric acid droplets created in the atmosphere from sulfur dioxide emissions. Four years earlier 20 immediate deaths and countless long-term casualties of a smog in Donora, Pennsylvania, did much to initiate pollution awareness and concerns in the US. Smog today is responsible for 1.2 million of the contemporary pollution deaths in East Asia, particularly in China (Lim et al. 2012). Aside from such extreme cases, urban pollution remains a problem even in countries with well-established legal restraints. In the US the EPA estimate that 126 million citizens live in counties where national air pollution standards are not being met (EPA 2013).

Outdoor: Industrial

Combustion

Air pollution by by-products of industrial pollution arose in line with industrialization and there continues to be a profound collateral damage accompanying the achievement of economic development, particularly in those countries still going though an industrial revolution. The long-range dimension of this became apparent in the recognition of the phenomenon of acid rain in the 1960s. Acid rain refers to the phenomenon whereby sulfur dioxide and other emissions from the burning of fossil fuels accumulate in the Earth's atmosphere and then return to the surface as precipitation, hundreds of miles from where they departed as fumes.

Heavy metals also feature in long-range transboundary pollution, particularly mercury. Whilst mercury emissions from North America and Europe have progressively fallen since the 1980s due to political actions, the growth of coal-fed power plants in China and other emerging markets has served to counter this and led to a continuation of contamination by long-range atmospheric transport. Like acid rain, pollution from mercury, too, can be transported in the air and then fall as snow in springtime, from where it can come to be ingested by seabirds and marine mammals.

The evolution of political action over the years in developed countries has seen the situation improve through more switching to non-fossil fuels or the attachment of electrostatic devices to smokestacks to remove pollutants. Localized poisoning in developing states, though, remains a major human security threat, both in terms of a gradual build-up of toxins in the atmosphere or through their sudden release due to industrial accidents.

Accidents

The world's worst-ever industrial accident occurred at Bhopal, India, on 3 December 1984. During the production of the pesticide carbaryl, the plant, run by the US-based multinational corporation Union Carbide, accidentally released 40 tonnes of the highly toxic chemical methyl isocyanate (MIC) used in the production process. At least 2,500 people living near the plant were quickly killed and around 180,000 other people have since suffered from a range of long-term health effects and birth defects. As an intermediate chemical, MIC did not feature on the world's foremost safety inventory of the time, UNEP's International Register of Potentially Toxic Chemicals, and Indian authorities were unaware that it was being stored. Investigations also proved that safety standards at the plant were weak and that previous fatal accidents had occurred. One worker had been killed and three others injured by exposure to phosgene, another chemical used in the processing of MIC, in 1981 during Bhopal's first year as a manufacturing unit (phosgene was one of the chemicals used on the battlefields of the First World War). In the following year a visiting safety team from Union Carbide's US headquarters described the plant's MIC unit in an internal report as possessing 'serious potential for sizeable releases of toxic materials' (Weir 1987: 40).

Added to the ignorance as to the nature of MIC and the negligence over safety precautions at the plant, was a third factor accentuating the Bhopal tragedy. Bhopal is a poor city and many thousands of people lived in crowded slums near to the Union Carbide plant. These people were powerless to protect themselves from the escaping fumes which spread over the ground (MIC is heavier than air). Estimates of the numbers of casualties vary, but it is believed that 200,000 people were exposed to the gas and 17,000 permanently disabled as a result. The immediate death toll could have been anywhere between 2,000 and 8,000, as most of the victims were not formally recorded in any way, and the killing of entire families hindered the identification process. Long-term health effects include various breathing and digesting disorders, along with birth defects and spontaneous abortions. After years of legal wrangling, Union Carbide USA and their Indian subsidiaries were finally made liable for prosecution in 1991, opening up the way for compensation payments to 500,000 people and for the setting up of a hospital in the city to deal with ongoing ailments.

Whilst Bhopal remains the worst case of pollution by industrial accident, nuclear leaks have provided perhaps the most infamous disasters. The two most significant nuclear accidents of the 20th century occurred in the two superpowers of that age whose unprecedented international political influences were built on that very power source. In 1979 at the Three Mile Island nuclear power plant in Pennsylvania a technical malfunction caused a release of radioactive gas from one of the reactors. There were no confirmed casualties from this accident but it attracted huge publicity which was seized upon by anti-nuclear protestors and, as a consequence, no new nuclear power plants have been built in the US since. The 1986 Chernobyl disaster in the former USSR was the worst-ever nuclear power plant disaster and, in line with the added 'fear factor' associated with this form of energy production, stands as the most notorious industrial disaster to date. Lax safety standards are generally held as the key reason for an explosion and fire which destroyed one of the plant's four power reactors and released huge amounts of solid and gaseous radioactive material into the surrounding area. Thirty-two plant and emergency staff were killed in the immediate aftermath of the explosion and in the following weeks some of this material was deposited over a large swathe of Northern Europe, prompting an unknown number of long-term deaths.

In 2011 nuclear safety was again put in the spotlight with the Fukushima Daiichi nuclear power station disaster, prompted by the devastating tsunami that struck Japan. Three workers were killed and thousands of residents moved out of the region and, whilst levels of public radiation exposure were initially reported as not being dangerous, many fear that further significant long-term health defects will yet emerge.

Agrochemical pollution

The most environmentally hazardous organic pesticides (along with some other organic chemical compounds created for industrial purposes) have, in recent decades, come to be known as persistent organic pollutants (POPs), defined by the UNEP as 'chemical substances that persist in the environment, bioaccumulate through the food web and pose a risk causing adverse effects to human health and the environment.' (UNEP 2009). Chemical droplets have been detected in the atmosphere over most parts of the globe. Clearly therefore, they are capable of falling to earth many miles from the areas where they were originally intended to be applied. Agrochemical vapours enter the atmosphere in many ways. A significant proportion of pesticides may be lost during spraying, through drifting in the wind, or evaporation. Some particularly persistent substances, such as DDT and dieldrin, remain long enough as surface residues after falling with rain that they are subject to evaporation again. Other routes by which pesticides enter the atmosphere include the escape of vapours from pesticide manufacture and formulation plants, and the introduction of residues within dust storms originating in agricultural areas.

Aside from such 'collateral damage' resulting from chemicals accidently missing their intended crop targets or wilfully being employed in ways for which they were not designed (such as in suicide), the chemical properties of POPs can cause them to be an environmental hazard well away from the fields where they have been applied. Since they are so slow to break down and tend to be stored in fat, POPs can end up deposited in animals thousands of kilometres from where they were used and passed down the food chain in the phenomenon of bioaccumulation. In another phenomenon known as the 'grasshopper effect' these chemicals can, after evaporating in the warmer climes where they tend to be used, then be carried around the globe in the atmosphere or water in a series of 'hops' of evaporation and deposition, and then build up in food chains remote from where they are used. Hence polar bears, at the top of Arctic food chains, have been found to be contaminated by POPs (Tenenbaum 2004).

Water pollution

Water pollution occurs from the input of molecules into water from human activities to a harmful level. This can occur in the form of pollution by mercury from mining, agrochemicals, organic waste from sewage and water treatment, acids from manufacturing industries, oil spills and also from the effects of heat or radiation on water sources. Pollution can be 'point source', resulting from the deliberate discharge of waste or 'non-point source' as a consequence of runoff, spillage during transportation, storage or use. Methods have gradually evolved for minimizing non-point-source water pollution. In most developed countries water treatment removes pollutants from domestic supplies and methods exist for the purification of industrial waste water.

Agrochemical source

Gross point source pollution by pesticides sometimes occurs in the form of illegal fishing but it is the unintentional contamination of groundwater from such chemicals that remains the more serious problem. Agrochemical residues can enter water through drift and atmospheric fallout in the same way as they do the soil, but also in a number of other ways. Chemicals in soil may enter nearby water through runoff or be carried there with eroded soil particles. On top of this, spills of pesticides into rivers have been known during the storage and transportation of the chemicals.

The effects of a cumulative input of pesticides into groundwater can be lethal to the organisms which live there. An increase in the mortality of bacteria, fungi, algae, aquatic invertebrates, amphibians, reptiles or fish will disrupt the food webs which exist between them and therefore upset the ecosystem in operation there. The fact that many pesticides concentrate in the tissues of aquatic organisms more readily than in terrestrial life forms exacerbates this problem. Of most concern to humanity is the effect on some fish populations through such pollution, either by direct poisoning or indirectly due to a depletion of their traditional prey. The presence of pesticides in groundwater can also have sub-lethal effects on aquatic life. The raising of the water temperature due to pesticide presence, or the entry of the chemicals into fish brains or nervous systems, can impact their behaviour and reproductive capacities. The most serious consequence of this behavioural change occurs when a species of fish develops a resistance to the pesticide it has been exposed to. When this happens, these fish become capable of carrying once-lethal amounts of chemicals within themselves, which can then be passed on to the next organism in the food web.

The run off of fertilizers into fresh water sources is another key cause of a particular form of pollution known as cultural eutrophication, resulting from the unnatural accumulation of phosphates, nitrogen and/or other plant nutrients. The consequent growth of algae, vegetation or micro-organisms on the water surface blocks light and increases oxygen absorption with sometimes devastating effects on underwater life in the creation of 'dead zones'. The world's largest 'dead zone' is in the Gulf of Mexico where the Mississippi empties, while others exist in the Baltic, the Black Sea and Lake Erie.

Industrial source

Eutrophication can also occur as a result of the accumulation of industrial emissions. Many lakes have acidified due to sulfur emissions from industrial smelting and mining. For example, studies have shown there to have been a progressive accumulation of sulfur in many lakes in Arctic Canada and Svalbard over recent decades. This is beyond a simple build-up of more pollutants since climate change exacerbates the phenomenon. Warming has increased the presence of algae in Arctic lakes which is altering the traditional sulfur cycle and trapping acidifying agents in the sediment and water (Drevnick et al. 2010, Smol & Douglas 2007).

Industrial spills into lakes, rivers or the sea can also prove deadly. A toxic shock to the European system occurred in 2010 when a spill of caustic waste at an alumina plant at Ajka, Hungary, led to toxic chemicals burning nine people to death and turning a stretch of the Danube across several countries red, making graphically apparent the physical and political interconnectedness of the EU.

Oil pollution

Oil spills can occur at various levels in the process of extraction, storage or transportation. The deliberate discharge of waste oils represents one way in which this can occur, although this is now less blatant than it once was due to regulatory actions. Accidental oil spills have also come to be better regulated, but the impact of these events remains acute. As discussed in Chapter 1, the 1967 *Torrey Canyon* ship-source oil spill had a huge impact on pollution awareness and environmentalism in general. Despite political action reducing the regularity of such disasters, two decades on, an even bigger spill occurred when the *Exxon Valdez* tanker hit a reef in Prince William Sound in Alaska in 1989, producing a slick that continues to affect fishing and wildlife in the region over 20 years later. Accidental oil spills can also result in the process of transporting the resource via pipelines such as in the 1998 disaster at Jesse which killed over a thousand Nigerians. More recently, the environmental and human impact that can accrue from rig-based oil spills was dramatically illustrated in the 2010 Deepwater Horizon disaster in the Gulf of Mexico. An explosion led to a massive oil spill which took five months to stop, by which time there had been 11 direct deaths and a huge environmental toll from a massive slick spreading hundreds of kilometres across the sea, along the coastline and on the sea floor.

Waste

Millions of tonnes of organic waste are dumped in the sea each year, with a variety of health consequences. Human sewage, agricultural manure and effluent from paper mills and food processing are not dumped as readily as in the past in many countries, but there are still human health consequences of this phenomenon and a danger of 'out of sight, out of mind' blinding us to the scale of the problem. Organic waste tends to deplete oxygen in water and so negatively affects, marine flora and fauna, which can have knock-on human consequences. Decomposing waste can also produce hydrogen sulfur emissions as a result of the actions of anaerobic bacteria. The international sale of waste from countries with rigid dumping standards to those without has subsequently evolved as a significant trade.

Soil pollution

The soil is a further vector for harmful pollution, which can occur from the accumulation of waste and the runoff from chemicals used in agriculture. Land pollution can occur through the deposition of solid waste in landfills or illegal dumping that does not readily biodegrade. Organic waste can also pollute the soil. Concentrations of heavy metals due to the addition of copper, cadmium and zinc to pig food can produce human health problems and the bacteria on farm animal excrement can be a source of diseases like cryptosporidia and giardiasis.

Additionally, the soil is the principal recipient of agrochemicals, the source of which may be deliberate or accidental. Unlike the intentional entry of pesticides into the soil, which is usually a precise procedure, accidental or collateral entry is indiscriminate and affects a much wider land area, including areas where their presence may be wholly undesirable. Many of the pesticides intended for crop application miss their target or run off the plants into the soil beneath. To this can also be added the entrance of pesticides into the soil from crop residues, leaf fall and root deposits. A less voluminous but more widespread source of pesticide soil pollution is by atmospheric fallout. Small amounts of pesticides have been detected in raindrops and atmospheric dust, which are absorbed into the soil on reaching the ground. Whether the presence of an agrochemical in the soil constitutes an environmental problem or not depends somewhat on its persistence. A quickly degrading chemical will not be likely to disrupt the ecosystem greatly, but a highly persistent chemical may have biological effects beyond the period of its usefulness. Four types of such biological effects can be environmentally damaging. The chemical residues may (i) survive long enough to affect succeeding crops, (ii) affect soil organisms, (iii) leach into water, or (iv) cause long-term damage to soil fertility. The effects of residues on living organisms within the soil can also be summarized into four categories. They may (a) be directly toxic, (b) cause genetic resistance, (c) be passed on to other organisms, or (d) have sub-lethal effects on behaviour or reproduction.

Food pollution

The direct contamination of foodstuffs, including via water pollution, is another source of human insecurity. Again this can arise as a result of agricultural or industrial waste. Industrial effluents entering water sources can lead to food poisoning via fish and seafood. In Japan it was discovered in the 1970s that over 900 people had been killed and thousands others harmed around Minamata Bay (by what is now known as Minamata disease) over the previous two decades as a result of eating seafood contaminated with mercury from a chemical plant on the bay (McCurry 2006).

Chemicals used as pesticides may also be responsible for damaging farm crops when the chemicals become volatile, or unintentionally come into contact with crops other than those they are intended to protect. The drift of vapour from neighbouring crop fields, the effects of herbicide residues which have remained in the soil after application on a different crop in a previous season, or changes in the nature of the pesticide due to the climate can all be causes of crop losses. Pimentel estimates that crop losses amounting to $1.5 billion occur every year in the US (Pimentel 2005). In the US alone, where restrictions on chemical use are amongst the most stringent in the world, it is estimated that every year between 6 and 14 million fish and around 5% of the honeybee population are killed as a result of exposure to pesticides (Pimentel 2005). Longer-term human exposure to harmful chemicals can also occur due to the consumption of residues of pesticides in foodstuffs after production.

Vulnerability to pollution

There are three main forms of exposure to pollution: dermal contact, inhalation and ingestion. Some suggest that exposure to pollutants via animal bites or deliberate injection can be considered further categories (Briggs 2003: 10). Exposure to harmful pollutants may be cumulative and long term (chronic) or short term (acute). Heath impacts may also be a delayed reaction after many years of latency, as with asbestosis. Long-term effects can also occur as a result of sensitization through exposure to allergens (such as dust mites) in early childhood, now understood as a factor behind rises in allergic airway diseases. A further complication for epidemiological studies comes from the 'harvesting effect' when a reduction in certain ailments is witnessed due to a previous upsurge having purged many of the otherwise vulnerable sections of the population (Briggs 2003: 11–12).

As with most causes of human insecurity, socio-economic factors are as significant, if not more so, than actual levels of environmental pollution in assessing vulnerability. In one of the many facets of environmental injustice it is poor people who tend to live in the most polluted places. Separating the impacts of pollution from other forms of insecurity is difficult, as is identifying the impact of specific forms of pollution since exposures are usually multiple. Whilst some pollutant-specific diseases exist, such as asbestosis, most result from several sources.

Industrialization, as well as creating much of the problem of pollution, also prompts the scientific advances and social changes that serve to control it. Rapid advances in medicine and epidemiology in the 19th century that occurred in the industrializing world allowed the new pollution to be better understood and then acted upon. Great social, as well as technological, change accompanied industrialization in Western Europe and North America in the late 19th century. The national importance of the new industries also served to empower the new 'working class' by giving them the leverage to demand political action from their governments to protect them at work. Later on, from the 1960s it was, again, a combination of scientific progress and social change that led to the further politicization of pollution. Further scientific advances exposed the longer-range and longer-term consequences of pollution, whilst the activism of 'new middle classes' put pollution firmly on the political agenda of developed democratic states. The new middle classes came to be deployed as a term by sociologists to refer to new social movements of people empowered by earned – rather than inherited – wealth, inclined – through education and their social mobility – to challenge established societal norms, and so be at the vanguard of environmentalism.

Awareness of the dangers posed by pollution, though, predates the 1960s or late 19th century. The domestic burning of 'sea coal' (which contains high levels of sulfur) in London was banned in the 13th century by King Edward I (Pickering & Owen 1994: 108). More systematic restrictions on pollution, though, were initiated in the 19th century and then deepened in the 1960s in the industrialized world. In the UK, for example, the Public Health Acts of 1848, 1872 and 1875 and the River Pollution Prevention Act of 1876 followed the establishment of the link between water pollution and cholera by Dr John Snow.

The US was at the forefront of environmental legislation in the 1960s. DDT and several other organochlorine pesticides were phased out in the aftermath of Carson's exposé of their polluting consequences in *Silent Spring* (Carson 1962) and the rise of environmental activism. Pollution concerns that had built up since the Donora smog of 1948 prompted legislative actions culminating in the Clean Air Act of 1963 which set national standards for carbon monoxide, sulfur dioxide, oxides of nitrogen, hydrocarbons and particulate matter. The US Clean Water Act was initiated in 1972 prompted by heightened environmental awareness and notable incidents such as the surreal ignition of the Cuyahoga River in Ohio on several occasions (Markham 1994: 162). Other Western states followed the US lead on pollution legislation in the 1970s and, elsewhere, China began introducing pollution legislation in 1982 as smog began to become a regularized, visible phenomenon in many cities.

'Risk society'

Legislation in developed states has served to cushion citizens from some of the harmful side-effects of the industrialization that had also enriched them, but the trade-off between growth and pollution is always apparent in politics. The inherent risks of modern living prompted sociologists in the 1990s to construct a new framework for thinking both about societies and industrial pollution and hazards, encapsulated in the term 'risk society' (Beck 1992). This idea posits that modern (or post-modern) society has gone beyond thinking of pollution and accidents as completely avoidable and accepts them as an inevitability. Hence insecurity becomes a part of life. Most of the conveniences and benefits of modern living come with some associated side-effects. The gamble of taking on some degree of risk in order to achieve greater reward than attainable by safe behaviour is, of course, simple to understand in terms of individual choices and is as old as history. What characterizes today's 'risk society' as different from previous generations, however, is the social dimension of risk-taking. Individuals can choose to play it safe by avoiding hazardous forms of transport or employment, but may have to accept the possibility of a radiation leak from their local nuclear power plant. Such an individual would probably gain a pay-off from cheaper electricity but would be a largely involuntary participant in the deal and more vulnerable as well as wealthy, whether they like it or not.

The perception of the social dimension of risk, then, is crucial in determining the political demands societies make of their authorities, beyond even the 'real' risk. Proponents of nuclear energy have long been irritated by the fact that the public in developed countries have demanded far greater restraints on their activities than other power stations with worse accident rates. A irony of the backlash against nuclear energy after the 2011 Fukushima disaster is that it could lead to a revival of electricity powered by coal, an industry which has a far worse pollution and accident track record. In this case, of course, the calculation is complicated by 'fear of the unknown', born not only of ignorance but of a genuine lack of clarity as to the hazard presented by nuclear radiation. Perception of the threats posed by pollution, as well as the science of the threat itself, is important in understanding the politicization and securitization of the problem.

International policy

Since 'pollution does not respect frontiers' international policy began to emerge from the recognition of long-range pollution in the 1960s. A set of distinct but interlinked international instruments have emerged over the past 40 years in relation to different forms and types of pollution.

Acid rain

Swedish scientists – most notably Svante Odén – were at the forefront of the discovery of the phenomenon of acid rain in the 1960s and the Palme government forcefully raised their concerns over this at the 1972 Stockholm Conference. The conference consequently authorized that a monitoring programme, under the auspices of the Organization for Economic Cooperation and Development (OECD), be set up that year to review the evidence. The 'polluter pays' principle was also signed up to by the parties at Stockholm, providing an obligation to compensate if acid rain were to be proven (which was doubted by many at the time). The case for acid rain was proven by the Cooperative Technical Programme to Measure the Long-Range Transport of Air Pollutants, paving the way for an international treaty to be opened for signature in 1979 (the LRTAP). The programme had become independent of the OECD a year earlier in the guise of the Cooperative Programme for Monitoring and Evaluation of the Long-Range Transmission of Air Pollutants in Europe, a body which would become the focal point of the new regime.

As the LRTAP has evolved, after coming into force in 1983, an initially generalized commitment to reduce emissions has been built upon by several protocols with specific reduction targets for compounds including sulfur dioxide (in 1985), nitrogen oxide (in 1988), heavy metals and POPs (in 1998) and ground-level ozone (in 1999). A funding mechanism was initiated in 1984 to aid compliance. By 2013 there were 51 parties including the US, Canada and all of Europe, although not all of these have ratified all protocols. The LRTAP regime is more than a one-off agreement and an Executive meets annually to discuss new protocols and implementation, whilst the United Nations Economic Commission for Europe (UNECE) serves as the secretariat.

The LRTAP regime was initially weak, committing parties only to limit pollution 'as far as possible' where 'economically feasible', but it has strengthened over time as the epistemic community has developed. The regime has had a significant and demonstrable impact on atmospheric quality in European and North America with sulfur dioxide emissions having reduced by over 75% between 1980 and 2004 and nitrogen oxide by around 30% (Agren 2009). These reductions have been monitored effectively by the European Monitoring and Evaluation Programme (EMEP), which produces annual tables on emissions in European countries, publicized by NGOs such as the Swedish Acid Rain Secretariat which publishes *Acid News*.

Several notable instances of the LRTAP being used for diplomatic leverage on governments have occurred and also aided its impact. The Swedish government was able to cite the LRTAP in order to convince the Norwegians to close a smelting plant at Bodo in the 1980s (Munton et al. 1999: 185). The initially sceptical chemical giant West Germany was persuaded on board by scientific evidence of the effect of acid rain on their forests and clever Nordic diplomacy which played on their desire to be good Europeans. The UK refusal to sign the sulfur dioxide protocol prompted a campaign against the 'dirty man of Europe' which succeeded in securing a U-turn from a Thatcher government notorious for declaring that 'the Lady's not for turning' (Munton et al. 1999: 194). The Soviets were brought on board in the context of improving relations with the West by presenting them with an opportunity to show themselves as being more environmentally friendly than the reluctant US and UK to the Germans and Nordic states. Swedish Cold War neutrality and the fact that they were largely pointing the finger of blame at the UK for acid rain, gave the Soviets an incentive to take up the cause of pollution they had notably appeared to forego in boycotting the Stockholm Conference in 1972 (Munton et al. 1999: 207). Later, in the age of post-communist transition, LRTAP standards came to be adopted by new regimes of Central Europe in order to curry favour with the European Union (Munton et al. 1999: 216). As a consequence, conflicting views and differing domestic policies on acid rain in the early and mid-1980s had, by the early 1990s, been largely ironed out over Europe and North America. Lidskog and Sundqvist concur that a combination of the backdrop of détente and the emergence of an epistemic community were key to the LRTAP regime's success (Lidskog & Sundqvist 2002).

Marine pollution

The International Maritime Organization (IMO) was established as a specialized agency of the UN for shipping safety reasons but has over time also come to deal with pollution concerns as environmentalism has evolved. This development began even before the real emergence of environmental concerns in the 1960s. Recognition that there was nothing to stop ships disposing of 'slops' (oil and water waste mixtures) on the high seas led to the International Convention for the Prevention of the Pollution of the Sea by Oil in 1954 which limited such dumping to areas of the sea over 50 miles offshore. This, though, was not a full solution since it was simply pushing pollution further out to sea from where it could still end up drifting back towards the land. Hence IMO delegates looked at taking international legislation further in two instruments in the early 1970s, strengthening the dumping regime and initiating a regime on accidental pollution. The 1972 Convention on the Prevention of Marine Pollution by Dumping of Wastes and Other Matter (London Convention) came into force in 1975 regulating a range of sources of marine pollution and, by 2013, had 87 parties. In 1996, under the 'London Protocol', which came into force a decade later, it was agreed to completely revamp the Convention and, eventually, replace it. Under the Protocol all dumping of hazardous substances is prohibited to some degree. The dumping of 'black' substances, such as high-level radioactive wastes, is completely banned and the dumping of 'grey' substances, such as low-level radioactive waste is limited by a permit system. A weakness though is that, as of 2013, the protocol only had 42 parties.

A London International Convention for the Prevention of Pollution from Ships was agreed in 1973 but did not come into force until a decade later after having been substantially modified by a 1978 Protocol. It is more universal than the dumping regime with 153 parties by 2013, accounting for over 99% of the world's shipping stock. Six annexes have subsequently been added, dealing with oil, noxious liquids, harmful substances, sewage, garbage and air pollution – the first two of which are obligatory for any new parties. The rules limit both operational and accidental pollution. There are regulatory standards for the construction of ships, such as the necessity of having a double hull, and limits for discharges. Other IMO agreements with environmental significance include treaty obligations on the transfer of invasive species via a ship's ballast waters, preparedness in the face of accidents and the environmentally sound recycling of redundant vessels.

Such IMO marine pollution measures have had some success. The average number of major oil spills (over 700 tonnes) declined from an average of 25.3 per year in the 1970s to 3.7 in the 2000s (IMO 2011: 4). As with much of international law, though, the ratification of treaties and tackling large-scale disasters is far from the whole story and there remains the problem of enforcement for smaller-scale incidents. Responsibility for the implementation of its treaties lies not with the IMO but with the 'flagship state' (the country responsible for the given ship). The weakness with this is the 'flagship of convenience' problem whereby countries take responsibility of ships of other nationalities for money, since these are usually developing states – such as Panama and Liberia – with weaker means of enforcement. There are huge disparities in the quality of implementation by flag states and procedures are known sometimes to be rushed or corrupted (Jacques 2011: 125).

The persistence of marine pollution problems in spite of the rise of IMO-led instruments has led to a trend for regional regimes to be established, particularly in response to high-profile disasters. The Oslo Convention for the Prevention of Marine Pollution of the North East Atlantic (OSPAR Convention) followed controversy surrounding dumping in European waters in the wake of the *Stella Maris* case in 1971 when public protests blocked a Dutch ship dumping waste in the North Sea. The OSPAR Convention commits most West European states to restriction on all forms of deliberate and accidental marine pollution. The *Exxon Valdez* accident of 1989 led to the Oil Pollution Act in the US the following year and also gave a spur to soft-law pollution measures under the auspices of the Arctic Council from the 1990s. As with the 1954 Convention, which initiated international marine pollution law, there is a danger that these regional regimes might still be a case of 'out of sight, out of mind' and simply pushing the problem away.

Hazardous waste

The trade in hazardous waste, from developed countries to less-developed countries, grew up in response to the rise of domestic legislator restrictions in Western states from the 1970s. The phenomenon of illegal dumping on an international scale also grew for similar reasons. Signed in 1989 and ratified in 1992, the Basel Convention on Transboundary Movements of Hazardous Wastes and Their Disposal regulates both phenomena. By 2013 the Convention had 180 parties but, notably, not the US, the world's largest generator of hazardous waste.

Measures adopted from the outset in 1989 include:

(a) A system of Prior Informed Consent (PIC), whereby the transboundary movement of hazardous waste can only occur after the notification of and consent from the 'competent authority' in the importing country.
(b) The export of hazardous waste to countries who have banned such imports domestically is illegal. Antarctica is included in this.
(c) Export of hazardous waste to non-parties is illegal unless they are subject to a comparable convention.

A subsequent measure, adopted in 1994, sought to ban the export of hazardous waste from OECD states to non-OECD states but has not yet secured enough ratifications to come into force. There is also no liability mechanism since a protocol of the convention to this effect has yet to come into force. On a regional scale, the Bamako Convention was agreed in 1991 by the Organization of African Unity (renamed African Union in 2002), banning the import into Africa of hazardous wastes, and came into force in 1998. That the problem of trading waste remains acute, however, was made evident in 2006 with the Abidjan disaster. A Panamanian-registered Dutch trading ship unloaded at the port 500 tonnes of what were claimed to be slops but turned out to include chemicals such as caustic soda and hydrogen sulfide which eventually caused over 100,000 injuries and at least ten deaths. The case illustrated fundamental weaknesses in the Basel and Bamako regimes, again focused on implementation in the global South. PIC may technically occur but assessments in developing counties may be inadequate, wastes might be smuggled in cases of sham recycling or – as also transpired in Abidjan – the implementation process may be corrupted (Andrews 2009).

Hazardous chemical trade

Similar to the Basel Convention is a sister instrument dealing with the trade in hazardous, non-waste chemicals; the 1998 Rotterdam Convention on the Prior Informed Consent Procedure for Certain Hazardous Chemicals and Pesticides in International Trade which came into force in 2004. The Rotterdam Convention sets out legally binding commitments constraining governments attempting to export chemicals banned in their own countries through the PIC regime. The Rotterdam Convention stands as an example of how private governance can form the basis of more stringent consumer-focused regulation since it made legally binding Article 9 of the FAO's 1986 International Code of Conduct on the Distribution and Use of Pesticides, a voluntary set of safety standards for the handling and transport of pesticides.

PIC was initially resisted by displays of corporate power but, eventually, was able to overcome such vested interests. The relevant PIC provision in Article 9 was withdrawn during the lead-up to the FAO Code's ratification in 1985 despite appearing on seven of its eight drafts in the face of strong UK and US persuasion, motivated by a chemical industry lobby alarmed at the prospect of restrictions on their trade. No national delegation officially requested the deletion of the PIC provision and 30 countries protested at its removal, but it appears that covert pressure convinced delegates at the ratifying conference that the Code as a whole would be at risk if a compromise over Article 9 was not accepted (Hough 1998: 113–120). Led by the Pesticides Action Network (PAN) and Oxfam, a campaign to reincorporate PIC into Article 9 of the FAO Code and advance the principle carried on regardless of the 1985 ratification. The Netherlands became the first country to formally embrace PIC into domestic legislation in 1985 and the EC made moves towards adopting the procedure for all its member states before eventually absorbing the whole FAO Code of Conduct, including PIC, into European law in the 1990s.[1]

The establishment of the principle of PIC as a binding international rule was sealed by eventually gaining the support of the chemical industry in the early 1990s. The agrochemical industry's global political mouthpiece at that time, the Groupement International Des Associations de Fabricants de Produits Agrochemiques (GIFAP), announced in its annual report for 1991 that one of its aims for 1992 would be to 'continue to cooperate with FAO/UNEP on the implementation of PIC' (GIFAP 1991: 11). The reason for this 'U-turn' on PIC appeared to be a fear of the alternatives, such as an outright prohibition of the export of certain pesticides. The drafting of a bill in the US during 1991–2 proposing the introduction of export controls for pesticides raised alarm in the agrochemical industry and prompted GIFAP to take the extraordinary step of criticizing the bill on the grounds that it was contrary to the very article of the FAO Code of Conduct it had so vehemently opposed. GIFAP here saw an opportunity to ensure that any chemical trade regulations that did emerge would be based only on import rather than export restrictions. In a choice between PIC and export restrictions of the sort discussed in the US Congress, the chemical industry came to accept the principle because it represented the lesser of two evils in the pursuit of their main goal of maintaining free trade. As with the ozone depletion regime, the chemical industry, mindful of the damage done to their reputation by the 1984 Bhopal disaster, could no longer afford to 'play hardball'.

The Rotterdam Convention obliges parties exporting any chemical restricted by their own domestic legislation to send Decision Guidance Documents (DGDs) to importing authorities detailing the basis of such restrictions. The process also ensures DGDs are automatically circulated to all parties for chemicals listed under Annex III of the Convention. A Chemical Review Committee (CRC) considers proposals from parties for including new chemicals in the automatically triggered PIC list (Annex III). By 2012 there were 43 chemicals, including 32 pesticides, contained in Annex III.[2] The CRC consider the reliability of the evidence provided and the significance of reported effects in comparison to the quantities used, and discern whether any reported ill-effects could be prevented by the proper application of the chemical. The Secretariat are able to take up reports from NGOs in addition to those from governments. This practice was established under a voluntary scheme due to PAN pressure in highlighting health problems peculiar to developing countries resulting from the use of some pesticides. The contentious issue of whether the rules of the Convention could be overruled by the World Trade Organization (WTO) provisions on free trade in the event of any clash was fudged by removing a get-out clause to this effect, which was supported by the US government (who have not ratified the Convention). In its place a number of governments were permitted to include in the preamble a statement that the Convention will not 'prejudice their respective positions in other international forums and negotiations addressing issues related to the environment and trade'. There was some opposition to including the word 'environmental' in the negotiating of the Convention but it was eventually agreed that PIC would be extended to any '… chemical formulated for pesticidal use that produces severe health or environmental effects observable within a short period of time after single or multiple exposures, under conditions of use' (Rotterdam Convention, Article 2d).

Even for those chemicals able to make Annex III, whether PIC lessens the problems associated with their trade is, though, open to debate. As with the Basel waste regime, the procedure provides for information to be provided to importers but does not actually prohibit the trade in hazardous chemicals. The enshrining of PIC as a rule for the trading of hazardous chemicals is an important step forward for global governance but does not, in itself, represent the realization of environmental- and consumer-focused safety standards comparable to those that have become established in many countries of the developed world since the 1960s.

Persistent Organic Pollutants (POPs)

Inspired by the progress achieved with the PIC regimes, but also by their practical limitations, a global campaign aiming to eliminate the use and production of the most toxic and persistent chemicals worldwide emerged following the ratification of the Rotterdam Convention. UNCED (Chapter 19, Agenda 21) raised the profile of a pressure group campaign, supported by a WHO-based epistemic community, culminating in a treaty similar to the ozone regime but for a range of chemicals including notoriously hazardous pesticides like DDT, aldrin and dieldrin. After endorsement by UNEP's Governing Council in 1997, the Intergovernmental Forum on Chemical Safety (IFCS), set up by UNCED, was charged specifically with the task of implementing the proposal which it duly adopted as the chief of its 'Priorities for Action' at its first meeting.

Once again, the development of a new regime can be seen to have emerged from a lengthy process of pressure group campaigning and UN agency-led epistemic cooperation. WHO Expert Committees have been at the forefront of developing global standards for measuring chemical toxicity since the 1950s and their 'Classification by Hazard Scheme', launched in 1975, is the key reference point for the Rotterdam Convention. On the back of their success in getting the FAO Code ready for signature, in 1985 PAN launched their 'Dirty Dozen' campaign calling for the outright prohibition of many of the same chemicals which subsequently formed the basis of the POPs. Sixteen years later many of the dirty dozen formed the basis of the International Legally Binding Instrument for Implementing International Action on Certain Persistent Organic Pollutants (POPs Treaty) which was signed by 127 governments at a diplomatic conference in Stockholm in May 2001 and entered into force in 2004.

Under Article 8 of the Convention a Persistent Organic Pollutants Review Committee appraises proposals to add new chemicals to the list (see Table 8.2). The Stockholm Convention is explicitly linked to its UNEP sibling the Basel Convention with measures

Table 8.2 Chemicals subject to the Stockholm Convention

The Original 12
Aldrin
Chlordane
Dieldrin
Endrin
Heptachlor
Hexachlorobenzene (HCB)
Mirex
Toxaphene
Polychlorinated biphenyls (PCB)
DDT
Dioxins
Furans
Additions in 2010:
Chlordecone
Lindane
Hexabromobiphenyl
Pentachlorobenzene
Alpha hexachlorocyclohexane
Beta hexachlorocyclohexane
Perfluorooctane sulfonic acid, its salts and perfluorooctane sulfonyl fluoride (PFOS)
Tetrabromodiphenyl ether and pentabromodiphenylether ('commercial pentabromodiphenyl ether')
Hexabromodiphenyl ether and heptabromodiphenyl ether ('commercial octabromdiphenyl ether')

calling on parties to minimize the generation and movement of waste POPs. The Convention is an example of 'soft international law' in that it is legally binding but contains no enforcement measures.

The production and use of the outlawed chemicals has long ceased in most developed countries but their properties ensure that they remain a domestic hazard to their populations. Due to their slowness to break down and propensity to travel, sterility, neural disorders and cancers in peoples of the developed world can be attributed to the use of POPs in other parts of the planet. The political significance of this is such that even President George W. Bush, shortly after his government's revocation of the Kyoto Protocol on Climate Change, in 2001 declared the US would support international environmental cooperation on POPs. That the POPs regime is not fundamentally driven by ecocentric values is evidenced by the fact the infamously environmentally unfriendly DDT is exempted from prohibition by governments signing up to the POPs regime who declare that they require the use of the chemical to combat mosquitoes in the fight against malaria. This qualification followed a concerted campaign by public health specialists.

The chemical industry, represented at Stockholm by GIFAP's successor the Global Crop Protection Federation (GCPF) and other global lobby groups, again gave their backing to an agreement which constrains their freedom of action in order to prevent something more restrictive emerging. The chemical industry presence at the Stockholm negotiations was more low-key than at other conferences on global chemical trade issues and they were largely receptive to environmental/consumer group demands. The POPs chemicals were not worth fighting for as they were by now rarely produced by the big agrochemical companies of the global North since their patent protection had mostly expired and cheaper generic versions were being produced by small companies in the global South. Hence a global ban on POPs could even serve the interests of the agrochemical giants since it would give them an opportunity to corner the market in new, alternative and patent-protected pesticides. Hence at Stockholm the chemical lobby concentrated on ensuring that the list of chemicals making up the POPs list be limited to the older organochlorine pesticides (Clapp 2003). The chemical industry and the US delegation at the negotiations of the Stockholm Convention fought hard to ensure that the term 'precautionary principle' did not appear in the final text and it was eventually replaced with the more ambiguous compromise phrase 'precautionary approach', which the industrialists hoped would open the door to less expansive 'scientific' toxicity assessments (Olsen 2003: 99–100). The significance of such semantics is clear from considering the Bush administration's pronouncements on the principle previously accepted by the US government at UNCED: 'the US government supports precautionary approaches to risk management but we do not recognize any precautionary principle' (Graham 2002). By 2013 the US had still not ratified Stockholm with Washington's initial enthusiasm curbed by the inclusion of furans and dioxins on the list which are significant by-products of the US's large chlorine industry.

Nuclear pollution

Global responsibility for nuclear pollution and safety lies with the International Atomic Energy Authority (IAEA), a UN Specialized Agency set up in 1957 to coordinate policy on both military and civilian uses of nuclear power. The IAEA has an International Nuclear Safety Advisory Group which has coordinated the establishment of a range of 'Safety Principles' and a 'Codes of Practice on the International Transboundary Movement of Radioactive Waste'. Prompted by the Chernobyl disaster and the end of Cold War secrecy, the IAEA codified their most extensive legal instrument to date in the 1990s with the Convention on Nuclear Safety, which came into force in 1996. The Convention covers a range of issues including the siting and construction of power plants and emergency preparation. However, despite the implied strengthening of IAEA standards with the use of the term 'convention' in place of 'principles' and 'codes of practice', this is not a robust piece of legislation. In the IAEA's own words, 'The Convention is an incentive instrument. It is not designed to ensure fulfilment of obligations by Parties through control and sanction' (IAEA 2012).

The high perception of risk attached to the production of nuclear power has made this a contentious issue of domestic politics in many countries but has also promoted a most literal form of spillover, inducing political cooperation between states. The Chernobyl disaster, more than Soviet–Western rapprochement, was the spur for the EC to launch the TACIS programme (Technical Assistance to the Commonwealth of Independent States) in 1991 which gives grants to the successor states of the Soviet Union[3] and has a strong focus on the modernization of the nuclear industry.

On the other side of the coin, concerns over the potential risk from nuclear accidents in other countries also served to sour relations between closely integrated countries. Chernobyl was a key factor in instigating independence movements in the Ukraine, where the plant was based, and in nearby Belarus. In both of these Slavic Soviet Socialist Republics anti-Russian nationalism was less of a spur for secession than the feeling of being treated as the USSR's industrial wasteland. Hence many of the Ukraine's large Russian minority voted for independence and Belarus has sought to maintain as strong as possible links with Russia since gaining independence.

Further west, the desire of former USSR satellite states to integrate themselves into the EU's integration project brought nuclear safety questions to the fore. The Austrian government, backed by public opinion, threatened to veto the Czech Republic's accession to the EU unless it halted the development of its Temelin nuclear power station located near the Austrian border. The EU, satisfied by an IAEA review in 2001 and a 2000 Austro-Czech bilateral agreement on safety (The Melk Protocol), did not make closing the new plant a condition of membership, but the issue remained contentious in Austrian civil society and party politics. The EU collectively in 2002 called upon Lithuania to close its Soviet-built nuclear plant, Ignalina, as a condition of membership, and in doing so agreed to provide substantial aid to assist in the project and compensate for the funding of alternative sources of energy production.

Even within the established ranks of the EU government, policies on nuclear power differ substantially and cause friction amongst the most integrated states on Earth. The avowedly non-nuclear Republic of Ireland's government has long complained about the UK's Sellafield nuclear power station, located on the Irish Sea coast, and in 2001 attempted to take legal action against the expansion of the plant. The case was dismissed by the International Tribunal for the Law of the Sea but the issue continued to be a source of diplomatic tension between the two states. Similarly, the Finnish government's declaration of its plans to expand its reliance on nuclear power in 2002 drew criticism from a number of its fellow EU member states, many of whom had begun to phase out this source of energy production.

The 2011 Fukushima leak caused a backlash against nuclear energy just as its stock was rising due to its relative attractiveness vis-à-vis fossil fuels in terms of mitigating climate change. Japan and Germany were at the forefront of countries reversing future reliance on nuclear power.

Conclusions

Pollution remains a very significant global problem but the polluters in the 'polluter's dilemma' can be persuaded to toe the line through epistemic consensus and civil society pressure. Scientific advances and public pressures saw pollution policies emerge in the world's first industrialized states in earlier ages and some currently industrializing states exhibit signs of following in this pattern, even in less democratic settings. China, for example, has witnessed a growing environmental social movement over recent years. In 2007 there were protests in Xiamen against the location of a chemical plant producing paraxylene which, ultimately, forced its relocation. A similar scenario unfolded again in 2012 over plans to construct a waste pipe for a paper factory in Qidong and, the following year, in a series of protests in Kunming in Yunnan province against the development of a petrochemical plant aiming to produce paraxylene. The Chernobyl disaster and wider pollution concerns were a factor in the break-up of the Soviet Union in 1991 and there is some evidence to suggest that the rise of environmentalism in North America and Western Europe in the 1960s could yet be replicated in China and other parts of the world where pollution problems are currently most acute.

In 2013 the Chinese government, clearly responding to rising protest, announced a package of significant anti-pollution policies aimed at reducing key emissions by 30% over the next four years, announcing that '… smog is visible and affects the life of everyone, rich and poor. It has been proven that environmental crises can stir controversy and greatly undermine social stability' (Coonan 2013). The local visibility of pollution allied to international knowledge of its consequences makes it a phenomenon that even the most opaque of governments can ill afford to ignore.

Key points

- Pollution kills over 8 million people a year.
- Air pollution is most deadly but fatalities also accrue from water, soil and food contamination.
- Domestic political measures to curb the health effects of pollution have evolved in industrialized countries but people in developing countries remain highly vulnerable.
- International regimes have evolved to restrict transboundary pollution, with demonstrable positive impacts in the global North, but often suffer from inadequate implementation in the global South.

Notes

1 EC Directive EEC2455/92.

2 List of pesticides subject to PIC procedure: 2,4,5-T; alachlor; aldicarb; Aldrin (HHDN); binapacryl (Endosan); captafol; dustable powder formulations containing a combination of at least 7% of benomyl, 10% of carbofuran, and 15% of thiram; chlordane; chlordimeform; chlorobenzilate; DDT; dieldrin (HEOD); DNOC and its salts; dinoseb and dinoseb salts; 1, 2-dibromoethane (EDB, ethylene dibromide); endosulfan; ethylene dichloride; ethylene oxide; flouroacetamide; HCH; heptachlor; hexachlorobenzene; lindane; mercury compounds; pentachlorophenol; monocrotophos; methamidophos; phosphamidon; methyl-parathion; parathion; toxaphene (camphechlor); tributyl tin compounds.

3 Latvia, Lithuania and Estonia are not included in TACIS. One non-former Soviet state, Mongolia, is included.

Recommended reading

Hough, P. (2011) 'Persistent Organic Pollutants and Pesticides', in G. Kutting (ed.) *Global Environmental Politics: Concepts, Theories and Case Studies*. London and New York: Routledge: 179–190.

Jacques, P. (2011) 'Marine Pollution', in G. Kutting (ed.) *Global Environmental Politics: Concepts, Theories and Case Studies*. London and New York: Routledge: 119–134.

Munton, D., Soroos, M., Nikitima, E. & Levy, M. (1999) 'Acid Rain in Europe and North America', in O. Young (ed.) *The Effectiveness of International Environmental Regimes: Causal Connections and Behavioural Mechanism*. Cambridge US: MIT: 155–247.

9 Running on empty

The human security consequences of resource depletion and biodiversity decline

A nation that destroys its soils destroys itself. Forests are the lungs of our land, purifying the air and giving fresh strength to our people.

(F.D. Roosevelt, Letter to all State Governors on a Uniform Soil Conservation Law, 1937)

As discussed in Chapters 3 and 4 and elsewhere, the implications of over-exploiting resources has periodically been framed in the context of national or global security. In spite of this, international political progress on tackling desertification, deforestation and biodiversity decline has been limited, even in the face of clear proof that the phenomena are occurring and having serious human security consequences. In these three broad policy areas the problems of national and corporate self-interest present barriers that have up until now proved more difficult to overcome than in the areas of pollution and ozone depletion.

Desertification

The expansion of many of the world's deserts is a clearly demonstrated form of environmental change with negative consequences but a lack of certainty and universality on the precise causes and effects of the underlying phenomenon has hampered international political action. Like many environmental problems, desertification is both a natural phenomenon and one caused by human activities, such as the harvesting of wood fuel. Also, like many other environmental issues, it is a problem exacerbated by the over-arching problem of climate change. Desertification is focused on – but not restricted to – five broad desert zones (UNCOD 1997).

1. Afro-Asian – Sahara, Arabian, Iranian, Touranian, Pakistan/India, Takla Makan, Gobi;
2. North American – Great Basin, Mojave, Sonoran, Chihuahan;
3. Atacama;
4. Namib and Kalahari;
5. Australian.

At UNCED desertification was defined as as 'land degradation in arid, half arid and dry sub-humid areas resulting from various factors including climatic variations and human activities' (UNCED 1992). Contrary to much popular assumption, then, the phenomenon is about persistent, irreversible land degradation rather than simply the advance of deserts. Desertification is a phenomenon that is more long term than droughts, which are symptoms of the wider problem of progressive land degradation. Hence a large proportion of the world, including much of North America, 13 EU states (principally in the Mediterranean region) and 110 countries overall are affected by desertification (WER 2009: 4).

The issue of desertification is far from new and neither is recognition of the phenomenon. As highlighted in Chapter 1, it was a feature of Roman expansion in the ancient world as recognized by Marsh at the birth of the science of ecology in the 1860s (Marsh 1864). The term itself was coined by French scientist Lavauden in the 1920s (Lavauden 1927, quoted in Brauch 2003) and then popularized by his compatriot Aubreville in the 1940s (Aubreville 1947).

Whilst long recognized, desertification is difficult to define and explain with precision. It has been suggested that there are over 100 academic definitions which differ in terms of the relative significance of three components: meteorological, ecological and human (Kannan 2012: 6). Early definitions focused on human over cultivation, epitomized by Lavauden's statement that 'It is only the result of man' (Lavauden 1927, quoted in Brauch 2003: 645). By the time of the UN Conference on Desertification (UNCOD) in Nairobi half a century later in 1977, convened in response to extensive drought in the Sahel over the proceeding decade, meteorological factors were also understood as being contributory. Droughts and more general periods of reduced rainfall were, by now, understood to sometimes be a cause, in addition to or instead of poor land management. The UNCED definition then added longer-term 'climatic variations' to a previous working UN definition to more clearly link the phenomenon with anthropogenic global warming.

Human security impact

It has been estimated that the annual economic cost of desertification is $65 billion (GEF & GM 2006). The UNCCD Secretariat have also sought to quantify the cost of the phenomenon and its consequences as summarized in Box 9.1.

Box 9.1 The costs of desertification

- 2.6 billion people depend directly on agriculture but 52% of the land used for agriculture is moderately or severely affected by soil degradation.
- Land degradation affects 1.5 billion people globally.
- Arable land loss today is at 30–35 times the historical rate.
- 12 million hectares are lost to drought and desertification each year (23 hectares per minute!), where 20 million tonnes of grain could have been grown.
- 74% of the world's poor (42% of the very poor and 32% of the moderately poor) are directly affected by land degradation.

Source: UNCCD 2013

Amongst the key human security implications of desertification are the following:

- *Food scarcity.* Degraded land can rarely be reclaimed for agriculture. In Haiti, for example, grain production is estimated to have halved between the 1960s and 1980s as a result of the progressive loss of fertile land (Brauch 2003).
- *Water stress.* Heightened difficulties in accessing that most vital of all resources in arid and semi-arid parts of the world represents an obvious human security problem.

- *Exacerbating climate change*. The loss of fertile soil exacerbates deforestation and so undermines the carbon sink effect and contributes to the accumulation of carbon dioxide in the atmosphere.
- *Health*. Greater food insecurity from the loss of productive land leads to increased vulnerability to malnutrition leading to growth retardation and anaemia (WER 2009: 5). In addition, heightened water scarcity tends to lead to the greater use of polluted water sources with many knock-on disease implications, such as cholera and tuberculosis.
- *Biodiversity decline*. Degraded land also destroys natural habitats which can have knock-on human effects. For example, 12% of mammals and 8% of birds in the arid zones of Australia became extinct in the 20th century, much higher rates than in the non-arid zones. This has undermined the hunting and food security of several aboriginal tribes (Pickup 1998: 56–57).
- *Natural disasters*. Desertification reduces the land's natural resilience to storms, wildfires and landslides. A very visible manifestation of this comes in the form of dust storms such as the dust bowl in the US in the 1930s and today where dust from the Gobi affects visibility in Beijing (IFAD 2010).
- *Migration*. Desertification is a key driver to many prominent migrant flows, such as the recent influxes of Mexicans and Haitians to the US. Whilst such movements may command greater political coverage and even be portrayed in national security terms, in Africa such environmental refugees and internally displaced persons are more significant in human security terms since they are likely to be pushed towards other vulnerable locations such as overcrowded cities.
- *Urbanization*. The social phenomenon of urbanization is encouraged by desertification, and in the global South this is a trend with many negative health consequences resulting from the rapid growth of shanty towns and slums. Many Chinese villages have been abandoned in recent years due to sandstorms and sand dune encroachment as the Gobi and Takla Makan have expanded in line with the strain on land created by the growth of the country's agricultural sector.

Just deserts? A history of political action

Reflecting the long-standing recognition of the problem, the British and French set aside imperial rivalry in the Sahel – the semi-arid zone south of the Sahara – to cooperate in the Anglo-French Forestry Commission – which included the prominent scholar Aubreville – set up in 1936 to investigate deforestation and the southwards advance of the Sahara. The Commission's report indicated that local mismanagement of the land, rather than weather patterns, was the cause (Kannan 2012: 6–7). 1936 was a particularly wet year which served to steer the Commission away from climatic factors (Spinage 2012: 176).

Forty years on, the UNCOD Plan of Action to Combat Desertification, whilst acknowledging meteorological contributions, still viewed the phenomenon as primarily human-caused, and this informed the guidelines and recommendations set out for the countries most affected. The Plan recommended the establishment of national institutions to tackle desertification and that UNEP work with other agencies and governments to fund projects. The impact of this plan was limited, aside from some localized initiatives prompted mainly by the International Fund for Agricultural Development (IFAD), established as a specialized agency of the UN in 1977 in response to the prolonged drought and food crises affecting the Sahel. In 1985 IFAD launched the Special Programme for Sub-Saharan African countries in response to the Sahel drought (by when Lake Chad had shrunk to a third of its previous size) providing $750 million for 45 projects in 25 countries (Tal & Cohen 2007: 174). However, despite such localized successes, desertification had worsened by the 1990s, with the further southern expansion of the Sahara into the Sahel representing the most striking evidence of this. Governments of countries affected by desertification did not respond as hoped and the issue generally was not prioritized by other governments and NGOs in their development policies. Recognition that the problem was worsening, together with the more benign international political climate, prompted greater political efforts. Scientific understanding of the problem improved, epitomized by the launch of the World Atlas of Desertification by UNEP in 1992 and UNCED then set up a negotiating process for a new international treaty, the United Nations Conference to Combat Desertification (UNCCD), which was concluded in 1994. Developing countries, empowered by the global North's desire to get them on board, were in a position to add their environmental political priorities to the international political agenda, and desertification, with its obvious economic implications, was prominent amongst them.

Developing countries, particularly in Africa, were very much behind the move for a convention at Rio, keen to focus on a regional issue more relevant to their economic development than climate change or biodiversity. However, there was a generally lukewarm response by developed countries who continued to view the phenomenon as a localized problem resulting from poor local governance. Over time though, evidence of the wider causal factors – and the advocacy of much-affected Spain – helped convince the EU and others of the need for a convention during the latter stages of the summit (Najarn 2006). In the end, the agreement arrived at was something of a sop by the North to get the South on board for the climate change and forestry conventions they were keen to conclude.

The UNCCD was adopted in Paris in 1994 and entered into force two years later. The convention advocates 'long term integrated strategies' aiming at the 'improved productivity of land and the rehabilitation, conservation and sustainable management of land and water resources' (Article 2). It is more decentralized than most global environmental regimes as it is based on the development of national action programmes. UNCCD is also notably bottom-up and relies on strong local and NGO participation. However, the impact of UNCCD has been limited and there is little evidence of improvements in combating desertification. Measurement is difficult given the ambiguity of desertification, but the progressive advance of the Sahara and other deserts and the shrinking of lakes such as Chad provide striking evidence of this (see Box 9.2). North–South differences have persisted and funds and technological assistance for

Box 9.2 Lake Chad

This once vast freshwater lake, spanning the borders of Chad, Cameroon, Niger and Nigeria, stands as a stark illustration of desertification, having shrunk by 90% from over 25,000 sq. km in the 1960s to just 2,500 sq. km today. The flow rates of the lake's two principal feeding rivers, the Chari and Logone, have fallen progressively over recent decades due to drought, a gradual overall decrease in rainfall and increased water demand. The region has suffered the consequences of declining fish stocks in the lake and the erosion of surrounding farmlands. The four countries, together with neighbouring Libya and the Central African Republic, have coordinated politically to combat this decline through the Lake Chad Basin Commission, and succeeded in improving the management of surrounding lands but, overall, their efforts have been undermined by climate change.

monitoring desertification have not been supplied as readily as with other regimes, and support from donors has been sporadic. Hence we see the importance of definition – if the human and climate dimensions are prioritized then the solutions will be assumed to lie in local land use policies and global climate policy, and this is what has happened. Tal and Cohen report that implementation of National Action Plans has been 'sluggish' and that 'actual progress on the ground remain sparse' (Tal & Cohen 2007: 166). Despite the seemingly empowering bottom-up strategies that underpin the UNCCD, they conclude that 'top down legislation is often the most cost effective if bitter medicine' (Tal & Cohen 2007: 167). Nevertheless, countries that have initiated National Action Plans incorporating clear new legislation, like China, Costa Rica and Chile, have made inroads in combating desertification (Tal & Cohen 2007: 183–190). In contrast to the climate change and pollution regimes, the UNCCD is notable for having developed only a limited epistemic community, hampering the production of evidence and a global consensus on the need to act. As a consequence the desertification regime is perceived in the North more as a development rather than environmental regime, and hence less scientific (Bauner & Stringer 2009). Northern ambivalence to the desertification regime was epitomized by the Canadian government's decision to formally withdraw from UNCCD 2013, even though they are amongst the many countries affected by the phenomenon.

Efforts to remedy this apathy have, though, persisted in the UN and in 2007 the General Assembly designated 2010–20 as the Decade for Deserts and the Fight against Desertification to heighten public awareness of the threat posed to sustainable development by desertification, land degradation and drought. The UN Secretary-General's speech launching the Decade, though, further emphasized the prevailing view that desertification is a consequence of human mismanagement and climate change rather than a meteorological issue, suggesting that mitigation strategies are still likely to focus on encouraging better local governance whilst seeing progress on tackling climate change as the key to improvements.

> Continued land degradation – whether from climate change, unsustainable agriculture or poor management of water resources – is a threat to food security, leading to starvation among the most acutely affected communities and robbing the world of productive land.
>
> (Ban Ki-moon 2010)

As with the associated problem of climate change, there is no magic bullet for desertification. In common with most environmental issues, responses need to address vulnerability whilst employing a range of mitigation strategies, including:

- *Reforestation.* Planting trees can replenish drying soil and, hence, such strategies have been employed by the Lake Chad Basin Commission and IFAD, the latter of whom have, for example, run a reforestation programme in Niger since 2000 (IFAD 2010).
- *Better water management.* Adaptive strategies in the face of increased aridity include saving and reusing treated water, storing rainwater and the use of seawater for desalination or for the cultivation of salt-tolerant plants.
- *Better soil management.* Soil can be managed more sustainably by protecting it through the use of sand fences and windbreaks or fertilizing the soil either naturally (by planting certain crops) or artificially.
- *Better land management.* Sustainable strategies employed in the face of desertification also include horticultural techniques such as selective pruning and the efficient use of mulch for feeding plants and trees.

However, building a consensus on the need to act on desertification has proved elusive and is indicative of the complexity and interconnectedness of environmental problems. Despite the obviousness of the problem and its negative consequences, desertification suffers from being viewed by the least-affected but most influential countries as a symptom of climate change and deforestation and therefore it suffers from being overshadowed by these concerns.

Deforestation

Like desertification – and indeed linked to it – deforestation refers to the progressive decline in the world's trees. Also like desertification it is a centuries-old phenomenon that is, to some extent, natural but has accelerated due to human exploitation, particularly in line with industrialization and industrial-scale agriculture. In the 2000s there was a net loss of 5.2 million hectares per year (equivalent to the size of Costa Rica), which, whilst shocking, does represent a reduction from an annual average net loss of 8.3 million hectares in the 1990s (FAO 2011a). Unsustainable agricultural practices, such as the growth in soy plantations, account for 80% of this global total with logging for timber, paper and fuel responsible for much of the rest (Kissinger et al. 2012: 5). Other contributory factors include the expansion of mining plants and urbanization.

Human security impacts

As with desertification the human security consequences of deforestation are numerous and interlinked.

Loss of habitat

70% of land animals and plants live in forests and they are also home to 300 million people (FAO 2011a).

Soil erosion

The removal of sun-blocking cover dries up soils and so exacerbates desertification. Tree roots also serve to bind the soil and so their depletion further increases soil erosion.

Water scarcity

The water cycle is disrupted by deforestation, prompting changes in patterns of precipitation and river flow which heighten water scarcity.

Carbon sink

The carbon cycle is also affected by deforestation, which accounts for 15% of greenhouse gas emissions through the loss of the carbon sink service provided by trees. The burning of logs also contributes to carbon accumulations.

Food security

Forests provide fruit and other foodstuffs. They also provide habitats for many animals useful for the human diet as well as other creatures important to agriculture, such as pollinating bees.

Medicines

In addition to food, many established internationally and locally sourced medicines originate in forest flora. Quinine is from the cinchona tree and novacaine is derived from coca plants, both native to South American jungles. Future medicinal formulations are also threatened by deforestation since many cancer-fighting chemicals being trialled are derived from rainforest plants and trees.

Natural disasters

Flooding and landslides are worsened in their human impact by deforestation since trees form natural barriers to rivers bursting their banks or to the mass movement of mud and rocks down mountainsides.

Conflict/abuse

Deforestation can disrupt the lives of hunter-gatherer tribes who inhabit woodlands. Many Amazonian Americans in Brazil are known to have been coerced into working under exploitative conditions on new soy plantations built in forest clearings (WWF 2013).

Loggerheads: International forestry politics

Like desertification, the international politics of deforestation has been characterized by a clear North–South dichotomy, although the roles of proponent and opponent are reversed. At UNCED there was a clear split between the global North, calling for a treaty committing countries to implementing sustainable forestry schemes, and the global South asserting their sovereign right to utilize their resources as they see fit. Attempts to portray forests as the common heritage of mankind – away from the formal negotiating process at least – were particularly resented by the global South and served to harden their stance (Humphreys 1996: 95). Tropical rainforests were used as a bargaining chip by G77 at Rio to try to extract environmental aid from the North but the 'logjam' occurred when they raised the stakes higher than the developed countries were prepared to pay (Humphreys 2011: 139). Consequently, the non-legally binding Forests Principles instrument that emerged from Rio was weak, as have been the several soft-law agreements negotiated since then, culminating in the suitably vague sounding 'Non-legally Binding Instrument on All Types of Forests' in 2007. By now, though, the geopolitics of global forestry negotiations had shifted, with the US switching sides and opposing a forests convention through fears of being committed to aid transfers and recognizing that they would also be bound by any binding instrument since it would apply not only to tropical woodlands. On the other hand, some developing states including Indonesia, Malaysia and Costa Rica have come to recognize the gravity of the situation and now favour a binding international treaty. There is, though, still no overall global consensus, only generalized platitudes and voluntary private schemes such as the Forest Stewardship Council certification system for notifying consumers of sustainably sourced timber.

As with desertification, local mismanagement and overpopulation can be cited as causal factors of deforestation, but wider patterns of global consumption cannot be ignored. For Humphreys, 'Deforestation is generated by the massive daily consumption of pulp, paper, timber and agricultural produce, the production of which places severe pressure on forest spaces. Deforestation is thus a crisis that is driven by global capitalism' (Humphreys 2006: 216).

Whilst there continues to be a progressive loss of tree cover and a political impasse, a recent slowdown in the phenomenon has occurred due to some successes in localized and private schemes. Amongst strategies employed to combat deforestation are the following;

Sustainable forestry management

Sustainably managing forests involves the implementation of schemes which ensure that a sustainable balance is found between the usage of forest resources and the maintenance of forest biodiversity. Technology can be harnessed to this effect. The satellite monitoring system Global Forest Watch, for example, was developed by the World Resources Institute and launched in 2013 at the UN Forum on Forests after having been used effectively in Gabon in combating deforestation.

Acting against illegal logging

Illegal logging is a growing phenomenon and one that is often poorly policed. Russia, for example, privatized their state-run forest industry in 1992, leading to an increase in both legal and illegal logging. The logging black market extends well beyond Russia, and Siberian wood has regularly found its way to Japan, China and Western Europe over the last two decades. The Chinese demand is particularly lucrative given her economic rise and the fact that it initiated a domestic ban on logging in 1998 due to the contribution of deforestation to flooding. As a consequence, several saw mills have brazenly sprung up near the Russian border (Humphreys 2006: 145–146). However, where countries have taken illegal logging seriously, significant improvement in combating deforestation has occurred, such as in Brazil where police and military units have been deployed over recent years in a crackdown on the black market in Amazonian timber.

Agroforestry

Agroforestry refers to the integration of trees into areas of cropland and livestock grazing. In 2013 the FAO produced a guide to advise on implementing such schemes because of their benefits in improving food yields. FAO enthusiasm resulted from World Agroforestry Centre research into how planting certain species of trees can improve soil quality. The Giricidia, for example, have been found to increase the absorption of atmospheric nitrogen and fix it into the soil as a natural fertilizer, boosting maize harvests in Malawi and Zambia (Saleshi et al. 2012).

Reforestation

Reforestation is the restoration of cleared forests. The World Bank's BioCarbon Fund established in 2004 assists in such programmes, as part of the Clean Development Mechanism set up under the Climate Change regime to facilitate carbon sequestration schemes. An example of this is a major scheme in Himachal Pradesh, India, that has been in operation in recent years.

Afforestation

Distinct from reforestation is the establishment of new forests on previously unforested areas. The EU, for example, from the 1990s introduced a 'set aside' scheme as part of the reform of its otherwise environmentally unfriendly Common Agricultural Policy, by which farmers were incentivized to convert some of their holdings to woodland.

Local empowerment

Decentralization is increasingly favoured in national politics to ease the burden on central government and is now seen as 'good governance' by the World Bank. This can be beneficial for land management – and environmentalism in general – by encouraging more localized, informed management. Indigenous forest dwellers often develop a culture of sustainability in adapting to their surroundings, making them better custodians of woodlands than outside corporate interests. In Indonesia, for example, the indigenous knowledge of tribes has been sought in efforts to conserve mangrove forest loss (Ferichani & Prasetya 2012).

Livestock management to control grazing

In contrast to the previous approach, schemes have been enacted that seek to limit over-grazing in order to protect woodlands. Botswana's National Policy on Tribal Grazing Land, for example, was introduced by President Khama in 1975 and sought to bring more control over agriculture. Some land was allocated for rent, some for communal grazing up to set limits, and some set aside for future use by those not yet possessing cattle or for wildlife conservation. In practice this led to much communal land being privatized in a classic response to a 'Tragedy of the Commons' scenario that was resented by some more nomadic herders. In fact the 'Tragedy of the Commons' notion rarely explains deforestation since it is often the selling-off of woodland 'commons' as private plots or pure 'land grabs' that has led to their over-exploitation, rather than abuse of the system by long-term users.

Protected area strategies

As with conservation schemes enacted by governments as far back as the 19th century, woodlands can be declared off-limits for economic development by government action. The Brazilian government extended areas of protected land from 5% to 28% from 2003 to 2009 and has pledged to expand on this under the auspices of the Convention on Biological Diversity (UN 2011).

Economic actions

Governments can also seek to disincentivize excessive tree clearance by the use of fiscal instruments and subsidies. In Argentina a prohibitive tax on soya bean exports whilst compensating land owners for forest preservation is estimated to have reduced deforestation by 60% (Kissinger et al. 2012: 18). The promotion of non-wood fuels is another economic disincentive to logging that governments can apply.

Loggers and environmentalists remain in stalemate in terms of global policy, and the securitization of deforestation has not occurred in spite of the clearly negative consequences. Nonetheless, awareness of the problem has increased and some improvements have occurred. The Brazilian government has reduced deforestation by two-thirds since 2004, equating to one billion tonnes of carbon dioxide emissions (UCS 2011).

Biodiversity

The world's food resources are facing the same problem as productive land and timber with economic interests tending to trump environmental and human security concerns. As introduced in Chapter 1, biodiversity is more than an ecocentric concern and there is a substantial human cost to the loss of other species. UNEP have suggested that the depletion of coral reefs comes at a cost of $43 billion per year in fisheries and tourism losses; a decline in bees due to insecticide poisoning costs between $2 billion and $8 billion in crop losses and $43 billion worth of herbal medicines are lost to deforestation (UNEP 2007).

Agricultural food insecurity

Although, as discussed in Chapter 3, fears of seeing the world's food supply overtaken by growing demand have subsided since the 1970s, regional hunger persists. 25,000 people every day die as a result of hunger and related ailments and over 1 billion in the world suffer from malnutrition. Some consider this a conservative estimate but this death toll undoubtedly outstrips any other threats to human existence. Why then does this relentless carnage persist in a world in which there is sufficient for every person in the world to consume the requisite 2,720 calories per day?

For Marxists this is 'structural violence' (Galtung 1969). *Developing* states are nothing of the sort, they are dependent states, systematically and deliberately exploited by their wealthy counterparts. The global economic system requires underdeveloped states in order to feed the voracious capitalist appetite for more wealth in the developed states. Hence, building on evidence that some Latin American states' economic fortunes improved rather than worsened when their principal trading partners were distracted in the Second World War, Frank and others advanced the notion that the poor states of the world would be better off by cutting themselves off from the global North and concentrating on developing their own resources (Frank 1971).

For Economic Liberals, hunger can be eradicated by those countries affected pursuing economic development of the kind experienced by Northern states. This view stands in direct opposition to the Marxist-Structuralist perspective by advocating that LDCs can best mimic Northern development by integrating themselves into the global economy to permit export-oriented industries to flourish and gain from the inward investment provided by multinational corporations (MNCs). In this way the conditions for modernization can be created – wealth, democracy, education, state-welfarism and smaller families – all of which can serve to alleviate poverty.

A reformist *Alter-globalist* (as opposed to being pro- or anti-globalization/capitalism) does not accept that hunger is inevitable in a capitalist world economy but argues that global political failings are still culpable for the persistence of poverty. Alleviating hunger is possible without abandoning global capitalism, by reforming international institutions and encouraging governments to act less selfishly in international trade. The 'Make Poverty History' campaign of the 2000s, for example, sought to increase public awareness of the daily death toll due to hunger and pressure governments into structural political actions to alleviate this tragedy. The agricultural industry in the global North, and particularly in the EU, has managed to remain largely exempted from the international trade liberalization of the last 60 years and, in many countries, enjoys heavy government subsidization and protection. This undermines the capacity of the global South countries to export their food produce to Northern markets. The losses resulting from this distortion of the free market – an estimated annual $100 billion – far exceeds the sums given to the global South in aid (Watkins 2002). Hence 'trade not aid' became a mantra of the Make Poverty History campaign, in contrast to the charity-focused Band Aid/Live Aid movement of the 1980s which had inspired it. Hence Alter-Globalists argue for a 'mixed economy' for the world in which more political intervention is required in some cases but, in other instances, the invisible hand of the free market should be allowed to do its work.

Overfishing

Like agricultural production, fishing and the consumption of the produce of this practice has accelerated with population growth and beyond, in line with consumption patterns over the past 70 years. The global market was 19.3 million tonnes in 1950 but had risen to 163 million tonnes in 2009 (FAO 2011b: 4). However, unlike agriculture, human ingenuity has only succeeded in terms of learning how to catch more fish and not increase or maintain the supply in a problem more akin to the Tragedy of the Commons: 57.4% of fish stocks are now 'fully exploited' and 29.9% 'over-exploited', meaning that less than 13% are being sustainably harvested (FAO 2011b). There are plenty of precedents for fisheries collapses on a regional scale, such as when cod fishing on the Grand Banks in Canada had to be abandoned in 1992 at the cost of 30,000 jobs. The Norwegian spring-spawning herring fishing industry also dried up through the 1950s and 1960s due to overfishing, directly analogous to the overgrazing of the village green commons. More politically driven was the Bering Sea Doughnut case a few years later when US and Soviet Exclusive Economic Zone (EEZ) declarations shrank the high seas and served to push international fishermen towards one particular fishery, which subsequently collapsed in 1972 (Jeffers 2010: 958–959).

Such a growth in fishing and fishing depletion is due to the industrialization of the practice from the 1950s with the deployment of much bigger 'factory vessels', more indiscriminate harvesting of 'bycatch' and the rise of aquaculture (fish farming). The underlying problem is that fishing tends, politically, to be treated as an economic and social issue rather than matter of conservation, even of a purely anthropocentric kind. Governments in domestic policy tend to focus on subsidizing the industry; in foreign policy they tend to play 'beggar thy neighbour' in the face of a collective goods problem and, in development policy, encourage the modernization of LDC fishing in aid programmes. Globally it is estimated that $26 billion per year is paid to the fishing industry, mostly encouraging modernization, including £6.4 billion on fuel subsidies (World Bank 2009). In this way the classic development policy maxim of 'giving a man a fishing rod rather than the fish' is undermined since 'the man with the rod' is, in reality, often put out of business by the focus on industrialization in aid programmes. In addition, the phenomenon of developing countries selling the rights to fish in their waters to industrialized countries has grown. West African states, like Mauritania and Senegal, have since the 1980s signed deals with the EU and then China granting them the right to fish within their Exclusive Economic Zones. Initially this seemed to satisfy both sides but over time local fishing industries have been undermined by competition able to utilize more sophisticated equipment and driving down prices because of their subsidization. Overall, the global fishing industry actually runs at a loss of around $5 billion per year whilst if run on an optimal, sustainable manner it could deliver a $45 billion profit (World Bank 2009).

The problem of overfishing is long recognized, particularly on the high seas where even the usually inadequate restrictions enacted by some governments are absent. UNCLOS Articles 116–119 call upon states to properly manage and conserve the living resources of the high seas but without any specific commitments. At UNCED in 1992 and then WSSD ten years later this message was reaffirmed and some targets set including that overfished stocks be restored to Maximum Sustainable Yield levels by 2015. The WSSD had a strong focus on overfishing and called on states to 'eliminate destructive fishing practices' and end 'harmful subsidies'. This momentum was maintained in 2011 when the Global Environmental Facility set aside

$50 million for better management and information-sharing on high seas fish, particularly tuna. Rio+20 in 2012 then reaffirmed the WSSD target and went further in calling for the closure of some fisheries in order to meet the previously asserted targets. The scale of this is such that the EU would need to close 40 of its 48 fisheries in order to meet this target (Froese & Quaas 2013). The EU quickly responded to this challenge by announcing reforms of its Common Fisheries Policy, acting to improve sustainability and end the problem of discards (discarded bycatch), but made no commitment to end subsidies amounting to over €1 billion per year.

As with deforestation, vested economic interests and sovereignty remain obstacles to achieving sustainability in fishing and agriculture. The Biodversity Convention, opened for signature at Rio in 1992, whilst committing parties to periodical reviews of their record in maintaining biological diversity also, in Article 3, acknowledges their 'sovereign right to exploit their own resources'. In the politics of biodiversity, as with many environmental issues, sovereignty and big business interests represent impediments to equitable, sustainable and rational cooperative strategies.

Conclusions

Forests, food and soil are – obviously – vital to humanity so their progressive depletion must be relevant to national and human security as well as environmental justice. The problems are nuanced but, at heart, represent classic collective goods/prisoner's dilemma scenarios but with a shifting cast of 'free riders' getting in the way of even purely anthropocentric solutions. With forests important elements in the global South (as well as some in the global North) are not prepared to sacrifice their short-term economic interests for the global good, but in desertification and questions of world food distribution it is much of the global North that is the barrier to progress. From a Structuralist, Critical or Eco-Anarchist perspective this failure is not one that can be dealt with by better governance of these resources since it is rooted in the exploitative nature of capitalism and, in particular, neo-liberalism. However, whilst it can scarcely be doubted that short-term economic interests are a barrier to effective, sustainable governance, it is possible to argue, from the opposite end of the political spectrum, that the problem is the lack of free enterprise distorting the market through the subsidization of food and fuel.

Key points

- The progressive loss of productive land through desertification continues in the face of an international political response limited by global North indifference.
- Deforestation has slowed but continues, with international policy stymied by continued sovereign assertions of a 'right to deforest'.
- The subsidization of agriculture and fishing in the global North has served to heighten localized scarcity in both areas and global scarcity in the latter.

Recommended reading

Humphreys, D. (2006) *Logjam: Deforestation and the Crisis of Global Governance*, London: Earthscan.

Kannan, A. (2012) *Global Environmental Governance and Desertification*, New Delhi: Concept.

10 Learning to expect the unexpected

Natural disasters

In many cases nature's contribution to 'natural' disasters is simply to expose the effects of deeper, structural causes.

(IFRC 2001: Introduction)

When the environment bites back

A distinct dimension of the environment–security nexus emerges from considering threats emanating from the non-human world itself. A major source of insecurity for much of the world's population is rooted in the natural, non-living world – from physical phenomena originating in the Earth's interior, its atmosphere and even from beyond our planet. The phrase 'Acts of God' encapsulates the notion of human helplessness in the face of such dangers which are out of our control, but the truth is that natural disasters are as much socio-political as geological or meteorological phenomena: '[A] disaster is the intersection of two opposing forces: those processes generating vulnerability on one side, and physical exposure to a hazard on the other' (Blaikie et al. 1994: 22). It is socio-political factors that make people vulnerable to hazardous natural events. The fact that people live, whether through their own choice, ignorance or compulsion, in places known to be prone to disaster is one such factor. Another is the capacity and/or willingness of governing authorities to take steps to alleviate the potential human cost of events known to be likely to occur.

Table 10.1 illustrates not only the horrific scale of human casualties that can accrue from natural disasters but also the importance of the socio-political component in such events. The Huang Ho and other Chinese rivers are more prone to dramatically bursting their banks than most of the world's waterways but this has been well known in China for centuries. Overpopulation, poor government and the human propensity to risk residing in such hazardous places for the benefits of farming on the fertile soils deposited by the flooding are major contributors to the shocking death toll that has accumulated over time. All of the drought-induced famines listed in the table can, at least partially, be explained by political failings in terms of not stockpiling food reserves.

Historically, floods and droughts have presented the greatest natural hazards to human life but, in the 1990s, windstorms claimed more lives. Statistics for recent years, however, differ from previous eras since three particular events, the 2003 and 2010 heatwaves in Western Europe and Russia and the 2004 Indian Ocean tsunami, were far and away the most calamitous incidents of their kind in history and have elevated these phenomena to a higher level of importance than ever before. Droughts are now much better 'managed' than in previous eras as is reflected in the recent data (see Table 10.2).

Table 10.1 The worst natural disasters in history

	Place	*Date*	*Type*	*Fatalities*
1	N. China	1876–8	Drought	12 million[ii]
2	Bengal	1770	Drought	10 million[iii]
3	C. India	1876–8	Drought	6 million[iv]
4	Huang Ho River, China	1931	Flood	3.7 million[i]
5	China	1928	Drought	3 million[i]
6	China	1959	Flood	2 million[i]
7	Bangladesh	1943	Drought	1.9 million[i]
8	Bihar, India	1965–7	Drought	1.5 million[i]
8	Rajputana, India	1869	Drought	1.5 million
8	India	1900	Drought	1.5 million[i]

Notes
i CRED (2013).
ii Becker (2000).
iii Davis (2001).
iv Sen (1981).
v Hazlitt (1973).

Table 10.2 Global deaths by natural disaster types 2009–11

	2009	*2010*	*2011*
Droughts	0	0	0
Earthquake (incl. Tsunamis)	1,888	226,735	20,946
Extreme temperatures	1,370	57,188	435
Floods	3,654	8,446	6,154
Mass movements	0	0	0
Storms	3,287	1,498	3,103
Volcanoes	0	323	3
Wildfires	190	135	10
Total	10,389	294,325	30,651

Source: CRED 2012.

Geological disasters

Geological events involving natural solid earth movements can have disastrous consequences in several ways.

Earthquakes

Earthquakes, more clearly than any natural hazard, demonstrate the centrality of the social component to a disaster. Though the scale of seismic shocks in the Earth's crust cannot be entirely predicted, the places where such shocks occur is well established. Seismic activity is most pronounced on the margins of the Earth's tectonic plates, such as along the San Andreas Fault Line which marks the point at which the Pacific plate meets the North American plate. Also, the threat to humanity posed by earthquakes is almost entirely due to the secondary effects of seismic waves destroying the man-made infrastructure built in such susceptible areas rather than the event in itself.

Surface faulting

Direct death by earthquake is rare but possible if someone is killed by a fall into a fault line, which has been widened or moved by seismic waves. More commonly, though still a relatively minor form of earthquake-related fatality, people can be killed by buildings being dislodged in this way.

Ground motion

Of far greater significance than faulting is the shaking effect of seismic waves on the Earth's surface. A combination of the waves' amplitude, frequency and duration determine how much ground motion occurs. This is generally most pronounced near the earthquake's *epicentre* (the point on the surface directly above the source of the seismic wave, the *focus*). Ground motion in itself is not especially hazardous but the effects it has on the human environment can be devastating:

- *Falling buildings*. The most common cause of death during an earthquake is as a result of the collapse of dwellings or other constructions. Recent history's most calamitous earthquakes, in Tang-shan in China in 1976 and Haiti in 2010, killed nearly a quarter of a million people in this way. Most of the cities' buildings were destroyed during the principal earthquake and many of those that survived were then toppled by the aftershocks that followed. Hence, the design and location of buildings in earthquake-prone areas is a critical factor in the scale of security threat they represent. In some cities in locations vulnerable to earthquakes, such as Tokyo and San Francisco, the security threat to citizens is significantly diminished by the implementation of regulations requiring particular safety-conscious engineering techniques in the construction of buildings.
- *Fire*. The structural damage caused by earthquakes can prove lethal in ways other than crushing victims with masonry or causing them to fall to their deaths. A common knock-on effect is the spread of fire through a town hit by an earth tremor. Most of the casualties of the famous earthquakes that hit San Francisco in 1906 and Tokyo in 1923 were killed in fires instigated by damage to cookers and heating equipment. The Tokyo fire was particularly devastating since it swept through wooden dwellings specifically designed to avoid the sorts of casualties associated with the fall of stone buildings.
- *Liquefaction*. Deaths may also result from earthquakes when geological conditions permit groundwater to seep to the surface due to seismic disturbance in a process known as liquefaction. This can result in major land subsidence or flooding. It is in this way that many of the victims of the 1985 Mexico City earthquake perished.
- *Landslides*. Earthquakes can also pose a hazard by prompting the fall of stones or soil from a hillside overlooking a town.

Avalanches/landslides

Sudden mass movements of snow and ice down a mountainside, known as avalanches, can kill by directly smothering people in a valley or, more commonly, by destroying buildings. 'Wet' snow avalanches, which tend to occur in Spring when mountain snows begin to melt, tend to be the most destructive. The biggest-ever avalanche disaster occurred in Peru in 1970 when nearly all of the 20,000 inhabitants of Yungay were killed when an earthquake triggered a wet 'slab avalanche' of ice and glacial rock to fall down the side of the country's highest mountain, Nevado Huascaran. Airborne-powder-snow avalanches are less hazardous but can also kill as they are frequently preceded by avalanche winds which can cause houses to explode as a result of rapid changes in air pressure (Whittow 1984: 45).

Landslides are a common knock-on effect of other geothermal and meteorological phenomena and are sometimes manmade, but can occur independently by the natural process of gravity acting on soil and rock accumulated on a hillside. Typically, rainwater is the catalyst for this process, and so it is possible to view landslides as hydrological rather than geological events. A period of torrential rainfall in northern China in 2010, for example, prompted mudslides in Gansu which led to 1,765 fatalities (CRED 2012).

Volcanic eruptions

The threats to human life from volcanic activity come in many diverse forms.

Lava flows

The most familiar threatening image of volcanicity is the sight of molten lava flowing down the hillside. Today, however, lava flows represent a minor threat to life since they are generally slow enough and well enough observed to permit the evacuation of nearby settlements. Hence volcanoes today tend not to kill in the numbers they have in the past, as is reflected in Table 10.2.

Pyroclastic flows

More deadly than lava flows is the movement of mixtures of volcanic gases and debris that can be formed on the side of a volcano. Most famously, the Roman city of Pompeii was destroyed in this way. The highest death toll by volcanicity in the 20th century was also accounted for in this way when 29,000 people were killed around Mont Pelee on the island of Martinique in 1902.

Lahars (volcanic mudflows)

Volcanic debris mixed with water can also form a deadly agent, principally since this moves further and more quickly than lava or pyroclastic flows. The 1985 Nevada del Ruiz eruption in Colombia killed 23,000 people in this way when a relatively small eruption produced pyroclastic flows which mixed with snow at the summit and flowed many kilometeres down the valley, engulfing the town of Armero.

Tephra

Various solid objects can be spat out at high speed during a volcanic explosion. Chunks of molten lava chilling in the air to form 'volcanic bombs', volcanic glass and ash may be showered onto residential areas. Eruptions of Mount Pinatubo in the Philippines in 1991 killed over 200 people principally as a result of tephra collapsing the roofs of houses in nearby settlements. Tephra may also create knock-on disasters by downing aeroplanes, instigating lightning and damaging infrastructure and crops. A famine occurred following the 1815 Tambora eruption in Indonesia, the largest and most deadly volcanic eruption in history, killing 82,000 people in addition to the 10,000 direct deaths from tephra and pyroclastic flows (University of North Dakota 2002).

Poisonous gases

Many toxic chemicals can be emitted by volcanic eruptions, including carbon dioxide, carbon monoxide, sulfur dioxide, hydrogen sulfide and gaseous forms of hydrochloric and sulfuric acid. It is even possible for poisonous gases to be released from a volcano without any eruption. In Cameroon in 1986, 1,700 people were killed by a cloud of carbon dioxide released from Lake Nyos, a crater on a dormant volcano (a caldera). The gas had seeped out of underground magma into the lake and was then released into the atmosphere owing to some sort of disturbance to the water (Coch 1995: 97).

Meteorological/climatological disasters

A wide range of disasters relate to events associated with atmospheric pressure and temperature changes.

Windstorms

Cyclones

Also known as hurricanes (in North America) or typhoons (in East Asia), cyclones are storm systems based on an area of low atmospheric pressure in tropical climes. Storm force winds circulate around the calm ‘eye’ of the storm (anti-clockwise in the Northern Hemisphere, clockwise in the South) accompanied usually by torrential rains. The most devastating consequence of a cyclone is coastal flooding caused by a storm surge, when winds create huge sea waves. It was in this way that upwards of 300,000 people were killed around the Ganges Delta in Bangladesh in 1970. Wind damage and riverine flooding can also result from cyclones and claim lives.

Tornadoes

Similarly to cyclones, tornadoes are storms which rotate around an eye of low atmospheric pressure. However, in contrast, they tend to be narrower and faster and generally originate inland rather than at sea. The world’s most deadly tornado occurred again in Bangladesh in 1989 when 1,300 people were killed around the town of Shaturia (Castello-Cortes & Feldman 1996: 27). Owing to their narrow, funnel-like shape the destruction caused by tornadoes tends to be quite localized, although they move across the surface in an unpredictable manner. Damage by tornadoes tends to be of three forms:

1. *High winds.* Extremely strong winds associated with tornadoes can cause significant damage to buildings, either directly or through the propelling of debris.
2. *Updraught.* The circulatory winds and low-pressure vortex can cause large objects and even people to be ‘sucked up’ the tornado funnel and deposited up to several kilometres away.

3. *Effect of low pressure*. The extremely low air pressure in the eye of the tornado is the most hazardous element of the phenomenon. Buildings caught in the eye are prone to explode because of the difference in pressure inside and outside of the walls.

Extreme temperatures

Both 'heatwaves' and 'cold waves' can kill. The deadliest recorded heatwaves hit Western Europe in 2003 and Russia in 2010, and both claimed over 50,000 lives (CRED 2012). Excessive cold represents the first and excessive heat the second biggest annual causes of death by natural hazards in the US (Goklany 2002). Short-term dramatic raises in temperature can kill through heatstroke and cold waves can kill directly by hypothermia or frostbite. Most cold wave deaths, however, are caused indirectly as a result of power lines freezing or heavy snow crushing dwellings. Unpredictability is the key danger in these extreme weather events. The 38ºC temperatures that Moscow and other Russian cities experienced in August 2010 would not have killed in other parts of the world, but there they were unprecedented, and the resultant heat and smog led to a sudden rise in heatstroke and served to exacerbate illnesses in the old and infirm.

Wildfires

Wildfires are prominent in woodland regions with an arid climate and strong winds. Droughts and hot winds can dry vegetation which may then be ignited by lightning or other forces, causing fires which spread to other trees or shrubs carried by the wind. The US and Australia are particularly prone to wildfire in the summer. The worst-ever disaster occurred in 1871 in the US states of Wisconsin and Michigan, when around 1,500 people perished (Smith 2001: 248). In Australia the bushfires of 1974–5 burned around 15% of the whole country (ibid.) and in 2009 claimed 180 lives (CRED 2012).

It is debatable, however, whether wildfires should be considered natural disasters at all since an estimated 80% of them ultimately are man-made, resulting from negligence or ignorance in forestry, farming or some other form of land use (Goldammer 1999: 69). Indeed, it has become increasingly apparent in recent years that many wildfires not only are not natural but are not accidents either. There was a public outcry in Australia in 2002 when it appeared that the 2001–2 'Black Christmas' fires that devastated large areas of New South Wales were deliberately started by a number of youths and young adults with no clear motive. The human aspect, whether deliberate or accidental, has become more significant with the increased encroachment of settlements into wooded areas and wildfires are becoming more common and even a regular phenomenon in certain places.

Drought

The most acute and immediate natural disaster threat to human security comes in the form of famines induced by drought. Estimating deaths by famine is extremely difficult for several reasons. Firstly, famines are functionally related to other threats such as disease, drought and flooding. Floods and droughts wipe out crops and can cause famine but they can also kill directly, whilst diseases are generally more virulent when infecting a malnourished population. Hence, determining the precise cause of death for people beset by such natural catastrophes is problematic and, as such, figures on famine fatalities are inexact. Secondly, even allowing for the blurring of the causal factors of death, disaster mortality statistics are notoriously unreliable. Governments tend to underestimate figures whilst anti-government voices often exaggerate them for opposing political purposes. Most of the figures quoted in Table 10.1 are contested and it is difficult to verify precise totals even with painstaking research. This problem is not solely one of authenticating historical records. Modern-day statistics also tend to be arrived at through educated guesswork. The highly secretive North Korean government denied any problem of starvation for a number of years and have subsequently admitted to 'only' around 200,000 deaths due to this. Natsios, though, estimates 2–3 million deaths, largely derived from making extrapolations based on interviews with refugees (Natsios 1999), but the true picture will probably never be known.

The causes of famine

Invariably there are a combination of factors which can explain famines. As with the mortality figures, the causes of famines are frequently disputed by analysts and politicians. Most famines are the result of a combination of both natural and political factors, and disputes on causation centre on determining the relative weighting of the two contributory factors. The famines in pre-independence India and Bangladesh, for example, had natural causes but are generally considered to have been exacerbated by an ignorance of the local situation borne of colonial rule. The North Korean famine of the late 1990s was initiated by intermittent periods of drought and flood in 1995 but was greatly worsened by the government's drive for economic self-sufficiency, which has seen food imports reduced at the same time as the domestic food supply has dwindled (hence it is not considered a 'natural' disaster here).

Marxist analysis argues that structural economic factors account for famines as much as the inadequate political responses of particular governments to crop failures. It is, indeed, striking that so many of the worst famines in history occurred in the late 19th century, an era of as-then unparalleled global economic liberalization when the trade in foodstuffs greatly increased. Marx himself considered the famines of his era to be the product of capitalism and his latter-day adherents, such as Davis, cite persuasive evidence that colonized or semi-colonized countries, like India and China, thrust into a global market economy, exported food to the developed world whilst their own nationals starved (Davis 2001: 27). The late 19th century, however, was also an era marked by extreme climatic conditions in Asia owing to an increased prevalence of the El Niño effect. El Niño is a periodically occurring phenomenon whereby equatorial areas of the Pacific Ocean warm up causing atmospheric disturbances which can manifest themselves in periods of drought and flood, in place of the characteristic seasonal changes in weather. It appears that a combination of profound changes in both the natural and economic environments transpired to kill millions in Asia and elsewhere in the late 19th century. Those deaths should serve as a powerful warning from history of the need to temper contemporary economic globalization with political measures in order to be ready to deal with the rise of unexpected threats to economic security.

There are three fundamental explanations for any particular famine related to the balance between the supply and demand for food:

1. A fall in the food supply.
2. An increase in the demand for food.
3. Disruptions to the normal distribution of food.

The third of these is most particularly influenced by politics and economics, and if considered from a global perspective, all famines can be attributed to it since there is demonstrably sufficient food in the world for all people to be adequately fed. We do not yet live by effective global governance, however, and all three explanations can variously be applied to the situation in states where famines are occurring. The food supply in countries can fall below the level sufficient to meet demand because of poor harvests or the population can grow at a rate that the food supply is unable to match.

Hydrological disasters

Water-related disasters can occur as floods or tsunamis, although the latter can also be argued to be geological since they are knock-on events prompted by seismic activity.

Floods

Floods historically represent a huge human security threat, as is evident from Table 10.1, and continue to do so as is clear from Table 10.2. Floods often occur as secondary effects of other natural phenomena but can present a direct hazard to human life in a number of ways.

Flash floods occur when heavy rainfall exceeds the capacity of the ground to absorb the water and causes a rapid, widespread deluge. Over 1,000 people were killed in Uttarkhand, northern India, in this way in 2013. *Riverine floods* occur when precipitation causes a river to burst its banks. This is the most dangerous type of flooding since it is relatively common and rivers frequently run through densely populated areas. The Huang Ho river system in China can lay claim to being the most hazardous natural feature on Earth having claimed millions of lives over the centuries. Additional flooding hazards can occur when an excessive inflow from rivers or as a result of snow melt causes lakes or seas to flood.

Drowning, obviously, is the major means by which floods can kill but this can happen in a number of ways. People may simply be engulfed by rising waters, become trapped in buildings or cars or caught in river sediment deposited by the waters. Collapsing buildings and trees form an additional significant hazard and structural damage may also lead to deaths by electrocution and even, with grim irony, fires. Hypothermia and water-borne diseases are also often associated with flooding. Flooding only represents a hazard when it is not predictable. The regular, seasonal flooding of rivers can not only be managed but utilized for its benefits to humankind since silt deposits from rivers bursting their banks provide fertile soils. This is revealed by the fact that the tongue of a region particularly blighted by the phenomenon, Bengali, has two, distinctive words for 'flood'. *Barsha* refers to the usual and beneficial floods, whilst the word *bona* is reserved for more infrequent and destructive large floods.

Tsunamis

The Japanese term tsunami (meaning literally 'harbour wave') is the more correct term for what are still sometimes referred to as 'tidal waves'. These giant sea waves are not produced by tides but by seismic activity, particularly volcanic eruptions and earthquakes. Tsunamis have a wavelength of between 100 to 150 km (around 100 times the size of an ordinary sea wave) and can travel hundreds of kilometres at speeds ranging between 640 and 960 km/h. On the high seas, however, they can be very difficult to detect since their height may be no more than a metre. By far the most devastating tsunami event in history occurred in December 2004 in the Indian Ocean, triggered by an earthquake along the margins of the Indian and Eurasian tectonic plates. Around 230,000 people were killed as a result of rapid coastal flooding in Indonesia, Sri Lanka, India, Thailand, Malaysia, the Maldives and Somalia (CRED 2012).

Human vulnerability to natural hazards

Natural disasters are as old as humankind, and even older if the risk posed to other animals from natural events, such as the fate that befell the dinosaurs, is considered. Although the overall historical trend has been downwards since the 1930s, the frequency and deadliness of natural disasters has increased since the early 1990s. A number of factors serve to render so many people vulnerable in today's world, as detailed in this Part 3.

Poverty

Between 1991 and 2005 the death toll by natural disasters in developing countries was ten times (pro rata) that in OECD countries (Ferris & Petz 2011). Clearly money can buy some degree of security from natural disasters. More particularly, it is the sort of well-evolved legal environment associated with economic development that brings security to people. 'It is not an "Act of God" that no more than 10 per cent of the multi-storey structures in Indian cities are built according to earthquake resistant norms' (Wisner 2000). Striking evidence of this was provided in 2010 when two major earthquakes struck the Americas. A month after the Haiti disaster devastated the Western hemisphere's poorest country, comparatively wealthy Chile was rocked by a earthquake that was 500 times as powerful but claimed only 500 lives.

Bankoff, however, cautions that shifting the focus for dealing with natural disasters from technical responses to tackling underlying vulnerability carries a danger of conflating securing those at risk with modernization and traditional notions of economic development. Designating large proportions of the population of the global South as 'vulnerable' reinforces the notion that such people can only be 'saved' by technical assistance from the North (Bankoff 2001). This is problematic since some aspects of economic globalization have served to make LDC populations more vulnerable, even if furthering their economic development. Prioritizing economic growth over safety has sometimes served to make LDC populations more vulnerable at the same time as advancing their 'development' by encouraging them to live in overcrowded cities. Additionally, the 2005 New Orleans flooding in the wake of Hurricane Katrina demonstrated that inadequate governance and social exclusion can render sections of the population of wealthy, developed countries insecure.

Better information

There is a case to be made that one key factor behind the rise in natural disasters is simply that more are being reported in the world's media. The ever-extending lenses of the global media and concerted efforts of a developing global epistemic community continue to bring more events than ever before into focus. The annual number of recorded natural disasters in the world was consistently in double figures in the 1970s and 1980s but has been in triple figures since 1990. (Swiss Re 2011).

Population growth

Since if no one is affected by a natural event it does not constitute a disaster the more people there are in the world the increased likelihood there is of a natural hazard having human security consequences and becoming a disaster. As significant population growth in the world is now largely confined to the global South, where disaster mitigation policy tends to be as underdeveloped as the economy, ever greater numbers of people are being exposed to natural hazards.

Urbanization

The burgeoning population of the global South in the main manifests itself in the growth of major cities. Around half of these new *megacities* which have emerged are located in areas prone to seismic or storm activity. Most of the quarter of a million people who perished as a result of the Haiti earthquake in 2010 were residents of shanty towns clinging to the hillsides that surround the capital, Port au Prince.

Land degradation

In many cases natural disasters are triggered or exacerbated by a lack of natural defences. Hence, changes in land use can have disastrous side-effects. For example, the loss of traditional vegetation on river banks can increase the likelihood of flooding, and on hillsides can make landslips more likely.

Refugees

Increased flows of refugees and internally displaced people over recent years has contributed to the increase in number and deadliness of natural disasters. Desperate and, frequently, unwelcomed people are likely to settle in insecure places. The exodus of around 2 million Afghans to neighbouring Pakistan over the last two decades has presented many of these people with a choice of relocating either in urban slums or rural margins, such as mountainsides (Matthew & Zalidi 2002: 74–75). Either option brings heightened vulnerability to natural hazards, the former from earthquakes and the latter from landslides.

Climate change

Natural disasters often occur for rational, natural reasons. Tropical cyclones can be understood as 'safety valves' which dissipate the build-up of excessive heat in the ocean or atmosphere (Ingleton 1999). This has led many climatologists to suggest that the increased prominence of the El Niño effect in the 1990s, associated with more frequent cyclones and other extreme weather phenomena, could be linked to global warming (Mazza 1998, Trenberth 1998). The 2003 and 2010 heatwaves in France and Russia seemed to offer further evidence of a correlation between global warming and natural disasters.

A lack of democracy and self-rule

Disasters tend to be more devastating in undemocratic states and colonies. An added factor behind the disparity in death toll between the 2010 earthquakes in Haiti and Chile, referred to earlier, is the democratization of the latter set against the political instability of the former. Stringent national building safety codes have evolved in the recent era of democratic stability in Chile and the Bachelet government responded rapidly and efficiently to the disaster (Smith & Flores 2010). There is good evidence that democratic citizenship provides some measure of security from natural disaster. Civil Society in Turkey was jolted into life by the 1999 earthquakes and a major pressure group campaign critical of the government and existing legislation of a kind not seen before emerged. Consequently, a crisis centre was created by the government and responses to a second earthquake that year were much more efficient (Smith & Flores 2010).

The argument is well established in relation to famines in the form of Amartya Sen's 'entitlements approach' which argues that all individuals should by rights be able to expect to be protected from famine by their government, regardless of changes in food supply or population (Sen 1999: 8):

> *Famines are easy to prevent if there is a serious effort to do so, and a democratic government, facing elections and criticisms from opposition parties and independent newspapers, cannot help but make such an effort. Not surprisingly, while India continued to have famines under British rule right up to independence ... they disappeared suddenly with the establishment of a multiparty democracy and a free press.*

Sen considered the deaths resulting from the 1965–7 drought not to amount to a famine–an assertion disputed by some (CRED 2012) – but the evidence of a correlation between democratic self-rule and effective mitigation of drought-induced famine does seem convincing (Sen 1999: 6–7):

> *Even the poorest democratic countries that have faced terrible droughts or floods or other natural disasters (such as India in 1973, or Zimbabwe and Botswana in the early 1980s) have been able to feed their people without experiencing a famine.*

Democratic governments are compelled to be responsive to the needs of ordinary people whose security is imperilled, whether directly or indirectly through the pressure of the media or other concerned citizens, in a way in which tyrannical dictators or neglectful colonialists are not. Democracy saves people as well as empowers them and further democratization in the world will help in the fight against natural disasters.

Global economic forces

In the same way that new health and environmental threats can be linked to social change prompted by global economic forces promoting modernization, so too can natural hazards. Changes to the human–environmental equilibrium can prompt natural hazards or make people more susceptible to 'regular' hazards. Lopez noted how subsistence farming tribes had, in the 1980s, become more at risk from tropical storms and landslides as a result of being pushed onto higher ground by the establishment of modern farmsteads (Lopez 1987). In addition, the traditional relationship between people and natural phenomena may be weakened by globalization. Societal coping mechanisms can develop over time in areas prone to extreme meteorological or geothermal events and these might be undermined by profound socio-economic changes related to modernization and development. Well-meaning outside interventions can sometimes even prove unhelpful. Traditional tactics for dealing with flooding in Bangladesh, which include building portable houses, burying precious possessions and responding to certain behaviour patterns in animals associated with an imminent cyclone, have tended to be overlooked by outside agencies. A report on NGO activity in Bangladesh found that well-equipped relief agencies were sometimes less prepared for a flood than the local population, with serious consequences since they had assumed control of response operations (Matin & Taher 2000).

Preparedness for coping with natural disasters might also be diminished by outside pressures in a more overt way. It has been suggested that the capacities of Nicaraguan and Honduran social services to deal with the effects of Hurricane Mitch in 1998 were diminished by Structural Adjustment policies put in place in both countries to meet the conditions of IMF loans (Comfort et al. 1999).

In thinking about natural disasters, then, 'vulnerable' should not simply be conflated with 'undeveloped' or 'poor', even though there is clearly some correlation. Various factors, natural and social and local and global, combine to render certain individuals vulnerable to natural hazards. From a 'horizontal' perspective, the strategy most effective for securing vulnerable people from the risks presented by natural hazards is by reducing their vulnerability through societal learning and empowerment. The less vulnerable of the world can assist in this with emergency assistance and technical applications to tame the effects of natural hazards but also by tackling their own contribution to exacerbating the effects of such hazards. Progress on the former has, to date, been much more impressive than the latter.

The securitization of natural disaster management

The horizontal versus vertical approaches debate seen in many human security issues hence resurfaces in the global politics of natural disasters. Traditional security responses have been invoked by natural disasters since they present a straightforward basis for governments to widen state security since armed forces can easily be utilized for relief operations. The post-Cold War 'peace dividend' in Europe has seen armies increasingly engaged in this non-military function, as illustrated by the increased prominence of NATO in this sphere of activity, highlighted in Chapter 2. However, the reflexive security policy instinct of sending in the troops can only achieve so much, and focusing on tackling underlying vulnerabilities (or a 'horizontal' approach) has become more prominent in recent years. This has served to challenge traditional assumptions that the best way to minimize human suffering from 'Acts of God' is by despatching soldiers to assist when disaster occurs or through the refinement and better application of technological predictions and solutions (a vertical approach). The appliance of science, indisputably, is vitally important in developing strategies to predict when disasters are likely to occur, lessen their human impact when they do occur and assist in the process of recovery from damages that do accrue. 'Horizontalists', however, contend that securing people from the effects of natural disasters is as much a social as a technical task. Security for people threatened by natural hazards cannot be achieved by tackling the physical causes of their risk if social factors making them vulnerable are not addressed.

The International Decade for Natural Disaster Relief (IDNDR)

The 1990s were designated as the International Decade for Natural Disaster Relief by UN General Assembly Resolution 46/182 in 1989, following the recommendation of a specially commissioned ad hoc group of experts. The decade inspired unprecedented levels of international cooperation in this policy area and the formation or deepening of numerous epistemic communities for particular disaster forms. The decade also, however, witnessed an upsurge in the number of fatalities from natural disasters, which served to illustrate that transnational scientific cooperation, though welcome, was not enough.

The IDNDR approach was largely technical and vertical. A number of sectoral initiatives were launched such as the Global Fire Monitoring Centre, Tsunami Inundation Modelling Exchange Programme and Tropical Cyclone Programme, which improved transnational early-warning capacities. A number of pilot studies were also activated during the decade by coordinating the work of existing international organizations. UNEP, WHO and the World Meteorological Organization (WMO), for example, collaborated in trial runs for a Heat/Health Warning System to better anticipate extreme weather.

The arch 'horizontalist' Ben Wisner says of the decade; 'Science was exchanged all right, but generally it has not been applied' (Wisner 2000). This view is echoed by Britton; 'There is little doubt that IDNDR was effective in encouraging nations to focus attention on the threat posed by natural hazards and in creating an environment wherein greater international collaboration was fostered. Nevertheless, the fundamental task of reducing societal consequences of disaster reduction remained' (Britton 2001: 45). As the Secretariat of the IDNDR itself admitted, 'The application of science and technology was recognized as being essential for reducing the risk of natural disasters, but in the early years of the decade, it became evident that this was not sufficient by itself' (Jeggle 1999: 24).

The International Strategy for Disaster Reduction (ISDR)

To continue the work undertaken under the IDNDR, a successor UN body was established in 1999 and launched in 2000. The ISDR was adopted at the 1999 IDNR Programme Forum and then ratified by both the UN General Assembly (54/219, 22 December 1999) and ECOSOC (E/1999/63, 30 July 1999). The ISDR has a small secretariat based in Geneva under the authority of the Under-Secretary-General for Humanitarian Affairs and a policy-making body, the Inter-Agency Task Force on Disaster Reduction (IATF/DR), chaired by the same person.

The ISDR declares that its overriding aim is 'To enable all societies to become resilient to the effects of natural hazards and related technological and environmental disasters, in order to reduce human, economic and social losses' (ISDR 2002a: 1). This aim is to be achieved in four ways: (i) stimulating public awareness, (ii) obtaining the commitment of public authorities, (iii) promoting interdisciplinary cooperation and (iv) fostering greater scientific knowledge (ISDR 2002a: 2). Notable from this is the fact that the ISDR has incorporated more horizontal, mitigation-based approaches in its overall strategy than did the IDNDR: 'Vulnerability to disasters should be considered in a broad context encompassing specific human, social/cultural, economic, environmental and political dimensions, that relate to inequalities, gender relations and ethical and racial divisions' (ISDR 2002b: 21).

At the global level, in a similar manner as seen in the politics of climate change, the horizontal approach to securing people against natural hazards has come to prominence from epistemic communities and operates alongside the more prominent vertical strategies. The ISDR maintains research on technical solutions to particular forms of hazard but has a far more holistic approach than that seen during the IDNDR. UN agencies have also shifted the emphasis towards a more horizontal strategy. From 2001 the UNDP began work on the first World Vulnerability Report, an annual index to aid disaster mitigation based on identifying where the world's most vulnerable populations, from a socio-economic perspective, are located. Whilst it might be expected that the UNDP would approach the problem of natural hazards from a socio-economic perspective, a more surprising convert is the World Bank, which has moved well beyond lending money just for post-disaster reconstruction. The Disaster Management Facility (DMF) established in 1998 aims to improve state preparedness through insurance and better public education (Arnold & Merrick 2001). In the sphere of global civil society the Global Disaster Information Network was launched in 1998 linking experts from academia, industry, IGOs, pressure groups and governments with the express purpose of providing information to potential victims rather than money to victims after the event. In 2005 the Central Emergency Response Fund (CERF) was then established after a resolution of the UN General Assembly to manage the dispersal of emergency aid (for war and disease as well as disasters).

Despite this advance of horizontal policy there is still a notable unevenness in international disaster aid donations, illustrated by the statistic that in 2010 eight times as much was spent on each earthquake-affected Haitian as on each flood-affected Pakistani. (Ferris & Petz 2011: 23). In addition, international responses to disasters still tend to be after the event rather than pre-emptive. This is not only ineffective but also often wasteful. In 2006 the government of Mozambique requested £2 million of emergency aid which would have been sufficient for them to prepare them against imminent floods but, shorn of tragic images to project to the world, no supply of funds was forthcoming. When the subsequent floods duly arrived the international community dug deep, but too late, to find £60 million (Ashdown 2011). The Haiti earthquake of 2010 prompted an unprecedented international relief operation but also logistical chaos with NGOs, government agencies and the UN treading on each other's toes and supplies struggling to enter a country with only one airstrip suitable for international aeroplanes. Hence there remains a problem with the capacity of the 'international community' to respond to disasters, and the ISDR and others in the 'natural disasters epistemic community', now focus on the need for more proactive responses in which the UN plays the leadership role (Ashdown 2011).

Conclusions

The horizontal approach to securing the lives of those most prone to natural disasters has steadily gained credibility in epistemic communities and in the global polity, but struggles to win the hearts and minds of governments and the general public of countries moved to help those people. Aid still tends to be after the event rather than pre-emptive. The long game of promoting education, economic development and local empowerment is less sexy than sending in relief workers and raising charitable donations. 'It is hard to gain votes by pointing out that a disaster *did not* happen' (Christopolos et al. 2001: 195). In 2013 Chancellor Merkel toured parts of Germany affected by serious flooding mindful of the political capital in recent German history from acts of 'disaster statesmanship'. When Gerhard Schroeder regained the Chancellorship at the 2002 German elections it was widely felt that his crisis management during recent devastating floods secured victory in a tight election. To put it another way, Schroeder won *because* German flood defences failed. Had they succeeded he would have been denied the opportunity to don his waders and demonstrate compassion and leadership in the media spotlight.

The 2004 Indian Ocean tsunami and 2010 Haiti earthquake prompted impressive global relief operation but also demonstrated how unnecessarily insecure large swathes of humanity are in the current world. Global governance, driven by human security rather than sporadic bouts of human compassion, could have saved most of the tsunami victims: specifically through the implementation of an early warning system of the kind operated in the wealthier Pacific rim and, more generally, through the appreciation of the way in which vulnerability turns natural hazards into human tragedies.

Inter-state competition and sovereignty have nothing to offer when it comes to dealing with natural disasters. Sharing security information in this context carries no risks and can only serve to make states more secure. A common non-human foe can forge human solidarity in the most unlikely of locations. The power rivalries of Turkey and Greece or India and Pakistan are irrelevant in the face of a threat from a higher power. Additionally, natural disasters present a straightforward basis for governments to widen state security since armed forces can easily be utilized for relief operations. The post-Cold War 'peace dividend' in Europe has seen armies increasingly engaged in this non-military function as illustrated by the increased prominence of NATO in this sphere of activity. As with other areas of security, however, widening rather than deepening can lead to a misallocation of resources. The concern that the 'war on terrorism' may be hampering governments in dealing with other threats to their citizens became apparent in 2005 with the US administration's response to the New Orleans disaster. The first batch of relief supplies sent to the area by the Federal Emergency Management Agency (FEMA) was made up of materials intended for dealing with the aftermath of a chemical terrorism strike.

Global problems require global solutions and natural disasters are global problems in both a geological and human sense. State borders are irrelevant in both regards. The natural dimensions can better be countered by a pooling of human efforts and ingenuity and the socio-economic dimensions of vulnerability can better be addressed by global action.

Key points

- Natural disasters are socio-political phenomena since it is human vulnerability to natural hazards, rather than the hazards themselves, which most accounts for the security threat they pose.
- Human vulnerability to natural hazards has increased in recent years due principally to population growth and movement in the global South.
- Global policy to mitigate the effects of natural disasters has traditionally been dominated by technical fixes, such as increasing predictive capacity, but recently has begun also to address the underlying socio-political issue of human vulnerability to hazards.

Recommended reading

Blaikie, M., Cannon, T., Davis, I. & Wisner, B. (2005) *At Risk: Natural Hazards, People's Vulnerability, and Disasters*, London & New York: Routledge.

Coppola, D. (2011) *Introduction to International Disaster Management* (2nd edition) London: Butterworth-Heinemann.

Sen, A. (1999) 'Democracy as a Universal Value,' *Journal of Democracy* 10(3): 3–17.

Smith, K. & Petley, D. (2009) *Environmental Hazards: Assessing Risk and Reducing Disaster*, 5th Edition, London and New York: Routledge.

Part 4

Conclusions

11 Conclusions

To securitize or not to securitize?

Protecting and preserving the earth's resources is not only the right thing to do it is fundamental to human life and well-being.

Report of the UN High-Level Panel of Eminent Persons on the Post-2015 Development Agenda (2013: 48)

As is regularly evident in the issues discussed in the previous chapters, the question of whether environmental problems merit the politically significant label of 'security' is a complex one and highly contested. On one hand, the complexity and uneven impact of environmental issues leads to disputes about the scale of threat they pose or an attitude of denial in the face of 'inconvenient truths' often geographically or chronologically distant. On the other hand, there is a lack of consensus on what 'security' actually means. For some, unable to break free of a militarized and state-centric view of IR forged in the three global wars of the 20th century, environmental challenges can only be considered the stuff of security if they can be seen to cause wars or threaten the sovereign apparatus of states. For others, receptive to ontological and epistemological challenges to the conventions of IR that emerged following the end of the Cold War, environmental threats can and should be securitized by abandoning the preoccupation with the state and the military and facing up to a different nature of threat. A third perspective agrees with the second in terms the scale of threat posed by environmental problems but resists securitization through concerns that this risks invoking inappropriate, militaristic 'national security' responses.

Objections to securitizing the environment

The environment is not a military concern

The notion that the politics of security must be a military concern and is not the appropriate domain of environmental problems persists. Hence Wirtz, after discussing a range non-military threats including environmental change, concludes that 'the fact that something is a threat to health and welfare does not make it a security problem in the sense that strategy or military force can minimize it' (Wirtz 2013: 339). This is a line of argument previously deployed by Deudney, a foremost challenger to the inclusion of environmental issues within the remit of security politics, in citing three key arguments for not extending the reach of security studies to incorporate issues, of which the first is because 'It is analytically misleading to think of environmental degradation as a national security threat, because the traditional focus of national security–interstate violence–has little in common with either environmental problems or solutions' (Deudney 1990: 461).

This widely held view gives an indication of how blinkered the mainstream study of security can be. Academia, rightly, often stands accused of semantic navel-gazing, but the importance of the use of words is apparent here. Why does an issue of security have to have a military solution? Why can a 'strategy' not minimize an environmental threat? Defining an issue as one of security on the basis of whether or not it involves military forces strips the term of any real meaning. Security is a human condition and this should be reflected in politics. To define it purely in terms of state bodies whose aim it is to help secure their state and people in a certain dimension, rather than the people whose security is at stake, is commonplace but, on examination, odd. This way of framing what is and what is not a security issue is akin to reasoning that a patient who is saved by a successful medical operation can only be deemed to have had their life secured if the medic was a military surgeon or that parents cannot protect their children from harm unless they hire state-approved security guards to look after them. A security issue, surely, is an issue which threatens (or appears to threaten) one's security. If people, be they government ministers or private individuals, perceive an issue to threaten their lives in some way and respond politically to this then that issue should be deemed to be a *security* issue.

Environmental problem-solving is not synonymous with the national interest

The second and third of Deudney's objections to environmental securitization are as follows:

> *2. The effort to harness the emotive power of nationalism to help mobilize environmental awareness and action may prove counterproductive by undermining globalist political stability.*
>
> *3. Environmental degradation is not very likely to cause interstate wars.*
>
> (Deudney 1990: 461)

Deudney's reasoning is more nuanced than that of refusenik military strategists irritated by greens encroaching on their turf (as in the Wirtz position) in that it comes from a sincere belief that securitizing the environment undermines rather than enhances the likelihood of finding appropriate political solutions to environmental problems. Point three is a direct rebuttal of the Homer-Dixon-led approach of coupling certain environmental issues with military security which, as discussed in Chapter 4, is certainly open to challenge. Point two rightly implies that global problems require global responses rather than relying on individual state calculations of rationality, a standard challenge presented by environmental problems to the traditional statist national interest-based model of how foreign policies should be constructed. The weakness in Deudney's argument, however, comes from a statist bias in another way. Nationalism is, indeed, an inappropriate political ideology to tackle most environmental problems but who has ever proposed this as a solution to climate change or pollution? Deudney, in common with most traditionalists, conflates 'security' with 'something that requires a military response by the state' rather than seeing it as a condition which relates to people's lives and which can be acted upon at various political levels. 'Both violence and environmental degradation may kill people and may reduce human well-being, but not all threats to life and property are threats to security' (Deudney 1990: 463). This represents an explicit admission that 'security' can have no meaning other than as a synonym for 'military defence against other states'. Real security needs of people and of the whole planet are excluded by such blinkered logic. The fact that a problem cannot be solved by conventional thinking and means does not indicate that the problem should be ignored but rather that the thinking should be improved and new types of solution sought.

The preoccupation of security studies with the state is very much a relic of the Cold War. In some ways this is understandable since the discipline of International Relations, and its sub-discipline security studies, only emerged in the 1930s and was thus very much forged in an era of unprecedented military threats. Realism was in the ascendancy at the close of the Second World War since the application of force had proved its worth in curbing aggression and restoring order in Europe and Asia. Pre-Second World War international cooperation, in the form of the League of Nations, and 'softly-softly' appeasement diplomacy vis-à-vis aggressors comprehensively failed to keep the peace. In addition, the total war of the Second World War and the 'total phoney war' of the Cold War, whereby whole populations were threatened by state quarrels in ways not seen before, bound individuals to the fates of their governments like never before.

Hence in the 1940s the twin concepts of 'national interest' and 'national security' took centre stage in International Relations and security studies. Walter Lippmann, an American journalist who popularized the term 'Cold War' also defined the nature of security that would characterize that era: 'A nation has security when it does not have to sacrifice its legitimate interests to avoid war and is able, if challenged, to maintain them by war' (Lippmann 1943: 32). The US's new pre-eminence and preparedness to act on the world stage in 1945 was an additional key factor in promoting this approach. The government of the US found itself in a position of unprecedented dominance and compelled to utilize its power in a way that it had shown little inclination to do in the past. The scale of the threat posed by nuclear war in the second half of the 20th century served to weld the security of individual people in the US and elsewhere to that of their governments. The state would assume the responsibility of protecting its citizens and demand their loyalty in return in a strengthened version of the 'Social Contract' relationship articulated by political philosophers such as Hobbes and Locke from the 17th century. Hobbes' advocacy of the need for the Leviathan (meaning a strong state) to save individuals from the dangerous anarchy that would otherwise result from the pursuit of their own selfish interests was a major influence on the Realists in IR. In the late 20th century the anarchy was the international state system and the dangers came, to a greater extent than ever before, from other states.

Hence the Realist approach to International Relations represented a revival of the understanding that the state was crucial to securing the lives of its citizens in a different guise. In between Hobbes and Morgenthau, however, political philosophy and state governance in Europe and North America was more influenced by Liberalism and a very different notion of security. Eighteenth century Liberal philosophers were alarmed that the social contract had become overbalanced and that the Leviathan was endangering rather than protecting its individuals. Paine, Montesquieu, Mill and Smith all referred to 'security' in their notable works and Bentham saw security and liberty as synonymous declaring that, 'without security equality could not last a day' (Bentham 1876: 96).

McSweeney observes that security over time had come to be defined in International Relations solely as an adjective rather than a noun or, as 'a commodity rather than a relationship' (McSweeney 1999: 15). The human part of a human condition had been lost and the term become synonymous with *realpolitik*, the interest of the state. Military might and the application of the 'national interest' can secure lives but it can also, of course, imperil them. Additionally, human lives can be imperilled by a range of issues other than military ones. In global politics issues of life and death frequently are not treated as priorities because they do not coincide with state gain or security. Governments tend to prioritize the rights and lesser interests of their own citizens over the fundamental rights of others and human rights are still routinely treated as secondary to 'national security' issues where the two are perceived to clash. The blinkered pursuit of profit can enrich some but imperil others. Agricultural protectionism in the global North keeps northern farmers and food producers wealthy but abandoning it would not imperil their lives. Lives in the global South, however, are threatened by the distorting effects of this protectionism. This illustrates clearly the failings of state-centricism in the pursuit of human security. The security of governments does not equate with the security of the people they are meant to represent. The scale of threats to people posed by environmental change are so far removed from the way in which issues are conventionally ordered on the political agenda by states that IR theory and international political practice needs to find ways of accommodating them, or cease to be connected in any meaningful way with human behaviour and needs. Eight million people a year already die from pollution and this is set to get much worse. War and terrorism set against this represent much lesser threats. A thorough application of security in the study of global politics must, surely, recognize this or else admit that it is a more limited field of enquiry – 'War Studies' or 'Strategic Studies', for example. The conceptualization of International Relations, like the conduct of International Relations, was very much frozen in time between 1945 and 1990.

Environmental harm is not deliberate

A further objection to environmental securitization is that, whilst there may be a significant death toll from problems such as air pollution, this cannot be compared to killings in war or terrorism because of a lack of direct human agency. Deudney has cited this as a further objection to coupling the environment and security (Deudney 1991) and, from the 'Copenhagen School', Wæver has argued that this is a basis for the 'desecuritization' of such issues and their treatment, instead, as 'ordinary' political matters (Wæver 1995). Dabelko and Simmons similarly reason that:

> *Military threats are most often targeted and intentional, two characteristics not commonly associated with environmental problems. Traditional military threats typically present an immediacy of danger in the form of direct violence. Environmental 'threats' are often, but not always, manifested over longer and incremental time scales and therefore differ fundamentally in how they should be addressed. With these differences in mind, the addition of such a diversity of 'threats' to security makes the concept boundless and therefore considerably less useful as an analytical tool.*
>
> (Dabelko & Simmons 1997: 21)

Even within human security circles the narrower 'freedom from fear' perspective excludes issues not resulting from direct and deliberate causes of harm, as discussed in Chapter 1.

Excluding indirect forms of insecurity from analysis, again, is a commonly held position which has the advantage of making demarcation straightforward but is based on flawed logic. As Galtung reasoned in the 1960s in his 'structural violence' thesis, why should deaths caused by global political failings not be equated with physical harm directly inflicted by another person (Galtung 1969)? Most deaths by pollution or disaster can be avoided by political action, therefore if steps are not taken to avoid them a political failing has occurred. Are people indirectly killed by a known problem not insecure? Again, there seems to be a military hang-up with this argument against environmental securitization. No one seems to question that collateral killings are war victims or that members of the public accidently caught up in a terrorist incident are not rendered insecure through such misfortune. Again this shows the significance of semantics in security politics. Long before security came to be seen as synonymous with military matters, the term 'social security' began to be deployed in the late 19th century to characterize the need for governments to protect their citizens from harm resulting from economic downturns or work-based hazards in an indirect and structural sense. If, as is now globally supported in the UN, there is a 'responsibility to protect' those imperilled by political violence, why should there not be for those imperilled by their government's political negligence? Indeed, it could be argued that the international community should feel a greater sense of responsibility when it comes to ozone depletion and climate change than human rights abuses since they are more clearly responsible for them.

Treating environmental questions as matters of security is analytically unhelpful

Another concern with securitizing the environment is the lack of consensus and subsequent confusion over what this actually means. De Wilde points out that there is a fundamental problem in the very different ideas coming to be conflated in the environmental security literature: (i) the environment as the referent object to be secured by urgent human action, and (ii) human civilization as the referent object to be secured against environmental change (De Wilde 2008: 598–599).

This argument has validity since, as has been detailed in the preceding chapters, securitization means different things to different thinkers, governments and international organizations. Civilizational security, as discussed in Chapter 6, can and has been invoked on occasion but risks accusations of exaggeration, particularly in light of the hysteria prompted by overpopulation concerns in the late 1960s. Securing the environment against human harm can be understood as the fundament of political ecology and, as such, could be accused of just giving a new and unnecessary label for ecocentric policy. However, whilst it has been criticized for its vagueness and comes in different strengths, human security does have a clear referent object – the human. Given the transboundary and global nature of environmental problems, the human is also a more clear-cut reference point for security than the state: 'Territorial security, for delimited groups may once have been fundamental to achieving "the good life", but it now seems more likely that the security of the global environment (incorporating localities) is the basic condition for human security' (Dyer 2001: 449).

Human security is still somewhat problematic from an environmentalist perspective since this is, by definition, an anthropocentric way of framing problems and the antithesis of an ecological approach. However, so long as human security is understood in the context of us being part of a global biosphere, the safeguarding of which enhances both human and non-human interests, this need not be a problem. Dalby argues that the key to safeguarding human security in issues such as climate change and resource depletion is to cease framing such problems in the context of 'environmental threats'. Dalby defines security in terms of a referent object which is the global totality: 'the assurance of relatively undisturbed ecological systems in all parts of the biosphere' (Dalby 2002: 106). Drawing somewhat on Lovelock's Gaia hypothesis, thinking in terms of ecological rather than environmental change means that social and economic transformations are not treated as distinct from atmospheric or biological developments in terms of their consequences. Human security can then be incorporated into this logic of ecological security: 'When people do not have enough options to avoid or adapt to environmental change such that their needs, rights and values are likely to be undermined, then they can be said to be environmentally insecure' (Mathew et al. 2010: 18). Appreciating that human phenomena like urbanization or increasing consumption have effects in the natural world with implications for human security can improve the management of threats. Security threats can be more subtle than the rapid emergence of a hole in the ozone layer and the solutions more complex than switching from the use of CFCs to replacement chemicals. A better appreciation of this complexity could help alleviate these difficulties before they become imminent crises. The traditional practices of international relations, though, are much better suited to responding to crises rather than tackling long-term, underlying causes of these sources of insecurity.

Box 11.1 UN High-Level Panel Post-2015 Development Targets on the Environment

5. ***Food Security***
   - c) focus on sustainably increasing smallholder yields
   - d) adopt sustainable agricultural and fishing practices
7. ***Sustainable Energy***
   - a) double the share of renewable energy in the global energy mix
   - c) double the global rate of improvement in energy efficiency
9. ***Manage Natural Resources Sustainably***
   - c) safeguard ecosystems and biodiversity
   - d) reduce deforestation and increase reforestation
   - e) improve soil quality and combat desertification
12. ***Create a Global Enabling Environment***
   - a) Reform international trade so that it helps LDCs, including reducing agricultural subsidies.
   - c) Hold temperature increases to below 2°C above pre-industrial levels.

(UN 2013)

Does securitization help prioritize environmental issues?

The meaning of 'security' is not just an arcane matter of academic semantics. The term carries significant weight in 'real-world' political affairs since threats to the security of states have to be a priority for governments and threats to the lives of people are increasingly accepted as more important than other matters of contention. The traditional, Realist way of framing security presupposes that military issues (and certain economic issues for neo-Realists) are security issues and as such must be prioritized by governments above other 'low politics' issues, important though these might be. Governments do tend to be somewhat Realist in their foreign policies and this high-politics/low-politics distinction is evident in the level of state expenditure typically allocated to the achievement of military security as opposed to other issue areas.

A further consequence of this residual Realism still permeating real-world international politics is that securitizing the environment for many still invokes a perception of militarization which, apart from some utility for deploying armed forces in the aftermath of a natural disaster, offers no solutions whilst presenting further problems. National securitization is welcome in terms of getting governments on board and giving environmental issues the spotlight they often deserve but old habits die hard and this tends to frame the issues in

Realist terms. The discourse of environmental change in venues of intergovernmental 'high politics' invariably becomes reduced down to the resource wars thesis or the apparent threat posed by a rise in environmental migration, as discussed in Chapters 2, 4 and 6. Environmental degradation is deemed important because it might be a cause of war and instability rather than because it *is* a threat to life in itself.

This militarization is not only unwarranted but, possibly, inaccurate. Environmental change may even be a source of peace rather than conflict. As discussed in Chapter 4, contrary to many assumptions, there is no real evidence of transboundary environmental problems or greater resource scarcity prompting war and, indeed, the environment can be 'used' in the context of peace building. Gorbachev's initial westward olive branches were to propose environmental cooperation in the Arctic and on tackling pollution. In a more concrete example of peace-building in 1998 the Peru–Ecuador Cordillera de Condor 'Peace Park' was consciously established by both governments to dampen the long-running border dispute between the Andean neighbours by consigning a contested mountainous region as a zone of conservation (Conca & Dabelko 2002).

An additional problem with securitization is that it fuels accusations of scaremongering and exaggeration from vested interests seeking to downplay environmental problems. The over-population hyperbole of the late 1960s and subsequent expansion of the food supply though technological innovation in the Green Revolution fed the dangerous climate change scepticism which stifles requisite urgent international action today. Concentrating on highly speculative and unproven links between environmental change and war rather than rigorously researched and already evident negative consequences of climate change, pollution or deforestation does not help in overcoming such accusations.

Where the military fetish can be overcome, national securitization can still tend to lead to inappropriate solutions. Technological quick fixes, reactive responses after a crisis or market solutions and headline grabbing stunts are often more politically attractive than the slow, unspectacular politics of tackling underlying causes of vulnerability. Low-key, gradual, technical solutions, however, are usually what are needed to address insecurities arising from environmental change. It was the careful, prolonged work of transnational scientists and civil society actors rather than grand government gestures that achieved the international political successes seen in combating ozone depletion and long-range atmospheric pollution and that hold the best hope for mitigating climate change.

Transnational politics holds the key to advancing environmental governance by overcoming the polluter's dilemma scenarios which inevitably emerge when global issues are tackled in a sovereign state system. Epistemic consensus and public opinion can overcome the short-term cost–benefit logic that tends to inform government and intergovernmental policy. From the birth of political ecology in the 1960s this was apparent when Carson's presentation of the facts on organochlorine pesticides overcame corporate attacks and led to ecocentric policies being enacted in the US. On an international scale this model of vested interests being overcome by public awareness of environmental problems came to be repeated in the areas of acid rain, marine pollution, hazardous chemical trading and ozone depletion. Initially this application of Sen's entitlements thesis seemed only relevant to developed democracies with prominent civil societies but the success of anti-pollution demonstrations in China over recent years demonstrates that even in undemocratic settings governments cannot ignore environmental concerns.

Governments can be shamed or persuaded to tow the line and respond to facts established by scientists (or, of course, they may reach such a conclusion themselves). Acid rain could not be ignored by polluting governments in the 1970s in the face of the facts and the reputational losses inherent in obstructing the progress of neighbouring countries. Governments can play on this by trumpeting their green credentials and leaning on others to tackle the 'free rider problem', as the Soviets were able to do by engaging in acid rain politics and pioneering policy on ecocide. However, there are limits to intergovernmental policy in the global interest. Tackling deforestation is a political priority for civil society, public opinion and many governments in the global North but has not yet been able to win over enough of the global South governments chiefly responsible for the problem. Desertification is a vital issue for people and government of arid countries but much less so for those in temperate climes. In addition, public opinion is not always green – democratic constituencies may recoil from the introduction of environmental taxes or ceasing to subsidize domestic farmers or fishermen. Apparent national interests can always get in the way of effective environmental governance in a world of sovereign states.

Global governance hence is a necessity for enhancing human security in the face of environmental degradation. As Dyer argues, global environmental change tends to be neglected because it is 'seen as an externality to the international system, rather than an internal variable which can be addressed in terms of familiar political structures and their supporting social values' (Dyer 2000: 139). Climate change potentially threatens the security of all life on Earth (and the states they inhabit) and it is a threat which does not emanate from any particular state and which cannot be averted by any particular state, regardless of its economic or military capabilities. Dyer refers to this conundrum as a new type of *security dilemma* soluble only by new, global political structures (ibid.). This has been recognized by all significant debates on the subject from the Brandt Commission to the Commission on Global Governance and then the UN's High-Level Panels. In 2013 the targets identified for taking governance beyond the 2015 deadline for the Millennium Development Goals notably set several environmental challenges in recognition that intergovernmental policy and law had not served the global interest in deforestation, desertification, climate change and the oversubsidization of farming and fishing (see Box 11.1).

Environmental problems are 'inconvenient truths' but just because they are not soluble by the application of security policies of sovereign states in the ways that we have grown accustomed to, it does not mean that they should be neglected. If received ways of thinking and tackling problems come to be inadequate then the response must be to find new ways of thinking and acting, rather than denying that there is a problem. However conceptually difficult it may be, IR needs to come to terms with environmental security or cease to have any real meaning as a discipline.

Key points

- Objections to securitization focus on the fact that environmental problems are: distinct from military concerns; may not be synonymous with the national interest; not comparable to deliberate threats and; dealt with ineffectively due to analytical confusion.
- Securitizing the environment in a conventional way is often unhelpful but global governance can enhance human and ecological security and is increasingly necessary.

Recommended reading

Dalby, S. (2009) *Security and Environmental Change*, Cambridge: Polity.

Dyer, H. (2001) 'Environmental Security and International Relations: The Case for Enclosure', *Review of International Studies* 27: 441–450.

Bibliography

Adams, W. (2004) *Against Extinction: The Story of Conservation*, London: Earthscan.

Agren, C. (2009) 'Long Range Transboundary Air Pollution, Conventions, Treaties and Other Responses to Global Issues–Volume 1', in G. Kutting (ed.) *Encyclopedia of Life Support Systems*, Paris: UNESCO, 253–281.

Almeida, M. (1974) Statement by Head of Brazilian delegation, *World Population Conference III*, Plenary Session, 26 August, Bucharest.

Andrews, A. (2009) 'Beyond the Ban–Can the Basel Convention Adequately Safeguard the Interests of the World's Poor in the International Trade of Hazardous Waste?' *Law, Environment and Development Journal*, 52, 167–184.

Anseeuw, W., Wily, L., Cotula, L. & Taylor, M. (2011) Land Rights and the Rush for Land. *Findings of the Global Pressures on Land Research Project*, Rome: International Land Coalition.

AP (2011) Associated Press, Manila, 31 October.

Arnold, M. & Merrick, P. (2001) 'Development for Disaster Reduction–the Role of the World Bank', *Australian Journal of Emergency Management*, 16(4) Summer 2001–2: 34–36.

Ashdown, P. (2011) *Humanitarian Emergency Response Review*, UK Department for International Development, http://www.dfid.gov.uk/emergency-response-review (Accessed 20 September 2011).

Aubreville, A. (1947) 'Erosion et "bovalisation" en Afrique noire française', *Agronomie Tropicale*, 2, 24–35.

Auer, M. (2004) *Restoring Cursed Earth: Appraising Environmental Policy Reforms in East Europe and Russia*, Oxford: Rowman and Littlefield.

Ban Ki-Moon. (2010) UN Secretary-General Ban Ki-moon at the launch of the Decade for Deserts and the Fight against Desertification in Fortaleza, Brazil.

Bankoff, G. (2001) 'Rendering the World Unsafe: "Vulnerability" as Western Discourse', *Disasters*, 25(1): 19–35.

Barnett, J. (2003) 'Security and Climate Change', *Global Environmental Change*, 13: 7–17.

Bauer, S. & Stringer, L. (2009) 'The Role of Science in the Global Governance of Desertification', *The Journal of Environment and Development*, 18: 248–267.

BBC (2003) 'Talking Point. Ask Boutros-Ghali', http://news.bbc.co.uk/1/hi/talking_point/2951028.stm (Accessed 1 July 2013).

BBC (2004) 'Scientist Renews Climate Attack', http://news.bbc.co.uk/1/hi/uk_politics/3584679.stm (Accessed 13 April 2009).

BBC (2004) 'WW2 Bombs Unearthed in China' 19 June, http://news.bbc.co.uk/1/hi/world/asia-pacific/3822007.stm

Beck, U. (1992) *Risk Society: Towards a New Modernity*, London, New Delhi and Thousand Oaks, CA: Sage.

Beckett, M. (2007) 'Speech at the UN Security Council', 16 April, UK Foreign and Commonwealth Office Press Release.

Bentham, J. (1876) *Theory of Legislation*, Translated from the French of Etienne Dumont by H. Hildreth, London: Trubner.

Biswas, A. (2000) 'Scientific Assessment of the Long-term Environmental Consequences of War', in J.E. Austin & C.E. Bruch (eds) *The Environmental Consequences of War: Legal, Economic and Scientific Perspectives*, Cambridge: Cambridge University Press.

Blaikie, M., Cannon, T., Davis, I. & Wisner, B. (1994) *At Risk: Natural Hazards, People's Vulnerability, and Disasters*, London and New York: Routledge.

Blaikie, M., Cannon, T., Davis, I. & Wisner, B. (2005) *At Risk: Natural Hazards, People's Vulnerability, and Disasters* (2nd edition), London and New York: Routledge.

Boas, G. & Schabas, W. (2003) *International Criminal Law: Developments in the Case Law of the ICTY*, Lieden: Martinus Nijhoff.

Bolivia (2011) *Law of Mother Earth*, Law 071.

Bookchin, M. (1971) *Post-Scarcity Anarchism*, Berkeley, CA: The Ramparts Press.

Borgerson, S. (2008) 'Arctic Meltdown', *Foreign Affairs*, 87(2): 63–77.

Brauch, H.G. (2003) 'Desertification: A New Security Challenge for the Mediterranean', in W.G. Kepner, J.L. Rubio, D.A. Mouat & F. Pedrazzini (eds) *Desertification in the Mediterranean Region*, Dordrecht: Springer.

Briggs, D. (2003) 'Environmental Pollution and the Global Burden of Disease', *British Medical Bulletin*, 68: 1–24.

Britton, N. (2001) 'A New Emergency Management for the New Millennium?' *Australian Journal of Emergency Management*, 16(4) Summer: 44–54.

Brock, L. (1997) 'Environment and Security: Conceptual and Theoretical Issues', in N. Gleditsch (ed.) *Conflict and the Environment: Proceeding of NATO Advanced Research Workshop on Conflict and the Environment*, Dordrecht: Kluwer: 17–34.

Brown, O. & McLeman, R. (2009) 'A Recurring Anarchy? The Emergence of Climate Change as a Threat to International Peace and Security', *Conflict, Security and Development*, 9(3): 289–305.

Bulloch, J. & Darwish, A. (1993) *Water Wars: Coming Conflicts in the Middle East*, London: Gollancz.

Buzan, B. (1991a) 'New Patterns of Global Security in the Twenty-First Century', *International Affairs* 67(3): 431–451.

Buzan, B. (1991b) *People, States and Fears, An agenda for International Security Studies in the Post-Cold War Era*, 2nd edition, Boulder, CO: Lynne Rienner.

Buzan, B., Wæver, O. & de Wilde, J. (1998) *Security. A New Framework for Analysis*, Boulder, CO and London: Lynne Rienner.

Canada (2002) *Foreign Affairs Agenda 2003*, Ottawa: Canadian Government.

Carson, R. (1962) *Silent Spring*, Harmondsworth: Penguin.

Carter, J. (1980) 'US President State of the Union Address' 23 January, Washington, DC.

Castello-Cortes, I. & Feldman, M. (1996) *Guinness Book of World Records 1997*, London: Guinness.

Cathcart, B. (2007) 'The Greening of Greenland', *New Statesman*, 13 September.

Chapman, J. (1992) 'The Future of Security Studies: Beyond Grand Strategy', *Survival*, 34(1): 109–131.

Chatterjee, K., Chatterjee, A. & Das, S. (2005) 'Community Adaptation to Drought in Rajasthan', *IDS Bulletin*, 36: 33–52.

Christopolos, I., Mitchell, J. & Liljelund, A. (2001) 'Re-framing Risk: The Changing Context of Disaster Mitigation and Preparedness', *Disasters*, 25(3): 185–198.

Clapp, J. (2003) 'Transnational Corporate Interests and Global Environmental Governance: Negotiating Rules for Agricultural Biotechnology and Chemicals', *Environmental Politics*, 12(4): 1–23.

Coch, N. (1995) *Geohazards: Natural and Human*, Englewood Cliffs, NJ: Prentice-Hall.

CoE (2011) 'Armed Conflicts and the Environment', Report of the Committee on the Environment, Agriculture and Local and Regional Affairs, Doc 12744 17 October; Parliamentary Assembly of the Council of Europe, Strasbourg.

Cohen, A. (2008) 'Russia's Race for the Arctic', *Heartland*, 2: 28–36.

Comfort, L., Wisner, B., Cutter, S., Pulwarty, R., Hewitt, K., Oliver-Smith, A., Weiner, J., Fordham, M., Peacock, W. & Krimgeld, F. (1999) 'Re-framing Disaster Policy: The Global Evolution of Vulnerable Communities', *Environmental Hazards*, 1: 39–44.

Conca, K. & Dabelko, G. (eds) (2002) *Environmental Peacemaking*, Washington, DC: Woodrow Wilson Press.

Conference III, Plenary Session, 26 August, Bucharest.

Connelly, J., Smith, G., Benson, D. & Saunders, C. (2012) *Politics and the Environment: From Theory to Practise* (3rd edition), London and New York: Routledge.

Connor, S. & Thomas, A. (1984) 'How Britain Sprayed Malaya With Dioxin', in *Pesticide Dilemma in the Third World: A Case Study of Malaysia*, Malaysia: Sahabat Alam.

Coonan, C. (2013) 'Beijing Orders its Industries to Cut Emissions', *Independent* 17 June: 33.

CRED (2012) Annual Statistical Review 2011. The Numbers and Trends http://www.emdat.be/

Dabelko, G. & Simmons, P. (1997) 'Environment and Security', In B.R. Allenby, T.J. Gilmartin & R.F. Lehman (eds) *Environmental Threats and National Security*, Monterey: Lawrence Livermore.

Dalby, S. (2002) 'Security and Ecology in the Age of Globalization', *The Environmental Change and Security Project Report*, 8, Summer: 95–108.

Dalby, S. (2009) *Security and Environmental Change*, Cambridge: Polity.

Davis, M. (2001) *Late Victorian Holocausts: El Niño Famines and the Making of the Third World*, London and New York: Verso.

De Wilde, J. (2008) 'Environmental Security Deconstructed', in H. Brauch (ed.) *Globalization and Environmental Challenges* (vol. 3), Berlin: Springer: 595–602.

d'Eaubonne, F. (1974) *Le Feminisme ou la Mort*, Paris: Pierre Horay.

Deudney, D. (1990) 'The Case Against Linking Environmental Degradation and Security', *Millennium*, 19(3): 46–76.

Deudney, D. (1991) 'Environment and Security: Muddled Thinking', *The Bulletin of the Atomic Scientists*, 47(3): 22–28.

Dinar, S. (2011) 'Conflict and Cooperation Along International Rivers: Scarcity, Bargaining Strategies and Negotiation', in S. Dinar (ed.) *Beyond Resource Wars. Scarcity, Environmental Degradation and International Cooperation*, Boston: MIT Press: 165–199.

Dixon, B. (1971) 'In Praise of Prophets', *New Scientist and Science Journal*, 16 September: 606.

Dobson, A. (1995) *Green Political Thought*, London and New York: Routledge.

Dodds, F., Strauss, M. & Strong, M. (2012) *Only One Earth: The Long Road via Rio to Sustainable Development*, London and New York: Routledge.

Drevnick, P.E., Muir, D.C.G., Lamborg, C.H., Hogan, M.J., Canfield, D.E., Boyle, J.F. & Rose, N.L. (2010) 'Increased Accumulation of Sulfur in Lake Sediments of the High Arctic', *Environmental Science and Technology*, 44(22): 8415–8421.

Dupont, A. & Pearman, G. (2006) *Heating up the Planet: Climate Change and Security*, Lowry Institute Papers 12, Sydney: Lowry Institute.

Dyer, H. (2000) 'Environmental Security: The New Agenda', in C. Jones & C. Kennedy-Pipe (eds) *International Security in a Global Age- Securing the Twenty-First Century*, London and Portland, OR: Frank Cass.

Dyer, H. (2001) 'Environmental Security and International Relations: The Case for Enclosure', *Review of International Studies*, 27: 441–450.

EC (2013) 'Population Statistics', Eurostat, Brussels: European Commission. http://epp.eurostat.ec.europa.eu/statistics_explained/index.php/Population_statistics_at_regional_level (Accessed 12 June 2013).

Ecuador (2008) 'Rights for Nature', *Constitution*, adopted 28 September.

Ehrlich, P. (1968) *The Population Bomb*, New York: Balantine.

Ehrlich, P. (1969) 'Eco-Catastrophe', *Ramparts* 8(3): 24–28.

Emmerson, C. (2010) *The Future History of the Arctic*, London: The Bodley Head.

EPA (2013) 'Human Health Impacts and Adaptation', http://www.epa.gov/climatechange/impacts-adaptation/health.html (Accessed 12 May 2013).

Falk, R. (1971) *The Endangered Planet*, New York: Random House.

Falk, R. (1995) *On Humane Governance, Toward a New Global Politics*, Cambridge: Polity.

FAO (2011a) 'Forestry', Rome: Food and Agricultural Organization, http://www.fao.org/forestry/30515/en/

FAO (2011b) 'Review of the State of World Marine Fishing Resources', FAO Fisheries and Aquaculture Technical Paper 569. Rome: FAO.

FAO (2013) *Advancing Agroforestry on the Policy Agenda: A Guide for Decision-Makers* (written by Buttoud, G.), Rome: FAO.

Ferichani, M. & Prasetya, D. (2012) 'Learning from the Grassroots: The Indigenous Knowledge on Mangrove Forest and the Social Economic Barriers in Fostering Local Green Economy of Ujung Alang Village Dwellers in Segara Anakan Lagoon Territory of Indonesia', *Proceedings of 17th International Forestry and Environment Symposium*, 17: 81–110.

Ferris, E. & Petz, D. (eds) (2011) *A Year of Living Dangerously: A Review of Natural Disasters in 2010*, London: Brookings Institute.

Fettweis, C. (2011) 'Is Oil Worth Fighting For? Evidence from Three Cases', in S. Dinar (ed.) *Beyond Water Wars: Scarcity, Environmental Degradation and International Cooperation*, Boston: MIT Press: 201–237.

Finland (2004) *Finnish Security and Defense Policy 2004*, Helsinki: Prime Minister's Office.

Floyd, R. (2010) *Security and the Environment: Securitisation Theory and US Environmental Security Policy*, Cambridge: Cambridge University Press.

Frank, A.G. (1971) *Capitalism and Underdevelopment in Latin America*, Harmondsworth: Penguin.

Franklin, H. (2003) 'Agent Orange and Cancer. An Overview for Clinicians', *Environmental Carcinogens*, 53(4): 245–255.

Frieman, W. (2004) *China, Arms Control and Non-Proliferation*, London & New York: Routledge.

Froese & Quaas (2003) 'Rio+20 and the Reform of the Common Fisheries Policy in Europe', *Marine Policy* 39: 53–55.

Galeotti, M. (2008) 'Cold Calling: Competition Heats Up for Arctic Resources', *Jane's Intelligence Review*, October: 8–15.

Galtung, J. (1969) 'Violence, Peace and Peace Research', *Journal of Peace Research*, 6(3): 167–191.

Gareau, B. (2008). 'Dangerous Holes in Global Environmental Governance: The Roles of Neoliberal Discourse, Science and California Agriculture in the Montreal Protocol', *Antipode* 40(1) January: 102–130.

Gareau, B. (2013) *From Precaution to Profit: Contemporary Challenges to Environmental Protection in the Montreal Protocol*, Yale: Yale University Press.

GEF & GM (2006) *Resource Mobilization and the Status of Funding of Activities Related to Land Degradation,*, Washington, DC: Global Environment Facility.

General Assembly. (2009) Climate Change and its Possible Security Implications Report of the Secretary-General, 11 September, New York: General Assembly 64/350.

Geneva (1977) Protocol Additional to the Geneva Conventions of 12 August 1949, and relating to the Protection of Victims of International Armed Conflicts (Protocol I), 8 June 1977.

GIFAP (1991) GIFAP Annual Report 1991, Brussels.

Gittings, J. (2002) 'Growing Sex Imbalance Shocks China', *Guardian*, 13 May.

Glasby, G. & Voytekhovsky, Y. (2010) 'Arctic Russia: Minerals and Mineral Resources', *Geoscientist*, 8. http://www.geochemsoc.org/publications/geochemicalnews/gn140jul09/arcticrussiamineralsandmin/ (Accessed 12 May 2011)

Gleick, P. (1994) 'Water, War and Peace in the Middle East', *Environment*, 36(3), April: 6–42.

Goklany, I. (2002) 'The Globalization of Human Well-being', *Policy Analysis*, 477, August: 22.

Goldammer, J. (1999) 'Wildfire', in J. Ingleton (ed.) *Natural Disaster Management: A Presentation to Commemorate the International Decade for Natural Disaster Reduction* (IDNDR), Leicester: Tudor Rose: 67–69.

Gorbachev, M. (1987) Speech at the 'Ceremonial Meeting on the Occasion of the Presentation of the Order of Lenin and the Gold Star to the City of Murmansk', *Murmansk*, 1 October.

Gore, A. (2006) *An Inconvenient Truth. The Planetary Emergency of Global Warming and What We can do About it*, Emmaus, PN: Rodale Press.

Gore, A. (2011) 'Climate Of Denial', *Rolling Stone*, 22 June.

Graham, J. (2002) 'The Role of Precaution in Risk Management', Remarks Prepared for The International Society of Regulatory Toxicology and Pharmacology Precautionary Principle Workshop, Crystal City, VA, 20 June 2002. Office of Information and Regulatory Affairs. Office of Management and Budget Executive Office of the President of the United States http://www.whitehouse.gov/omb/inforeg/risk_mgmt_speech062002.html (Accessed 13 March 2008).

Grant, S. (2010) *Polar Imperative: A History of Arctic Sovereignty in North America*, Vancouver: Douglas and McIntyre: 418.

Haas, P. (1989) 'Do Regimes Matter? Epistemic Communities and Mediterranean Pollution', *International Organization*, 43(3): 377–403.

Haas, P. (1992) 'Epistemic Communities and International Policy Coordination', *International Organization*, 46(1): 1–35.

Haeckel, E. (1866) *Generelle Morphologie der Organismen*, Berlin: Georg Reimer.

Hardin, G. (1968) 'The Tragedy of the Commons', *Science*, 162: 1243–1248.

Hardin, G. (1996) 'Lifeboat Ethics: The Case Against Helping the Poor', in W. Aitken & H. LaFollette (eds) *World Hunger and Morality*, Englewood Cliffs, NJ: Prentice-Hall.

Harrison, G. (1978) *Mosquitoes, Malaria and Man: A History of the Hostilities Since 1880*, New York: Dutton.

Hague Convention (1907) *Convention IV respecting the Laws and Customs of War on Land and its annex: Regulations concerning the Laws and Customs of War on Land. The Hague, 18 October 1907.* Annex to the Convention: Regulations respecting the laws and customs of war on land–Section II: Hostilities–Chapter I: Means of injuring the enemy, sieges, and bombardments–Regulations: Art. 23.

Hay, A. (1982) *The Chemical Scythe – Lessons of 2,4,5, T and Dioxin*, New York: Plenum Press.

Higgins, P. (2010) *Eradicating Ecocide: Laws and Governance to Prevent the Destruction of our Planet*, London: Shepheard-Walwyn.

HLP (2013) *A New Global Partnership. Eradicate Poverty and Transform Economies Through Sustainable Development*, Report of the UN High-Level Panel of Eminent Persons on the Post-2015 Development Agenda 2013.

Homer-Dixon, T. (1994) 'Environmental Scarcities and Violent Conflict: Evidence from Cases', *International Security*, 19(1): 5–40.

Homer-Dixon, T. (2007) 'Terror in the Weather Forecast', *New York Times*, 24 April.

Homer-Dixon, T. & Percival, V. (1996) *Environmental Scarcity and Violent Conflict: Briefing Book*, Population and Sustainable Development Project, American Association for the Advancement of Science and University of Toronto.

Hough, P. (1998) *The Global Politics of Pesticides: Forging Consensus from Conflicting Interests*, London: Earthscan.

Hough, P. (2013) *International Politics of the Arctic: Coming in from the Cold*, London and New York: Routledge.

Hsiang, S. Meng, K. & Cane, M. (2011) 'Civil Conflicts are Associated with Global Climate', *Nature*, 476: 438–441.

Hughes, B.B., Kuhn, R., Peterson, C.M., Rothman, D.S. & Solorzano, J.R. (2011) 'Improving Global Health: Forecasting the Next 50 Years', in B. Hughes (ed.) *Patterns of Potential Human Progress*, Boulder, CO: Paradigm.

Humphreys, D. (1996) *Forest Politics: The Evolution of International Cooperation*, London: Earthscan.

Humphreys, D. (2006) *Logjam: Deforestation and the Crisis of Global Governance,* London: Earthscan.

Humphreys, D. (2011) 'International Forest Politics', in G. Kutting (ed.) *Global Environmental Politics: Concepts, Theories and Case Studies*, London and New York: Routledge: 135–150.

Hungary (1998) Resolution No. 94/1998. (XII. 29.) of the Hungarian National Assembly on 'The Basic Principles of the Security and Defence Policy of the Republic of Hungary'.

IAEA, Convention on Nuclear Safety (2012) http://www-ns.iaea.org/conventions/nuclear-safety.asp (Accessed 13 June 2012).

ICIDI (1980) *North-South: The Report of the International Commission on International Development Issues*, London: Pan Books.

IFAD (2010) *Desertification*, Rome: International Fund for Agricultural Development.

IFRC (2001) *World Disasters Report 2001. Focus on Recovery*, Geneva: International Federation of Red Cross and Red Crescent Societies.

Ilulissat Declaration (2008) The Ilulissat Declaration, Governments of Denmark, Norway, Russia, US and Canada, 28 May, http://arctic-council.org/filearchive/Ilulissat-declaration.pdf (Accessed 12 May 2011).

IMO (2011) *IMO and the Environment*, London: International Maritime Organization.

Ingleton, J. (ed.) (1999) *Natural Disaster Management: A Presentation to Commemorate the International Decade for Natural Disaster Reduction (IDNDR)*, Leicester: Tudor Rose.

IPCC (2001) *Third Assessment Report Climate Change*, Geneva: Intergovernmental Panel on Climate Change.

IPCC (2007) *Fourth Assessment Report Climate Change*, Geneva: Intergovernmental Panel on Climate Change.

ISDR (2002a) 'ISDR Vision', http://www.unisdr.org/unisdr/aboutvision.htm (Accessed 27 February 2002).

ISDR (2002b) *Living With Risk: A Global Review of Disaster Reduction Activities*, Geneva: International Strategy for Disaster Reduction.

Jacques, P. (2011) 'Marine Pollution' in G. Kutting (ed) *Global Environmental Politics. Concepts, Theories and Case Studies*, London & New York: Routledge: 119–134.

Jeffers, J. (2010) 'Climate Change and the Arctic: Adapting to Changes in Fisheries Stocks and Governance Regimes' *Ecology Law Quarterly*, 37, 917–978.

Jeggle, T. (1999) 'The Goals and Aims of the Decade', in J. Ingleton (ed.) *Natural Disaster Management: A Presentation to Commemorate the International Decade for Natural Disaster Reduction (IDNDR)*, Leicester: Tudor Rose.

Jensen, E. (2005) 'The International Law of Environmental Warfare: Active and Passive Damage During Armed Conflict', *Vanderbilt Journal of Transnational Law*, 38: 145.

Kalpers, J. (2001) Armed Conflict and Biodiversity in Sub-Saharan Africa: Impacts, Washington, DC: Biodiversity Support Program.

Kannan, A. (2012) *Global Environmental Governance and Desertification*, New Delhi: Concept.

Kaplan, R. (1994) 'The Coming Anarchy', *The Atlantic Monthly*, 273: 44–76.

Karunaratne, W. (1959) 'The Influence of Malaria Control on Vital Statistics in Ceylon', *The Journal of Tropical Medicine and Hygiene*, 62: 79–85.

Kelman, I. & Koukis, T. (eds) (2000) 'Disaster Diplomacy', *Cambridge Review of International Affairs*, special section, XIV(1), Autumn–Winter: 214–294.

Kennan, G. (1985) 'Morality and Foreign Policy', *Foreign Affairs*, 64: 205–218.

Keohane, R. & Nye, J. (1977) *Power and Interdependence: World Politics in Transition*, Boston, MA: Little, Brown.

Ker-Lindsay, J. (2000) 'Greek–Turkish Rapprochement: The Impact of Disaster Diplomacy?' *Cambridge Review of International Affairs* 14(1) Autumn–Winter 2000, special section, Disaster Diplomacy: 215–232.

Kissinger, G., Herold, M. & De Sy, V. (2012) *Drivers of Deforestation and Forest Degradation: A Synthesis Report for REDD+ Policymakers*. Vancouver: Lexeme Consulting.

Kitchin, C. (2001) '"Early Discoveries" Part of Feature; "Focus: Asteroids"', *Astronomy Now*, 15(1), January: 54–55.

Krech, S. & McNeill, J.R. (2004) *Encyclopedia of World Environmental History*, London and New York: Routledge.

Lappé, F. & Schuman, R. (1988) *Taking Population Seriously*. San Francisco: Institute for Food and Development Policy.

Laurance, J. (2006) 'Climate Change Blamed for Legionnaire's Disease Surge', *Independent*, 18 October: 4.

Lavauden, L. (1927) 'Le Forets du Sahara', *Revue des Eaux et Forets*, 65(6): 265–277.

Lawson, N. (2008) *An Appeal to Reason: A Cool Look at Global Warming*, London and New York: Duckworth.

Levy, M. (1995) 'Time for a Third Wave of Environment and Security Scholarship?' *The Environmental Change and Security Project Report*, 1, Spring: 44–64.

Libiszewski, S. (1995) 'Water Disputes in the Jordan Basin Region and their Role in the Resolution of the Arab-Israeli Conflict', ENCOP Occasional Paper No. 13. Zurich/Berne: Centre for Security Policy and Conflict Research/Swiss Peace Foundation.

Lidskog, R. & Sundqvist, G. (2002) 'The Role of Science in Environmental Regimes: The Case of the LRTAP', *European Journal of International Relations*, 8(1): 77–101.

Lim, S. et al. (2012) 'A Comparative Risk Assessment of Burden of Disease and Injury Attributable to 67 Risk Factors and Risk Factor Clusters in 21 Regions, 1990–2010: A Systematic Analysis for the Global Burden of Disease Study 2010', *Lancet*, 380: 2224–2260.

Lippmann, W. (1943) *US Foreign Policy*, London: Hamish Hamilton.

Lomborg, B. (2001) *The Skeptical Environmentalist*, Cambridge: Cambridge University Press.

Lomborg, B. (2007) *Cool It: The Skeptical Environmentalist's Guide to Global Warming*, London: Random House.

Lomborg, B. (2008) 'A Time for Clarity' Copenhagen Consensus Center http://www.copenhagen consensus.com/sites/default/files/A_TIME_FOR_CLARITY.pdf (Accessed 3 July 2013).

Lopez, M. (1987) 'The Politics of Lands at Risk in a Philippine Frontier', in P. Little & M. Horowitz (eds) *Lands at Risk*, Boulder CO: Westview Press: 230–248.

Lovelock, J. (1971) 'Atmospheric Fluorine Compounds as Indicators of Air Movements', *Nature*, 230 (5293): 379.

Lovelock, J. (1991) *Gaia: The Practical Science of Planetary Medicine*, London: Gaia Books.

Lynge, A. (2011) *Encyclopedia of Climate Change* (2nd edition), Oxford: Oxford University Press.

Maathai, W. (2004) *Nobel Peace Prize Winner Acceptance Speech*, Oslo City Hall, 10 December.

MacFarlane, N. & Foong Khong, Y. (2006) *Human Security and the UN: A Critical History*, Bloomington, IN: Indiana University Press.

Malthus, T. (1798) *An Essay on the Principle of Population*, London: J. Johnson.

Markham, A. (1994) *A Brief History of Pollution*, New York: St Martins.

Marsh, G. (1965) *Man and Nature* (reprint), Cambridge, MA: Harvard University Press.

Mathew, R.A., Barnett, J., McDonald, B., O'Brien K.L. & Dabelko, G.D. (eds) (2010) *Global Environmental Change and Human Security*, Boston: MIT.

Mathews, J. (1989) 'Redefining Security', *Foreign Affairs*, 68(2): 162–177.

Matin, N. & Taher, M. (2000) 'Disaster Mitigation in Bangladesh: Country Case Study of NGO Activities', Report for Research Project *NGO National Disaster Mitigation and Preparedness Projects: An Assessment of the Way Forward*, ESCOR Award no. R7231.

Matthew, R. & Zalidi, A. (2002) 'People, Scarcity and Violence in Pakistan', in R. Matthew, M. Halle & J. Switzer (eds) *Conserving the Peace: Resources, Livelihoods and Scarcity*, Geneva: International Institute for Sustainable Development: 57–98.

Mazza, P. (1998) 'The Invisible Hand: Is Global Warming Driving El Niño?' *Sierra Magazine*, 83, May/June.

McCurry, J. (2006) 'Japan Remembers Minamata', *Lancet*, 367(9505): 99–100.

McSweeney, B. (1999) *Security, Identity and Interests: A Sociology of International Relations*, Cambridge: Cambridge University Press.

Meadows, D.H., Meadows, D.L., Randers, J. & Behrens, W.W. (1972) *The Limits to Growth: A Report for the Club of Rome's Project on the Predicament of Mankind*, London: Earth Island.

Mearsheimer, J. (1990) 'Why We Will Soon Miss the Cold War', *The Atlantic Monthly* 226(2): 35–50.

MSV (2012) 'Many Strong Voices' http://www.manystrongvoices.org/ (Accessed 5 August 2012).

Munton, D., Soroos, M., Nikitima, E. & Levy, M. (1999) 'Acid Rain in Europe and North America', in O. Young (ed.) *The Effectiveness of International Environmental Regimes: Causal Connections and Behavioural Mechanism*, Cambridge, MA: MIT: 155–247.

Myers, N. (1996) *Ultimate Security: The Environmental Basis of Political Stability*, New York: Norton.

Naess, A. (1973) 'The Shallow and the Deep, Long-Range Ecology Movement. A Summary'. Inquiry, 16(1): 95–100.

Najarn, A. (2006) 'Negotiating Desertification', in P.M. Johnson, K. Mayrand & M. Paquin (eds) *Governing Global Desertification*, Farnham: Ashgate.

Namibia. (2007) *Statement by H. E. Dr Kaire Munionganda Mbuende Ambassador and Permanent Representative at the Open Debate on the Relationship Between Energy, Security and Climate*, New York: Security Council April 17.

National Academy of Sciences. (1974) *The Effects of Herbicide in South Vietnam, Part A Summary and Conclusion*, Washington, DC: NAS.

NATO (2013) *Environmental Security*, http://www.nato.int/cps/en/natolive/topics_49216.htm

Natsios, A. (1999) 'The Politics of Famine in North Korea', Special Report, Washington, DC: US Institute of Peace, http://www.usip.org/oc/sr/sr99082/sr990802.html (Accessed 2 April 2002).

Netherlands (2006) *Policy Agenda 2006*. Amsterdam: Ministry of Foreign Affairs.

Nixon, R. (1969) Speech, 18 July, White House, Washington, DC.

Nordas, R. & Gleditsch, N. (2007) 'Climate Change and Conflict', *Political Geography*, 26(6): 627–638.

Nye, J. (1990) *Bound to Lead: the Changing Nature of American Power*, New York: Basic Books.

O'Brien, K. & Leichenko, R. (2008) *Human Security, Vulnerability and Sustainable Adaptation*, Human Development Report 2007/2008, New York: United Nations Development Programme.

Olsen, M. (2003) *Analysis of the Stockholm Convention on Persistent Organic Pollutants*, Dobbs Ferry: Oceana.

Oneshes, N. (2004) 'Beyond the Ivory Tower: The Scientific Consensus on Climate Change', *Science*, 306(5702): 1686.

Osborn, F. (1948) *Our Plundered Planet*, New York: Grosset & Dunlap.

Ostling, K. (1992) 'The Impact of Militarism on the Environment', *Peace Magazine*, May/June.

Paddock, W. & Paddock, P. (1967) *Famine 1975*, London: Weidenfield & Nicolson.

Palme, O. (1982) *Common Security: A Programme for Disarmament*, London: Pan Books.

Paris, R. (2001) 'Human Security: Paradigm Shift or Hot Air?' *International Security*, 26(2): 87–102.

Pearce, F. (2005) 'Climate Warning as Siberia Melts', *New Scientist*, 11 August.

Peiser, B. (2001) '"Impact Scares and How to Avoid Them", in "Focus: Asteroids"', *Astronomy Now*, 15(1), January: 64–65.

Peluso, N. & Vandergeest, P. (2011) 'Taking the Jungle Out of the Forest', in R. Peat, P. Robbins & M. Watts. *Global Political Ecology*, London and New York: Routledge.

Peterson, I. (2009) 'The Natural Environment in Times of Armed Conflict: A Concern for International War Crimes Law?' *Leiden Journal of International Law*, 22(2): 325–343.

Pew (2010) 'Wide Partisan Divide Over Global Warming', http://www.pewresearch.org/2010/10/27/wide-partisan-divide-over-global-warming/

Pickering, K. & Owen, L. (1994) *An Introduction to Global Environmental Issues*, London: Routledge.

Pickup, G. (1998) 'Desertification and Climate Change–the Australian Perspective', *Climate Research*, 11: 51–63.

Pimentel, D. (2005) 'Environmental and Economic Costs of the Application of Pesticides Primarily in the United States', *Environment, Development and Sustainability*, 7: 229–252.

Porritt, J. (1984) *Seeing Green: The Politics of Ecology Explained*, New York: Basil Blackwell.

Prins, G. (2002) *The Heart of War. On Power, Conflict and Obligation in the Twenty-First Century*, London & New York: Routledge.

Preston, S. (1975) 'The Changing Relationship between Mortality and Level of Economic Development', *Population Studies*, 29(2): 231–248.

Prins, G. & Stamp, R. (1991) *Top Guns and Toxic Whales: The Environment and Global Security*, London: Earthscan.

Reuveny, R. (2007) 'Climate Change-Induced Migration and Violent Conflict', *Political Geography*, 26 (6): 656–673.

Reuveny, R., Mihalache-O'Keef, A.S. & Quan Li. (2010) 'The Effect of Warfare on the Environment', *Journal of Peace Research*, 47(6): 749–761.

Roberts, A. & Guelff, R. (2000) *Documents on the Laws of War* (3rd edition), Oxford: Oxford University Press.

Rogers, P. (2000) *Losing Control. Global Security in the Twenty-First Century*, London & Sterling, VA: Pluto Press.

Roosevelt, F.D. (1937) 'Letter to all State Governors on a Uniform Soil Conservation Law', 26 February.

Ruether, R. (1975) *New Woman/New Earth: Sexist Ideologies and Human Liberation*, New York: Seabury.

Russia (1996) *Environmental Security of Russia*, issue 2, Moscow: The Security Council of the Russian Federation, 13 October, 1994.

Salehyan, J. (2008) 'From Climate Change to Conflict: No Consensus Yet', *Journal of Peace Research*, 43(3): 315–326.

Saleshi, G.W., Debusho, L.K. & Akinnifeso, F.K. (2012) 'Can Integration of Legume Trees Increase Yield Stability in Rainfed Maize Cropping Systems in Southern Africa?' *Agronomy Journal*, 104: 1392–1398.

Sanders, B. (2009) *The Green Zone*, Oakland: AK Press.

Schettler, T. (1995) 'Reverberations of Militarism: Toxic Contamination, the Environment, and Health', *Medicine and Global Survival*, 2(1): 7–18.

Sen, A. (1981) *Poverty and Famines: An Essay on Entitlement and Deprivation*, Oxford: Clarendon.

Sen, A. (1999) 'Democracy as a Universal Value', *Journal of Democracy*, 10(3), 1999B: 3–17.

Sheehan, N. (2003) 'The Aftermath of an Invasion: A Field Report from Nasiriyah', *Warchild*, 1 May.

Shiva, V. (1988) *Staying Alive: Women, Ecology and Development*, London: Zed Books.

Simon, J. (1981) *The Ultimate Resource*, Princeton: Princeton University Press.

Simon, J. (1996) *The Ultimate Resource II*, Princeton: Princeton University Press.

Simon, J. (1999) *Hoodwinking the Nation*, New Brunswick, NJ: Transaction.

Singer, P. (1979) *Practical Ethics*, Cambridge: Cambridge University Press.

Singh, K. (1974) Statement of Head of the Indian Delegation, World Population Conference III, Plenary Session 26 August, Bucharest.

Smith, A. & Flores, A. (2010) 'Why Earthquakes Rock Democracies Less', *Foreign Affairs*, 15 July.

Smith, D. (1994). 'Dynamics of Contemporary Conflict: Consequences for Development Strategies', in N. Græger & D. Smith (eds) *Environment, Poverty, Conflict*, Oslo: International Peace Research Institute (PRIO) Report 2/1994: 47–89.

Smith, K. (2001) *Environmental Hazards: Assessing Risk and Reducing Disaster* (3rd edition), London and New York: Routledge.

Smith, R., Corvalan, C. & Kiellstrom, T. (1999) 'How Much Global Ill Health is Attributable to Environmental Factors?' *Journal of Epidemiology*, 10(5): 573–584.

Smith-Spark, L. (2013) 'Injured Russians Leave Hospital, Analysis of Meteorite Fragments Begins', *CNN*, 22 February.

Smol, J. & Douglas, M. (2007) 'From Controversy to Consensus: Making the Case for Recent Climate Change in the Arctic Using Lake Sediments', *Frontiers in Ecology and the Environment*, 5(9): 466–474.

Sopoanga, S. (2002) 'Statement by Tuvalu', *Johannesburg: World Summit on Sustainable Development*, 2 September.

Spinage, C. (2012) *African Ecology: Benchmarks and Historical Perspectives*, London and New York: Springer.

Sprout, H. & Sprout, M. (1971) *Toward a Politics of the Planet Earth*, New York: Van Nostrand Reinhold.

Starr, J. (1991) 'Water Wars', *Foreign Policy*, 82, Spring: 17–36.

Stern, N. (2006) *The Economics of Climate Change.* The Stern Review, Cambridge: Cambridge University Press.

Store, J. & Lavrov, S. (2010) 'Joint Communique', *Globe & Mail*, Canada, 21 September.

Sukhdev, P. (2008) *Economics of Ecosystems and Biodiversity–TEEB*, Germany: Helmholz Association.

Swiss Re (2012) *Natural and Man-made Catastrophes in 2011*, Sigma Study.

Tal, A. & Cohen, J.A. (2007) 'Bringing "Top Down" to "Bottom Up": A New Role for Environmental Legislation in Combating Desertification', *Harvard Environmental Law Review*, 31: 163–216.

Tenenbaum, D. (2004) 'POPs in Polar Bears: Organochlorines Affect Bone Density', *Environmental Health Perspectives*, 112(17): A1011.

Thatcher, M. (1989) Speech, United Nations General Assembly, New York, 8 November.

Trenberth, K. (1998) 'El Niño and Global Warming', *Journal of Marine Education*, 15(2): 12–18.

UCS (2011) *Brazil's Success in Reducing Deforestation*, Washington, DC: Union of Concerned Scientists http://www.ucsffdusa.org/assets/documents/global_warming/Brazil-s-Success-in-Reducing-Deforestation.pdf (Accessed 12 May 2013).

UKOA (2013) Ocean Acidification, http://www.oceanacidification.org.uk/ (Accessed 20 June 2013).

Ullman, R. (1983) 'Redefining Security', *International Security*, 8(1): 29–153

UN (2004) *A More Secure World: Our Shared Responsibility*, United Nations Secretary-General's High-Level Panel on Threats, Challenges, and Change, New York.

UN (2013) 'A New Global Partnership: Eradicate Poverty and Transform Societies Through Sustainable Development', *Report of the UN High Level Panel of Eminent Persons on the Post 2015 Development Agenda*, New York: United Nations.

UN (2011) MDG Indicators, http://unstats.un.org/unsd/mdg/SeriesDetail.aspx?srid=616 (Accessed 18 June 2012).

UNCCD (2013) Brochure Desertification, Land Degradation and Drought. Some Global Facts and Figures.

UNCED (1992) United Nations Conference on the Environment and Development, Rio de Janeiro (quoted in Brauch 2003: 13).

UNCOD (1997) *United Nations Conference on Desertification* New York, 29 August–9 September.

UNDP (1993) *Human Development Report: People's Participation*, Oxford: Oxford University Press.

UNEP & Environmental Law Institute *Protecting the Environment During Armed Conflict: An Inventory and Analysis of International Law* Merma, Bruch & Diamond (eds) Nairobi: UNEP.

UNEP (1992) *Synthesis Report on the Methyl Bromide Interim Assessment*, Nairobi: UNEP.

UNEP (2002) GEO3 Chapter 3 *Human Vulnerability to Environmental Change*, http://geo.unep-wcmc.org/geo3/ (Accessed 3 October 2002).

UNEP. (2002) *GEO-3: Global Environment Outlook 3*, London: Earthscan.

UNEP (2007) Geo-4 http://www.unep.org/geo/geo4.asp (Accessed 8 April 2009).

UNEP (2009) 'Persistent Organic Pollutants', http://www.chem.unep.ch/pops/ (Accessed 7 July 2009).

UNEP (2012) South Sudan Joins Montreal Protocol, http://www.unep.org/Documents.Multilingual/Default.asp?DocumentID=2666&ArticleID=9010&l=en (Accessed 12 May 2013).

UNEP Grid-Arendal (2007) 'Vital Ozone Graphics–Resource Kit for Journalists', http://www.grida.no/publications/vg/ozone/page/1393.aspx (Accessed 21 June 2011).

UNHCR (2009) 'Report of the Office of the UNHCR on the Relationship Between Climate Change and Human Rights', UN document A/HRC/10/61/15 Geneva: United Nations High Commission for Refugees.

UNHSU (2013) *Lessons from the Field: Applying the Human Security Approach*, New York: Human Security Unit, Office for the Coordination of Humanitarian Affairs.

University of North Dakota (2002) *Volcano World*, http://volcano.und.nodak.edu/vwdocs/volc_images/southeast_asia/indonesia/tambora.html (Accessed 3 October 2002).

UNSC (2007) Letter Dated 5 April 2007 from the Permanent Representative of the United Kingdom of Great Britain and Northern Ireland to the United Nations addressed to the President of the Security Council 5 April S/2007/186.

USA (1994) *National Security Strategy Document*, Washington, DC: US State Department.

USDC (2005) ' "Agent Orange" Product Liability Litigation', Memorandum Order and Judgement, MDL no. 381 10 March, New York: United States District Court.

Usher, M.B., Callaghan, T.V., Gilchrist, T.V., Heal, O.W., Juday, G.P., Leong, H., Muir, M.A.K., & Prestrud, P. (2010) 'Human Impacts on the Biodiversity of the Arctic', *Encyclopedia of the Earth*, http://www.eoearth.org/article/Human_impacts_on_the_biodiversity_of_the_Arctic (Accessed 15 December 2010).

Wæver, O. (1995) 'Securitization and Desecuritization', in R. Lipschutz, ed., *On Security*. New York: Columbia University Press: 46–86.

Walt, S. (1991) 'The Renaissance of Security Studies', *International Studies Quarterly*, 35(2): 211–239.

Waltz, K. (1979) *Theory of International Politics*, Reading, MA: Addison-Wesley.

Warren, M. (1985) *Gendercide: The Implications of Sex Selection*, Totowa, NJ: Rowman & Littlefield.

Westing, A. (1974) 'Proscription of Ecocide', *Bulletin of the Atomic Scientists* 30(1): 24–27.

Watkins, K. (2002) *Rigged Rules and Double Standards: Trade Globalization and the Fight Against Poverty*, Oxford: Oxfam.

Weinstein, T. (2005) 'Prosecuting Acts that Destroy the Environment: Environmental Crimes or Humanitarian Atrocities?' *Georgetown International Law Review*, 17: 607–722.

Weir, D. (1987) *The Bhopal Syndrome- Pesticides, Environment and Health*, Earthscan: London.

Weir, D. & Schapiro, M. (1981) *Circle of Poison*, San Francisco: Institute for Food and Development Policy.

WER (2009) 'Desertification. Its Effects on Land and People', *World Ecology Report* 21(1): 1–5.

Westing, A. (1974) 'Proscription of Ecocide', *Science and Public Affairs*, 26: 24–27.

Westing, A. (1980) *Warfare in a Fragile World: Military Impact on the Human Environment*, London: Taylor and Francis.

Westing, A. (1984) *Herbicides in War-the Long Term Ecological and Human Consequences*, London: Taylor and Francis.

Westing, A. (1989) 'Herbicides in Warfare: The Case of Indochina', in P. Bourdeau, J.A. Haines, W. Klein & C.R. Krishna Murti (eds) *Ecotoxicology and Climate*, Chichester: Wiley, 337–357.

Wetterstad, J. (1997) 'Acid Lessons? LRTAP Implementation and Effectiveness', *Global Environmental Change*, 7: 235–249.

WHO (1999) *World Health Report. Part 1 Health and Development in the Twentieth Century*, Geneva: WHO.

WHO (2012) *Climate Change and Health Fact Sheet 266*, Geneva: World Health Organization.

Whittow, J. (1984) *The Penguin Dictionary of Physical Geography*, London: Penguin.

WikiLeaks (2010) 'Canadian PM and NATO S-G Discuss Afghanistan, the Strategic Concept and the Arctic', cable no. 244500, 20 January 6.49pm, US Embassy Ottawa.

Wille, C., Kutzbach, L., Sachs, T., Wagner, D. & Pfeiffer, E. (2008) 'Methane Emission from Siberian Arctic Polygonal Tundra: Eddy Covariance Measurements and Modelling', *Global Change Biology*, 14: 1385–1408.

Wirtz, J. (2013) 'A New Agenda for Security and Strategy?' in J. Baylis, J. Wirtz & C. Gray, *Strategy in the Contemporary World*, Oxford: Oxford University Press: 323–340.

Wisner, B. (2000) 'Disasters. What the United Nations and its World Can Do', *United Nations Chronicle* (online edition) XXXVIII, 4, http://www.un.org/Pubs/chronicle/2000/issue4/0400p6.htm (Accessed 13 August 2002).

Wolf, A. (2007) 'Shared Waters: Conflict and Cooperation', *Annual Review of Environmental Resources*, 32: 241–269.

World Bank (1993) *World Development Report: Investing in Health*, Washington, DC.

World Bank (2009) *The Sunken Billions*, Washington, DC: World Bank Publications.

World Bank (2011) Multilateral Fund, http://web.worldbank.org/WBSITE/EXTERNAL/TOPICS/ENVIRONMENT/EXTTMP/0,,contentMDK:20502611~menuPK:1246963~pagePK:148956~pi PK:216618~theSitePK:408230,00.html (Accessed 3 June 2013).

World Meteorological Organization/United Nations Environmental Programme. (2006) *UNEP/WMO Scientific Assessment of Ozone Depletion: 2006*. Global Ozone Research and Monitoring Project. Report no. 50. Geneva: WMO.

WWF (2013) Threats Deforestation, http://worldwildlife.org/threats/deforestation.

Wyn-Jones, R. (1999) *Security, Strategy and Critical Theory*, Chapter 4, Boulder, CO: Lynne Rienner, http://www.ciaonet.org/book/wynjones/wynjones04.html (Accessed 14 March 2003).

Young, O. (1989) *Building Regimes for Natural Resources and the Environment*, Ithaca, NY: Cornell University Press.

Index

Note: Locators in bold refer to heading.

Abidjan disaster, 100
accidents, 91–2
acid Rain, 6–7, 68, 90–1, **97–8**, 139
aforestation, 113
Agent Orange, 27, 56–7, 66
agroforestry, 113
Alexander the Great, 50
Alter-globalization, 115
Antarctic Treaty, 5
anthropocentricism, 6, 17–18, 20, 25, 39, 137
Arab-Israeli dispute, 51, 59, 65
Arctic, 27, 51–3, 58, 60, 64, 81–2, 86, 92, 93, 99, 138
ASEAN, 32
avalanches, 120–1

Bali, Climate Change Conference, 16
Basel Convention, 99–100, 102
Beckett, M., 29
Bentham, J., 135
Bhopal disaster, 17, 91, 101
biodiversity, 11, 14, 16, 25, 27, 45, 60, 61, 106, 108, 109, 113, **114–17**, 140
Bookchin, M., 18
Boundary Water Treaty, (1909), 5
Boutros-Ghali, B., 46
Britton, N., 130
Brock, L., 26
Brundtland, G.H. 12
Buddhism, 17
Bush, G (Jr.), 15, 16, 52, 70, 84, 103
Bush, G. (Snr.), 84
Buzan, B., 23, 25

Camacho, D.M., 37
Cameron, D., 87
carbon sink effect, 12, 14, 108, 111
Carson, R. 6, 17, 89, 139
Carter Doctrine, 46–7
Cem, I., 31
Central Emergency Response Fund, 131
Chemical Weapons Convention, 61
Chernobyl disaster, 92, 103–4, 105
Chiang Kai-shek, 58
Chinese anti-pollution protests, 105
CITES, 11, 14
Climate Change, 16–17, 19, 21, 22, 23, 24, 27–8, 29–30, 32, 45, 49–50, **70–2**, 73–5, **79–88**. 92, 103, 104, 106, 108, 109–11, 127, 134, 137, 138–9, 140
Clinton, B. 16, 26
Club of Rome, 9
Cold War, 20, 21, 22, 23, 27, 29, 30, 46, 49, 50, 51, 53, 60, 63, 65, 67, 71, 98, 132, 133, 135
Commission for Sustainable Development, 14
Common Heritage of Mankind, 10, 112
Confucianism, 18
Convention on the Protection of Birds Useful to Agriculture (1902), 4, 5
Copenhagen Consensus, 84
Copenhagen School, 23–5, 136
Cordillera de Condor Peace Park, 138
Cornucopians, 41–2, 45, 72, 84
Council of Europe, 66
Cretaceous/Tertiary Impact, 3, 73

Dabielko, G. & Simmons, P., 136
Dalby, S., 137
Darfur Crisis, 49, 50
Darre, R., 4
Darwin, C., 5
DDT, 6, 15, 39, 92, 96, 102, 103

deforestation, 12, 14, 22, 24, 28, 45, 57–8, 60, 61, 106, 108, **111–14**, 115, 139, 140
democracy, 19, 20, 25, 50, 51, 53, 67, 96, 105, 115, 127–8, 139
desertification, 12, 14, 17, 24, 45, 58, **106–11**, 117, 139, 140
Deudney, D. 133–4, 136–7
De Wilde, J. 23, 137
Deep Green Ecology, 18
Dinar, S, 51, 54
Dobson, A. 18
Donora smog, 96
Drought, 50, 80, 86, 87, 106–7, 108, 118–19, **123–4**, 128
DuPont, 72
Dupont, A. & Pearman, G., 49
Dyer, H., 137, 139–40

earthquakes, 31, 50, 75, **119–20**, 121, 125, 126, 127–8, 131
d'Eaubonne, F., 18
EC/EU, 25, 38, 51, 86, 94, 98, 104, 109, 113, 115, 116, 117
Eco-Anarchism, 18, 117
ecocentricism, 5, 6, 17–18, 19, 20, 26, 28, 103, 137, 139
ecocide, 27, **55–67**, 139
Eco-Feminism, 18
Economic Liberals, 115
Economics of Ecosystems & Biodiversity (TEEB), 25
Edward I, King, 96
Ehrlich, P., 40, 42, 45
El Niño, 25, 49, 50, 81, 124, 127
El Salvador Civil War, 57–8, 61
ENMOD, 62–2, 64
ENVSEC, 30, 65
Epistemic community, 8, 9, 10, 14, 15, 16, 19, 32, 79–80, 98, 102, 104, 110, 126, 129, 130, 131, 139
Euphrates agreement, 51
Exclusive Economic Zones (EEZ), 10, 116
Extinctions, 3, 73, 108
Extra-Terrestrial collision, 72
Extreme temperatures, 80, 118, 119, **123**

Falk, R., 22, 24, 64
Famine, 38, 40–1, 118–19, 122, 124–5, 128
Fishing, 7, 8, 10, 11, 16, 19, 25, 48, 52, 61, 72, 81, 93, 94, 95, 109, 115, **116–17**, 139, 140
Floods, 4, 24, 30–1, 58, 63, 80, 81, 112, 113, 118–19, 120, 122, 123, 124, 123, 124, **125**, 126, 127, 128, 131
Food security, 40–1, 107, 111, 114–17, 124–5
'Football War', 50
Ford, G., 66
Foreign Affairs (Journal), 22, 51
Founex Report, 9
Framework Convention on Climate Change, 14, 71, **83,** 86
Fukushima disaster, 92, 97, 104

G7, 70
G77, 71
Gaia hypothesis, 18–19, 137
Galtung, J., 115, 136
Gandhi, I., 9, 12
Gandhi, M., 3
Geneva Conventions, 61–2
Gleick, P., 50
Global Crop Protection Federation, 103
Gorbachev, M., 27, 52, 138
Gore, A., 16, 26, 71, 79, 84
Grant, S., 53
Greenpeace, 17
Gulf Cooperation Council, 32
Gulf War, 48, 51, 55, 58, 63

Haas, P., 10
Haeckel, E., 3, 5
Hague Conventions, 61
Haiti earthquake (2010), 50, 75, 127, 131
Hammond, A., 72
Hardin, G., 8, 39–40
Harper, S., 52
hazardous chemical trade, 100–3
hazardous waste, 17, 60, 92–3, 99–100
Helmand River agreement, 51
Higgins, P., 64
HIV/AIDS, 38, 74, 75, 84
Hobbes, T., 135
Homer-Dixon, T., 22, 26, 48–9, 71, 74, 134
Huang-Ho floods, 24, 118
human security, 16, 23–4, 79–131, 136–8
Human Security Unit (UN), 86
Humphreys, D., 24, 112, 113, 117
hunger, 37, 115

IAEA, 103
ICRC, 64
International Criminal Court (ICC), 64, 65

International Criminal Tribunal for Yugoslavia (ICTY), 64
illegal logging, 113
ILO, 28
IMO, 98–9
Indian Ocean Tsunami, 24, 80, 118, 131
indigenous people, 28, 53, 87, 114
Indonesian Civil War, 57
International Decade for Natural Disaster Relief (IDNDR), 129–30
international regime, 5, 10–11, 19, 65
International Strategy for Disaster Relief, 130
International Whaling Commission (IWC), 5, 11
IPCC, 71, **79–80**, 81, 82, 84
Iraq War, 59, 60, 85
IUCN (IUPN), 5, 8, 11, 66

Just War, 61–2

Kaplan, R., 49
Kennan, G., 22
Keohane, R., 46
Ker-Lindsay, J., 31
King, D., 21
Kosovan War, 31, 59, 64
Kyoto Protocol (1997), 14, 16, 83, 85, 103

Lake Chad, 108–9
Lake Nyos disaster, 122
landslides, 60, 108, 112, **120–1**, 127, 128
Lawson, N., 84
League of Nations, 62, 135
Levy, M., 49, 105
Liberals, 18, 22, 23–4, 46, 135
Limits to Growth, 9, 13, 18
Lomborg, B., 84, 85
London Smog (1952), 5, 90
Lopez, M., 128
Lovelock, J., 18–19, 29, 69, 137
LRTAP, 11, 14, **97–8**

Maathar, W., 55
MacFarlane, N. & Foong Khong, Y., 25
Malayan Emergency, 56
Malthus, T., 5, 37–8
Manchurian War, 58, 59, 62, 66
MARPOL, 10, 17, 66
Marsh, G.P., 3–4, 5
Marxism, 115, 117, 124
Matthews, J., 22
Mbuende, K., 71
McSweeny, B., 135
Mearsheimer, J., 22
Mediterranean Action Plan (MAP), 10
Medvedev, D., 52
Merkel, A., 131
methane, 24, 72, 82, 86
methyl-bromide, 70
Military-industrial complex, 60, 67
Millennium Development Goals (MDGs), 16, 44, 140
MNCs, 12, 46, 53, 115
Montreal Protocol (1987), 15, 68. 69–70
Morales, E. 28, 64
Morgenthau, H., 135
Mussolini, B., 62
Myers, N., 24

Naess, A., 18
Napoleon Bonaparte, 58
NATO, 30–2, 52, 59, 60, 64, 129, 132
natural disasters, 24–5, 41, 108, 112, **118–32**
Nazis, 4
Neo-Malthusians, **39–42**, 44, 45, 50
Nixon, R., 27, 40
Non Aligned Movement, 71
North Pacific Fur Seal agreement (1911), 5
North Sea Convention, 10
nuclear pollution, 19, 29, 60, 91–2, **103–4**
Nuremburg War Trials, 62
Nye, J., 26, 46

Obama, B. 17, 71, 79
Ocean acidification, 81
Odėn, S., 97
OECD, 97, 100, 126
oil, 6–7, 10, 18, 28, 45, 46–8, 50, 51, 53, 58–9, 63, 93, 94, 98–9
OPEC, 46–7
Oregon State University, 51
Osborn, F., 22
overpopulation, 8–9, 17, 22, 26, 29, **37–45**, 47, 48, 49, 53, 112, 116, 118, 125, 126–7, 137, 138

Paddock, W. & P. 40
Palme, O., 27, **29**, 56, 97
Papandreou, G., 31
People's Task Force for Bases Clean Up, 66
Persistent Organic Pollutants (POPs), 15–16, 92, 97, **102–3**

Peru, Civil War, 48–9, 50
pesticides, 6, 15, 41, 69, 91, 92–3, 94–5, 96, 100–2
phylloxera, 4
pollution, **6–7**, **10–11**, 12–13, 15, 17, 23, 27, 28, 30, 31, 45, 59–60, 61, 63, 81–2, 85, 87, **89–105**, 106, 110, 134, 136, 138, 139
  air, 6–7, 89–90
  food, 95
  marine, 10–11, 98–9
  oil, 94
  soil, 94–5
  water, 92–6
Porritt, J., 18
polluter's dilemma, 7, 13, 19, 104, 139
poverty, 71, 82, 84–5, 115, 126
precautionary principle, 13, 14, 16, 19, 42, 103
pressure groups/NGOs, 3, 5, 8, 9, 11, 13, 18, 19, 32. 43, 86, 98, 101, 102, 109, 127–8, 130, 131
Prevention of Major Accidents Convention, 64
Prins, G., 32, 74
Prior Informed Consent (PIC), 100–2

Reagan, R., 41, 70
Realism/neo-Realism, 10, 22–3, 25, 26, 46, 48, 51, 53, 74, 135, 138
reforestation, 113
Regional Greenhouse Gas Initiative, 86
Rendulic trial, 62
resource curse theory, 50
resource depletion, 8–9, 21, 22, 46, 48, 59–60, 106–17, 137
resource wars, 26, 31, **46–54**, 74, 138
risk society, 96
Rogers (US Secretary of State), 62
Rogers, P., 50
Roosevelt, F., 106
Rotterdam Convention, 100–1
Rowland, S. & Molina, M., 68–9
Royal National Park (Sydney), 5
RSPB, 4, 5
Ruether, R., 18

Saddam Hussein, 58, 64, 67
Schroeder, G., 131
scorched earth policy, 57–8
Sellafield Nuclear power plant, 104
Sen, A., 128, 139
Senegal River Conflict, 48–9
Shiva, V., 18
Sierra Club, 3, 4, 5
Simon, J., 41–2, 45
Small Island Developing States (SIDS), 86
smog, 5, 90, 96, 105, 123
Smuts, J., 5
Snow, J., 96
Sprout , H.& M. 22
Stern, N. (Report), 12, 29–30, 72, 74
Stockholm Convention (2001), 102–3
Strong, M., 9
Subic Bay, 60, 66
Sustainable Development, 12–13, 15–17, 24, 27, 65, 110
Sustainable forestry management, 113

TACIS, 104
Talbot, S., 26
Temelin Nuclear Power plant, 104
Thatcher, M., 68, 98
Three-mile Island disaster, 91–2
Tokyo War Trials, 62
Torino Scale, 72
Torrey Canyon disaster, 7, 17, 94
Tragedy of the Commons, 8, 10, 39–40, 114, 116
Tsunamis, 24, 80, 92, 118, **125**, 129, 131

Ullman, R., 21–2
UN Biosphere Conference (1968), 8, 17
UNCCD, 14, 106–10
UNCED (1992 Rio Summit), **13–15**, 19, 65, 70, 82, 102, 103, 106, 109, 112, 116
UNCHE (1972 Stockholm Conference), **8–10**, 12, 13, 17, 27, 29, 56, 97, 98
UNCLOS, 10, 51–3, 116
UNCOD, 106–8
UNDP, 24, 25, 30, 65, 130
UNESCO, 5, 8
UNEP, 56, 64–5, 66, 69–70, 79, 86, 91, 92, 101, 102, 108, 115, 130
UNFPA, 40–1
UN General Assembly, 12, 13, 30, 62, 63–4, 65, 68, 71–2, 79, 82–3, 110, 129–31
UNHCR, 87
UN High Level Panel (Post 2015 Development Goals), 133, 140
UN Secretary General, 29, 30, 56, 64, 71, 83, 110
UN Security Council, 29, 63, 71–2, 74–5
urbanization, 12, 108, 111, 127, 138
US National Security Strategy, 26, 49

Vienna Convention (1985), 15, 68
Vietnam War, 27, 46, 55–8, 59, 62, 63, 66
volcanic eruptions, 119, **121–2**

Waever, O., 25, 136
Waltz, K., 46
Washington Consensus, 29, 41
Wellington, Duke of, 58
Westing, A., **55–6**, 57, 61, 64
WHO, 38, 80, 81, 102, 130
Wikileaks, 53
wildfires, 80. 108, 118, **123**
William the Conqueror, 56
windstorms, 81, 118, **122–3**, 128
Wisner, B., 126, 130, 132
Wirtz, J., 133
Wyn Jones, R., 25
World Bank, 38, 51, 56, 69, 113, 114, 116, 130
World Commission on the Environment and Development (WCED), 12
World Population Conferences, 40–1
World Summit on Sustainable Development (WSSD), 16, 116–17

Yellowstone Park, 3, 5